$3

D0072597

Manifest Destiny

Manifest Destiny

DAVID S. HEIDLER
AND JEANNE T. HEIDLER

Greenwood Guides to Historic Events 1500–1900
Linda S. Frey and Marsha L. Frey, Series Editors

GREENWOOD PRESS
Westport, Connecticut • London

Library of Congress Cataloging-in-Publication Data

Heidler, David Stephen, 1955–
   Manifest destiny / David S. Heidler and Jeanne T. Heidler.
     p. cm—(Greenwood guides to historic events 1500–1900, ISSN 1538–442X)
   Includes bibliographical references and index.
   ISBN 0–313–32308–9 (alk. paper)
   1. United States—Territorial expansion. I. Heidler, Jeanne T. II. Title. III. Series.
E179.5.H45 2003
   973.5—dc21   2002192774

British Library Cataloguing in Publication Data is available.

Library of Congress Catalog Card Number: 2002192774

ISBN: 0–313–32308–9
ISSN: 1538–442X

First published in 2003

Greenwood Press, 88 Post Road West, Westport, CT 06881
An imprint of Greenwood Publishing Group, Inc.
www.greenwood.com

Printed in the United States of America

The paper used in this book complies with the
Permanent Paper Standard issued by the National
Information Standards Organization (Z39.48–1984).

10 9 8 7 6 5 4 3 2 1

To
Darrell and Kathleen Hagar
Friends when it counted, and
now, forever.

CONTENTS

A photo essay follows page 116

MAPS

SERIES FOREWORD

American statesman Adlai Stevenson stated that "We can chart our future clearly and wisely only when we know the path which has led to the present." This series, Greenwood Guides to Historic Events, 1500–1900, is designed to illuminate that path by focusing on events from 1500 to 1900 that have shaped the world. The years 1500 to 1900 include what historians call the Early Modern Period (1500 to 1789, the onset of the French Revolution) and part of the modern period (1789 to 1900).

In 1500, an acceleration of significant trends marked the beginnings of an interdependent world and the posing of seminal questions that changed the nature and terms of intellectual debate. The series closes with 1900, the inauguration of the twentieth century. This period witnessed profound economic, social, political, cultural, religious, and military changes. An industrial and technological revolution transformed the modes of production, marked the transition from a rural to an urban economy, and ultimately raised the standard of living. Social classes and distinctions shifted. The emergence of the territorial and later the national state altered man's relations with and view of political authority. The shattering of the religious unity of the Roman Catholic world in Europe marked the rise of a new pluralism. Military revolutions changed the nature of warfare. The books in this series emphasize the complexity and diversity of the human tapestry and include political, economic, social, intellectual, military, and cultural topics. Some of the authors focus on events in U.S. history such as the Salem Witchcraft Trials, the American Revolution, the abolitionist movement, and the Civil War. Others analyze European topics, such as the Reformation and Counter Reformation and the French Revolution. Still others bridge cultures and continents by examining the voyages of discovery, the Atlantic slave trade, and the Age of Imperialism. Some focus on intellectual questions that have shaped the modern world, such as Darwin's *Origin of Species,* or on turning points such as the Age of Romanticism. Others examine defining economic, religious, or legal events or issues such as the building of the railroads, the Second Great Awakening, and abolitionism. Heroes (e.g., Lewis and Clark), scientists (e.g., Darwin), military leaders (e.g., Napoleon), poets (e.g., Byron), stride across these pages. Many of these events were seminal in that they marked profound changes or turning points. The Scientific Revolution, for example, changed the way individuals viewed themselves and their world.

The authors, acknowledged experts in their fields, synthesize key events, set developments within the larger historical context, and, most important, present a well-balanced, well-written account that integrates the most recent scholarship in the field.

The topics were chosen by an advisory board composed of historians, high school history teachers, and school librarians to support the curriculum and meet student research needs. The volumes are designed to serve as resources for student research and to provide clearly written interpretations of topics central to the secondary school and lower-level undergraduate history curriculum. Each author outlines a basic chronology to guide the reader through often confusing events and a historical overview to set those events within a narrative framework. Three to five topical chapters underscore critical aspects of the event. In the final chapter the author examines the impact and consequences of the event. Biographical sketches furnish background on the lives and contributions of the players who strut across this stage. Ten to fifteen primary documents ranging from letters to diary entries, song lyrics, proclamations, and posters, cast light on the event, provide material for student essays, and stimulate a critical engagement with the sources. Introductions identify the authors of the documents and the main issues. In some cases a glossary of selected terms is provided as a guide to the reader. Each work contains an annotated bibliography of recommended books, articles, CD-ROMs, Internet sites, videos, and films that set the materials within the historical debate.

These works will lead to a more sophisticated understanding of the events and debates that have shaped the modern world and will stimulate a more active engagement with the issues that still affect us. It has been a particularly enriching experience to work closely with such dedicated professionals. We have come to know and value even more highly the authors in this series and our editors at Greenwood, particularly Barbara Rader and Kevin Ohe. In many cases they have become more than colleagues; they have become friends. To them and to future historians we dedicate this series.

Linda S. Frey
University of Montana

Marsha L. Frey
Kansas State University

INTRODUCTION

When newspaper editor John L. O'Sullivan coined the phrase "Manifest Destiny" in 1845, he summarized as well as defined a national mood. The wide acceptance of O'Sullivan's phrase at the time and the currency given it since can lead to the false perception that a spirit of American expansionism was not apparent—or "manifest"—until the 1840s. True enough, in that decade the administration of President James K. Polk undertook to secure a clear title to the vast Pacific Northwest and to pry from Mexico the rich California coast. Yet, the idea that American expansion did not achieve a robust dynamism until the middle of the nineteenth century ignores the forces that promoted territorial expansion as early as colonial times. Advocates of Manifest Destiny were in full voice by the War of 1812, and though they lacked the label, they understood its implications well enough. The events of the 1840s, then, were more a continuation of a trend that stemmed from the earliest days of American settlement and existed as a constant force over the entire span of the Early Republic.

A better understanding of this important aspect of the period is crucial to comprehending how the American political system functioned under the stresses imposed by expansionism and why such stresses ultimately disrupted politics, leading to civil war. This book will explain the origins of territorial expansion and trace the course of Manifest Destiny to its culminating moment, the conquest of Mexico and the acquisition of the western territories. It will also weigh major historical interpretations of Manifest Destiny as they have evolved over the years, spanning from those that praise expansionism as an expression of American altruism to recent ones that condemn it as imperialistic and racist.

The book begins with a chronology that starts at the land ordinances of the 1780s and includes major diplomatic, military, and political events for each year through 1850, the year that the first part of the Mexican Cession was admitted to the Union.

Seven essays follow that analyze chronologically and topically various aspects of American expansionism. The first serves as a starting point for the more detailed analyses of succeeding essays by providing an overview of American expansion, including its causes and consequences from colonial times to 1848. It also examines the view held by many white Americans in the first half of the nineteenth century that their "manifest destiny" was to extend their influence to the Pacific Ocean and evaluates the range of historical interpretations that have sought to explain this phenomenon.

Chapter 2 describes the evolution of U.S. land policy and analyzes how the War of 1812 fueled American expansionism. When the postwar land rush transformed the frontier into what would become the South's cotton belt and the Midwest's wheat belt, such changes only whetted the appetite of American expansionists to protect what they had already acquired and also to set their eyes on additional lands to sustain the postwar economic boom.

Chapter 3 describes the 1818 invasion of Spanish Florida by Major General Andrew Jackson. Dispatched to "discipline" marauding Indians, Jackson instead evicted Spanish military garrisons from St. Marks and Pensacola, thus violating orders from the U.S. government, and established U.S. control over the western regions of Florida. This essay analyzes the international crisis Jackson triggered and explains why in the aftermath Spain not only conceded its ownership of Florida but also accepted a treaty that delineated United States and Spanish territory to the Pacific Ocean. The Transcontinental Treaty, or Adams-Onís Treaty, set the stage for U.S. claims in the Pacific Northwest, but the final resolution of those claims would not occur until America's Manifest Destiny would compel the resolution of the Oregon question in the 1840s.

Chapter 4 considers how white encroachment on Indian lands led to increasing pressure on the national government to remove Indians from all lands east of the Mississippi River. The result was the adoption of a sweeping Indian Removal Act, renewed Indian conflict in the 1830s and in the case of the Seminoles, the most protracted Indian war in United States history. Having accomplished Indian removal, white Americans began gazing at lands west of the Great River and cultivating the idea that an obvious fate had decreed they should own them.

Chapter 5 explains why the Mexican government began inviting United States citizens to settle in Texas to establish a buffer between hostile Native Americans and the more populated parts of Mexico. It was an ill-conceived plan, however, for the growing American presence in Texas led to a rising desire to separate from Mexico. This chapter traces those events and concludes with Texas's revolution for independence and its eventual annexation by the United States.

Chapter 6 illustrates how the United States established a serious claim to the Pacific Northwest. American explorations beginning with the voyage of the *Columbia,* the subsequent journey of Lewis and Clark (1804–1806), and the establishment of fur-trading posts on the Columbia River placed American interests in the region. Diplomacy by way of the Rush-Bagot Agreement of 1817 and the Transcontinental Treaty of 1819 further advanced the United States as a contender for this potentially vast region. It was precisely the size of the American claim, however, that caused a serious disagreement with Great Britain in the 1840s. This essay examines the Oregon question and how the burgeoning spirit of Manifest Destiny colliding with sectional tensions over slavery nearly hurled President James K. Polk's administration into war with Great Britain.

Chapter 7 traces how President Polk's determination to acquire California ports from Mexico led first to American purchase offers and then American threats of war to take them. This essay considers the ensuing Mexican-American War and how U.S. victory realized the view of many Americans that it was their destiny to expand to the Pacific. In addition, the essay concludes with an examination of how disagreements over the war and its results would prove deeply troubling. The status of slavery in newly acquired territories came to dominate national discussion and finally sparked the most cataclysmic event in United States history—the American Civil War.

Following the essays are brief biographies of ten people pertinent to the subject of American expansion. We have included primary documents with accompanying explanations that supply historical background. A glossary lists military, political, and social usage made cryptic because of its arcane nature or its peculiarity to the period. An annotated bibliography subdivided into categories covering general histories, military topics, biographies, diplomacy, diaries and letters, Native Americans, politics, agriculture, slavery, and films/electronic media, provides a broad overview of the current literature on this subject. Finally, an index for easy reference to specific items in the text concludes the book.

We are grateful to Marsha and Linda Frey for the chance to contribute to this series and to Kevin Ohe of Greenwood Press for his encouragement and support. Several colleagues have read parts of the manuscript, and Dr. William J. Astore read it all. We are indebted for their helpful suggestions, every one of which marked an improvement.

CHRONOLOGY

May 20, 1785	Confederation Congress enacts an ordinance "for ascertaining the mode of disposing of the lands in the Western territory," a scientific method of surveying trackless wilderness and laying out boundaries.
July 13, 1787	Another Confederation Ordinance provides for representative government in the area northwest of the Ohio River and sets the procedure for admitting designated territories to the Union as co-equal states.
May 11, 1792	American merchant sea captain Robert Gray discovers the Columbia River in the Pacific Northwest.
April 30, 1803	The Louisiana Purchase doubles U.S. holdings in North America.
1804–1806	To explore the northern reaches of the Louisiana Purchase, Meriwether Lewis and William Clark lead an expedition to the Pacific Coast gathering information about the terrain and its inhabitants.
1805–1807	An expedition led by Zebulon Pike explores the Southwest, including the front range of the Rocky Mountains.

1806	The conspiracy led by Aaron Burr allegedly aims to conquer Spanish territory west of the Mississippi, and possibly includes a plan to separate Louisiana from the Union, but it collapses upon Burr's arrest.
1811	Georgia filibusterers wage the abortive "Patriot War" in Spanish and East Florida with tacit approval of the United States government but abandon the venture as the prospect of war with great Britain forces the Madison administration to withdraw its support.
1811	The Cumberland Road is begun, speeding settlement of the Ohio and Upper Mississippi valleys. By 1852 it stretches to Vandalia, Illinois.
1811	Americans seize part of West Florida with tacit government sanction.
March 1811	John Jacob Astor's Pacific Fur Company establishes Astoria on the southern bank of the Columbia River; an overland expedition will arrive the following year.
April 30, 1812	Louisiana admitted to the Union.
June 1812–Feb. 1815	The War of 1812 fails to promote American expansionism in either Canada or Florida but does establish U.S. dominance over northwestern and southeastern Indians.
April 15, 1813	U.S. forces occupy Spanish Mobile.
December 24, 1814	Envoys sign the Treaty of Ghent, ending the War of 1812 and returning all property seized during the war to its original owners.
December 11, 1816	Indiana admitted to the Union.
July 4, 1817	The Erie Canal is begun, and by 1825 it will link New York City to Buffalo.
December 10, 1817	Mississippi admitted to the Union.

March–May 1818	Andrew Jackson invades Spanish Florida and captures weak garrisons at St. Marks and Pensacola.
October 20, 1818	Negotiations between the United States and Great Britain result in a treaty for joint tenancy in the Oregon Country.
December 3, 1818	Illinois admitted to the Union.
February 22, 1819	The Adams-Onís Treaty is signed in Washington, D.C., providing for the cession of Florida and the establishment of the forty-second parallel as the border between Spain and the United States in the Pacific Northwest.
December 14, 1819	Alabama admitted to the Union.
1820	The Missouri controversy is settled by a compromise, but slavery will remain an unresolved problem regarding future western expansion.
1821	Mexico grants land in Texas to the Austin family.
February 22, 1821	The Adams-Onís Treaty is ratified by both the United States and Spain.
September 18, 1823	Treaty of Moultrie Creek relocates Seminoles to southern Florida.
February 12, 1825	Treaty of Indian Springs cedes a large area of Creek territory to the United States.
1827	Revisiting the Oregon question, the United States and Great Britain fail to reach a boundary agreement but extend the 1818 treaty indefinitely with the option to end its terms with one year's notice.
May 28, 1830	Indian Removal Act
September 28, 1830	Treaty of Dancing Rabbit Creek begins Choctaw removal.
December 12, 1830	The Cherokee Nation seeks an injunction against the state of Georgia that will result in

	Cherokee Nation v. *Georgia* that rules the Cherokees could not sue before the U.S. Supreme Court because they were not U.S. citizens.
1832	In *Worcester* v. *Georgia,* the Supreme Court rules that the Cherokee Nation is not subject to Georgia state law.
May 9, 1832	Treaty of Payne's Landing begins Seminole removal from Florida.
August 2, 1832	The Battle of Bad Axe ends the Black Hawk War.
October 20, 1832	Treaty of Pontotoc Creek begins Chickasaw removal.
December 29, 1835	Treaty of New Echota begins Cherokee removal.
December 29, 1835	The Dade Massacre begins the Second Seminole War.
March 2, 1836	Texas declares independence from Mexico.
March 6, 1836	Mexican forces overrun the Alamo after a thirteen-day siege.
March 27, 1836	Mexican forces massacre Texas revolutionaries at Goliad.
April 21, 1836	Battle of San Jacinto successfully concludes the Texas war of independence.
June 15, 1836	Arkansas admitted to the Union.
January 16, 1837	Michigan admitted to the Union.
March 1837	United States recognizes the Texas Republic.
November 1844	Expansionist Democrat James K. Polk defeats Whig nominee Henry Clay for the presidency.
March 1, 1845	Congress passes a joint resolution annexing Texas, which President John Tyler signs just before leaving office.
March 3, 1845	Florida admitted to the Union.
December 29, 1845	Texas admitted to the Union.

April 26, 1846	Congress authorizes President Polk to advise Britain of the one-year notice for ending the 1827 convention regarding Oregon.
May 8, 1846	Battle of Palo Alto
May 9, 1846	Battle of Resaca de la Palma
May 13, 1846	United States declares war on Mexico.
June 15, 1846	The United States and Great Britain sign the Oregon Treaty, establishing the boundary at the forty-ninth parallel; the Senate ratifies the treaty three days later.
August 8, 1846	The Wilmot Proviso, which seeks to ban slavery from any territory acquired from Mexico, is introduced in the House of Representatives.
September 21–23, 1846	Battle of Monterrey
December 28, 1846	Iowa admitted to the Union.
February 22–23, 1847	Zachary Taylor defeats Mexican forces at the Battle of Buena Vista.
September 13, 1847	Battle of Chapultepec
February 2, 1848	The Treaty of Guadalupe Hidalgo is signed, ending the Mexican War; the Senate ratifies it on March 10, 1848.
May 29, 1848	Wisconsin admitted to the Union.
September 9, 1850	California admitted to the Union.

CHAPTER 1

HISTORICAL OVERVIEW

In the fifth decade of the nineteenth century, the United States embarked on expansionist enterprises that extended the country to the forty-ninth parallel in the Pacific Northwest, to the border of Mexico in the southwest, and to the Pacific Ocean. Fewer than seventy-five years after declaring its independence from Great Britain, the American republic had transformed itself from a motley collection of thinly populated colonies into a vigorous and proud country. That transformation partly occurred because of rapid westward expansion stretching first to the Mississippi River, then to the Rockies, and finally to the Pacific.

Some Americans, marveling over this spectacular achievement, both encouraged and proclaimed it as an obvious event. It was, they said, the predictable result of unparalleled liberty and was fated by God for a special people as they multiplied and prospered. Other Americans were not so sure. They decried the expansion as an enormous mistake and predicted it would have an extravagant price. It is a testament to the vagaries of the American experience that both sides were right: the realization of this manifest destiny was a stunning triumph; the consequences of realizing it would be appalling.

Roots of Manifest Destiny (1607–1815)

Material growth, increasing population, and spreading settlement were part of the American story from the start. The English colonists who came to North America during the seventeenth and eighteenth centuries were a restless people. Whether starting in the marshes of Jamestown or on the rocky coasts of New England, they had no sooner set down homesteads than they were casting their eyes westward, planning ways for today's frontier to become tomorrow's farm. A southern colony such as Virginia expanded because planting tobacco quickly exhausted the soil and compelled settlers westward to tap the fertility of new lands. From the Chesapeake region, rivers became languid avenues of access to this first "West," which was really only the interior just beyond the sea-scent of the Atlantic. Meanwhile New Englanders, driven to American shores to escape religious persecution, migrated in a more systematic fashion to meet a growing population's need for farmland or to continue habits of dissent by breaking away to found new colonies. Though the reasons for this incessant restiveness differed for different regions, the result was invariably the same. The habit of moving toward the western horizon became a fixed constant in the American chronicle.

Foreshadows: Indian Conflicts

Another constant of this restless urge was conflict with native peoples in North America. Problems broke out in the Virginia Colony within three years of its 1607 founding, and New England Puritans in Massachusetts Bay Colony would echo the tragic tale.

In 1622, just fifteen years after Jamestown's founding in Virginia, Indians launched a series of attacks to stop the growing and increasingly intrusive English presence. The colony's retort was continuous war to eliminate the Indians. Intermittent reprisals steadily diminished Indian numbers, and they eventually retreated to the interior. Yet, as they and their descendants would discover, they could never move far enough away. In fact, following a second war in 1644, a 1646 treaty essentially expelled the Indians from the Chesapeake region, a deed that anticipated the Indian removal policy of two centuries later.

In New England, the Pilgrims arrived in 1620 to find that the Indians of the coastal region had been ravaged by a mysterious illness. By some estimates, the plague killed as much as 80 percent of their population. Suffering from such diminished numbers, the Wampanoag Indians initially helped white settlers because they were too weak to resist them, but as in Virginia, the increasing white presence eventually sparked quarrels. When war broke out in 1637, white settlers waged it with a brutal ferocity that intimidated the Indians for almost forty years. In 1675, however, a Wampanoag chieftain named Metacom, known to the English as King Philip, led an intertribal coalition that left a dozen Puritan settlements in ruins and put more than fifty on the frontier under siege. A flood of white refugees streamed into Boston, but the initial Indian success united the colonists to pursue counterattacks of extraordinary savagery. At the end of the year-long war, colonists had multiplied Indian casualties beyond their own and ended by killing King Philip, mutilating his body and displaying his severed head on a pike in Plymouth for years.[1]

The conflicts in these two regions established the pattern wherein Indians fell victim to the twin white weapons of disease and organized, systematic warfare. Whether in Virginia or New England or the other colonies that came in their wake, when Indians blocked access to land, whites either killed them or shoved them out of the way.

Foreshadows: Victory and Ruin

English colonization of North America continued into the early eighteenth century, concluding with the establishment of Georgia in 1733. In every instance, colonial charters asserted English ownership of all territory to the west, theoretically to the Pacific Ocean. In addition to the resistance of native inhabitants, however, Britain found other European powers vying for portions of North America as well. Starting in 1688 and continuing with brief interruptions through the mid-1700s, no fewer than four wars shook both Europe and the colonies. The last struggle broke out when France moved south from Canada to claim the Mississippi River and challenge British power in the Ohio Valley. Known as the French and Indian War (in America) and the Seven Years' War (in Europe), this local contest rapidly expanded into a world war that one historian has aptly dubbed the Great War for Empire.[2] It ended in a British victory that was nothing short of stupendous. With the Treaty of Paris in 1763, King George III doubled his North American possessions by acquiring all of French Canada. As it happened, however, the vast scope of this triumph proved a mixed blessing.

King George III's attempts to organize and finance his newly expanded empire were in large part responsible for the policies of taxation and commercial control that increasingly alienated his thirteen original North American colonies. When those colonies banded together to resist British policy, the result was heightened tensions that finally erupted into the American Revolution.

In this way, these events established another pattern that would trouble territorial expansion. In the case of the British colonies, the drive to the west was accomplished by population surges working in concert with occasional military operations. The same formula propelled American expansion in the nineteenth century. Yet, the scope of Britain's great victory held the very seeds of imperial ruin in North America. Similarly, American progress to the Pacific Coast aggravated the political discord over slavery that divided the American people and ended in civil war.

The Expanding American Republic

The American Revolution was more than the war that gained the colonies their independence and established the United States as a republic. It was also the logical result of a fermenting freedom born when English settlements were first established in the New World. The first generation of people who settled those colonies did so because of their displeasure with the ways of the Old World. In Europe, many of them had been socially outcast, politically disenfranchised, economically deprived, or religiously oppressed. Their descendants did not lose the defiance that balked at social inequality and challenged political discrimination; instead, they became independent in mind long before they were willing to assert their sovereignty with guns and governments. In fact, that mental independence was necessary before they could seek that sovereignty.

While English colonists secured a level of self-government unmatched by any other European colonies, America's isolated wilderness further encouraged an independent spirit; everything about the frontier was extraordinary and demanding. The strain of pioneering cultivated vigor and poise, courage and self-sufficiency. The same fortitude that fueled America's revolutionary fervor continued to draw its citizens westward even while they were fighting the British.

The Land: Problems and Solutions

As Americans moved westward, state governments asserted their expansive territorial claims inherited from colonial charters. States that had no territory west of the Allegheny Mountains—Vermont, New Hampshire, New Jersey, Delaware, Maryland, and Pennsylvania—blocked the formation of a national government until the other states ceded their vast western claims to the common ownership (or public domain). The first quarrel over western territory would not be the last, but it had a happy resolution. In two innovative legislative enactments, Congress promised to distribute the new public domain for the benefit of all the states and establish new states in it that could become equal members of the Union.

The donation of these public lands by Massachusetts, Virginia, New York, Connecticut, North Carolina, and Georgia removed potentially serious boundary disputes among the landed states. It also helped to cement the existing bonds of the new republic while launching an intelligent way to extend it. As pioneers continued to move westward, their growing numbers necessitated an innovative land policy. Its creation challenged the ingenuity of the republic's founders.

Simply put, the same problem that had baffled George III and his government before the Revolution now troubled the new United States. How did one resolve the thorny riddle of governing a colonial establishment (such as the pioneer settlement in the wilderness) without stifling its autonomy, provoking its rebellion, and risking its separation?

In 1785, the Confederation Congress passed an ordinance to survey the nation's vast western wilderness. Once mapped, an orderly system of townships in ranges[3] would be auctioned and opened to settlement. Two years later, another ordinance established a systematic procedure for setting up local governments in these territories. The Ordinance of 1787, sometimes called the Northwest Ordinance, placed territories under the initial control of Congress and its agents. Subsequently, a territorial legislature elected by the territory's inhabitants would enact local law subject to review by Congress. This arrangement closely emulated the relationship between colonial legislatures and the British Parliament, but the brilliance of the American plan lay in its culmination. When a territory filled with 60,000 inhabitants, it could apply for statehood. After meeting the minimal requirements of establishing a republican government, it would gain admission to the Union on the same footing as the original states.

By limiting the time of territorial status, the procedure averted the possibility that pioneer settlements would mount another American war of independence pitting the West against the East. The system was not perfect, however. The slow pace of surveyors could not always keep up with the rapid advance of settlers, and pricing and procedural details of land sales would require numerous revisions. In addition, when increasingly unmanageable arguments over slavery began to jam the machinery of government, the policy governing the admission of western territories would accordingly suffer.

The Louisiana Purchase

In 1803, Thomas Jefferson acquired the huge North American heartland, the trans-Mississippi River region collectively known as Louisiana. The circumstances leading up to the Louisiana Purchase were in themselves complicated and merit explanation to illustrate this first occurrence of American expansion.

At the close of the American Revolution, Great Britain and France ceded to Spain lands bordering the United States' western and southern border. Spain had lost Florida to Britain at the close of the Great War for Empire in 1763, but after the Revolution, Britain regarded the peninsula as hard to defend and of little value. A similar situation existed for Louisiana's owner, France, whose interests in a North American Empire had waned after losing Canada in 1763. While of relatively little importance to France and England, the assignment of Florida and Louisiana to Spain was of great consequence for both Spaniards and Americans. For the Spanish king, it made his imperial possessions in the Caribbean and western North America seem more secure by providing a large frontier buffer between them and the upstart United States. On the other side, the United States now had a feeble neighbor to its west and south, for Spain was a fading empire soon to be racked by its own colonial rebellions.

This situation threatened to change in 1800, however, when the French emperor Napoleon Bonaparte laid plans to recreate a New World empire for France. He began by persuading Spain to transfer Louisiana back to France. French ownership of Louisiana would give Napoleon not only much of the North American interior but most importantly control of the Mississippi River's gateway to the gulf at New Orleans. Before this transfer went into effect, in fact, Spanish authorities removed the American right of deposit at New Orleans, an important commercial privilege granted by a treaty with Spain in 1795.

This closing of New Orleans to American commerce revealed how much American westward migration had swelled after the Revolution. Because the mushrooming numbers of American farmers on this west-

Map 1.1
U.S. Expansion, 1783–1848

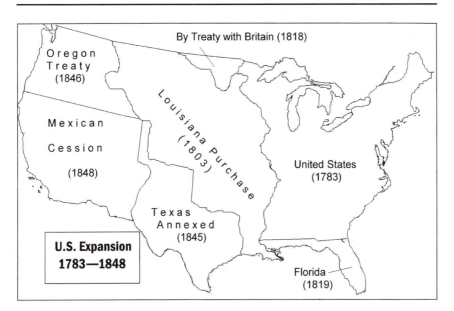

ern frontier relied on the Mississippi River to transport their produce to markets, closing off New Orleans promised to strangle their livelihoods. Their reaction was rapid, loud, and violent, including the pledge to reopen New Orleans, even if it meant war between the United States and Spain, and possibly France.

Thomas Jefferson, in spite of his commitment to peace and preference for isolationism, realized the perils of French ownership of Louisiana. Napoleon would not be a weak neighbor. If the United States had to fight France, it needed stronger allies, such as Britain, and such an arrangement would have been most distasteful to Jefferson. Nonetheless, he anxiously remarked, "The day that France takes possession of New Orleans, we must marry ourselves to the British fleet and nation."[4]

The western uproar spurred Jefferson to decisive diplomatic action. He sent envoys to Napoleon to attempt to purchase New Orleans at the least. When Napoleon abruptly abandoned his plans for empire in the western hemisphere—a slave revolt in the French Caribbean island of Santo Domingo proved impossible to suppress—instead electing to revive his war with Britain, he sold the whole of Louisiana to the United States on April 30, 1803.

The Louisiana Purchase was an event of immense historic significance for the United States. Without shedding a drop of blood, the new nation laid claim to the entire expanse of the most fertile river valley in the world, dubbed by Jefferson the "Valley of Democracy" that ensured the spread of his "Empire of Liberty." (See Map 1.1.) Aside from the constitutional questions the purchase raised—Jefferson himself was troubled that the president did not explicitly possess the authority for such a major exploit—it established a diplomatic model for obtaining foreign territory and also legitimated the American people's urge to expand their borders and extend their dominion. The immediate dispatch of an exploratory party under Meriwether Lewis and William Clark furnished a greater knowledge of the region that in part showed the practicality of overland migration to the Pacific Northwest. In the years to come, a slow trickle of pioneers became a steady stream that surged over the Oregon Trail, strengthening the United States claim to that far country. In 1805–1807, an expedition led by Zebulon Pike likewise probed the southern regions of the Louisiana Purchase and laid the foundations for American travel over the Santa Fe Trail into the arid Southwest.

The War of 1812: A Quest for Canada and Florida?

Jefferson's purpose for purchasing Louisiana was to isolate the United States from European problems, especially a disagreement with France that would have compelled an Anglo-American alliance. Yet, less than two years after the purchase, Americans found themselves drawn into the titanic final phase of the Napoleonic Wars, the contest that pitted England and its allies against the seemingly invincible French Empire. As the British Royal Navy waylaid American shipping, the final act of that struggle saw the United States declare war against Great Britain in 1812, stating its reason as the need to resist impressment and to protect neutral rights on the high seas. Paradoxically, the United States proceeded to mount a series of campaigns that mostly focused on invading British Canada, a fact that immediately raised questions about actual American motives for waging this fight. Was the claim of protecting neutral rights in fact only a veil to disguise a plan to acquire additional territory by force of arms?

Most historians agree that the War of 1812 was not caused by expansionism but instead reflected a real concern of American patriots to defend the United States' neutral rights from the overbearing tyranny of the British navy. That is not to say that expansionist gains would not potentially result from the war. Jefferson himself remarked that conquering Canada would be a "mere matter of marching," and the United States in April 1813 swiftly occupied Spanish Mobile on the Gulf of Mexico to keep it out of British hands.[5] Late in the war, redoubtable General Andrew Jackson invaded Spanish Florida when it appeared that Britain had breached the province's neutrality.

The War of 1812, however, did not offer a realistic opportunity for extending the American empire of liberty. Instead, U.S. military forces struggled from the outset, failing repeatedly to invade Canada and finally having to stave off a major British invasion in New York. In the South, Jackson's foray into Florida was preemptive rather than acquisitive, especially when he was forced to defend New Orleans from a major British assault. Finally, in 1815, the treaty ending the war reestablished borders as they had existed before the conflict.

Preamble to Expansion (1815–35)

The United States emerged from its war with Britain brimming with enthusiasm, and that zeal accelerated western migration. The most notable achievements of the war resulted from William Henry Harrison's shattering of a northwestern Indian confederation and Andrew Jackson's crushing defeat of the Creek Indians in the South. These operations prepared the way for the government's policy of Indian removal in the 1820s and 1830s, but they immediately opened up extensive lands for settlement. The cutting of roads—such as the Cumberland Road that would span from Maryland to Illinois—eased travel into the Ohio Valley. In 1811, the year the Cumberland Road project started, steamboats began straining against the swift currents of western rivers, turning that natural network of one-way avenues into two-way streets.

Countless pioneers rapidly peopled western lands that speedily passed through territorial status to statehood. By 1819, nine additional states had joined the first thirteen, a burst of expansion fueled by cheap land on the frontier and its allure to immigrants from Europe. Tobacco and cotton's tendency to deplete soil fertility also pushed southerners westward, and efficient entrepreneurs worked the land sale system with expanded credit that enriched them (at least on paper) as it attracted homesteaders to the frontier.

While westward expansion fueled a major economic boom, it also began to alter the nature of American politics. The West became an important ally courted by the North and the South to decide presidential elections and influence important legislation. Less happily, the question of western statehood at last stumbled on slavery, an issue that soon posed insoluble political problems. The years after the War of 1812 would be dubbed "The Era of Good Feelings" because political consolidation and an apparent lack of controversy produced noteworthy harmony. Yet, beneath that wide accord lay abrasive frictions. The virtually complete domination by the Republican Party briefly veiled significant disagreements over a broad array of matters, but rancorous arguments soon emerged. The most troubling interwove national expansion and slavery. The most ignominious deprived Indians of their land.

Oregon and Florida

Expansion after the War of 1812 placed new tensions on American foreign policy and prolonged old conflicts with Indians. Under the leadership of Secretary of State John Quincy Adams, President James Monroe's administration negotiated an important treaty in 1818 with Great Britain that in part set the forty-ninth parallel as the United States-Canadian boundary from the Lake of the Woods to the Rocky Mountains. The agreement also established equal access to the Pacific Northwest for ten years, a region collectively known as the Oregon Country. Because the accord relinquished neither British nor American claims to the area, final resolution regarding its ownership would be postponed until the 1840s when the growing American population finally required a conclusive settlement for Oregon.

The fate of Spanish Florida, however, was resolved in the short term. Many Americans believed geography dictated that Florida would become part of the United States. From Thomas Jefferson's administration onward, the United States government insisted the Louisiana Purchase included at least West Florida (the panhandle). Spain disagreed, but torn by the European war, Madrid could do little when unwelcome American settlers hoisted the Stars and Stripes along the Perdido River in 1810. The following year, the Madison administration secretly endorsed an unsuccessful filibustering expedition into East Florida. In 1812, Congress sanctioned the seizure of West Florida, and once the war with Britain was underway, sent General James Wilkinson from New Orleans to take control of Mobile. Although Andrew Jackson briefly occupied West Florida's capital at Pensacola, he quickly withdrew to defend New Orleans.

The greater part of Florida remained under Spanish rule after the war, but not for long. As revolutions erupted in Spain's South American colonies, Madrid stripped Florida of soldiers, sending them south to suppress the rebellions and leaving only a shadow of Spanish power in the peninsula and panhandle. Meanwhile, fugitive slaves from Georgia and the Mississippi Territory sought refuge there, and American raiding parties plundered across the border both to reclaim them and loot Indian villages. The Florida Indians retaliated by marauding into Georgia, afterward retreating across the Spanish border. As the level of violence on this unstable frontier increased, the Monroe administration finally responded to the plaintive cries of settlers for action by sending General Andrew Jackson into Florida to punish the Indians there.

Although the government expressly told Jackson to stay clear of all Spanish posts in Florida, his 1818 invasion was both sweeping and inclusive. Ignoring his instructions, he captured Spanish garrisons first at St. Marks and then at Pensacola, where he raised the United States flag and established an American customs house.

The diplomatic uproar caused by Jackson's unauthorized actions embarrassed the Monroe administration and challenged the talents of Secretary of State Adams. Nonetheless, Adams successfully insisted that the country's response should be to remind Spain of its obligations under the Spanish-American treaty of 1795, especially its failure to restrain the Florida Indians. If Spain could not control Florida, Adams contended, it should be ceded to the United States.

Under such pressure and still coping with Latin American revolutions, Madrid gloomily agreed to the latter solution in the Transcontinental Treaty of 1819. Usually labeled the Adams-Onís Treaty, this agreement saw Spain not only ceding Florida to the United States, but also surrendering claims to the Oregon Country in exchange for the United States' surrender of similar claims to Texas.[6] By finally defining the Louisiana Purchase's border as running along the Rocky Mountains to the forty-second parallel and then west to the Pacific, the Adams-Onís Treaty not only separated the Pacific Northwest from New Spain, it also bolstered the American claim to the Oregon Country.

The Missouri Crisis

In the same year as the Adams-Onís Treaty, the Missouri territory requested admission to the Union and sparked the nation's first great political controversy over slavery. When New York congressman James Tallmadge introduced a measure that required Missouri's gradual elimination of slavery as a condition of its statehood, southerners raised violent opposition. In 1819, the United States consisted of eleven free and eleven slave states. Because Missouri's admission would tip that balance North or South, congressional debate over the issue became especially intense.

Finally in 1820, a compromise admitted Missouri as a slave state and Maine as a free state. Seeking to avoid the reemergence of this debate, Congress established the so-called Missouri Compromise Line of 36°30' as the northern limit of slavery in the Louisiana Purchase. The arrangement had few enthusiastic supporters but deeply disappointed only the extremists in both camps. Slavery, for the time being, was laid to rest as a political issue—or so the mainstream political establishment hoped.

The Monroe Doctrine

In the early 1820s, the United States confronted another troubling issue, but this one was of international origin. Old Europe seemed eager to suppress South American rebellions and restore Spain's colonial empire. Americans sympathized with the struggling South American republics, in part because the reinstatement of European colonization would endanger U.S. frontier borders. Secretary of State Adams had already challenged a Russian attempt to extend the tsar's influence in the Pacific Northwest, and rumors of South American intervention further alarmed the government.

Because their commercial interests were profiting from trade with Latin American republics, the British in 1823 proposed a united front against any European plan to restore Spanish authority there. The U.S. government chose instead to make an independent declaration in President James Monroe's 1823 annual message. The Monroe Doctrine put

Europe on notice that the United States would permit neither additional colonization nor interference in the Western Hemisphere.

Although this brash statement depended on the coincidental support of Britain's Royal Navy for potential enforcement, the Monroe Doctrine did put on record the belief that America considered itself the dominant power in its part of the world. In 1845, President James K. Polk would recall Monroe's sentiments, which, by then, had been woven into the larger fabric of Manifest Destiny.

Indian Removal

After the War of 1812, American numbers multiplied with remarkable speed. By 1830, natural increase and immigration more than tripled the country's population to nearly thirteen million. During that time, most of the land east of the Mississippi River had been carved into territories that were subsequently admitted as states. Scattered throughout this disappearing frontier, clusters of Indians numbering at least 125,000 remained on lands that white neighbors increasingly wanted.

By the mid-1820s, white pressure had persuaded the United States government that Indian removal was the only permanent solution. Among the many hardships this new policy imposed, the fate of Georgia's Cherokee Indians was among the most chilling. In spite of their efforts to accommodate and embrace white culture, the Cherokee were squeezed onto marginal land. Even then, when gold was discovered in the Cherokee nation, the Georgia state government began a systematic effort to establish jurisdiction over Cherokee lands. Cherokee legal efforts were rewarded with a meaningless victory in the U.S. Supreme Court.

In fact, President Andrew Jackson's administration rigorously urged removal under the rationale that it was necessary in part to protect eastern Indians from both cultural and physical devastation. Although Indian participation in removal was supposed to be voluntary, the 1830 Indian Removal Act resulted in a forced migration. More than a hundred thousand Indians were driven like cattle to the plains beyond the Mississippi. Countless numbers of them perished either on harsh journeys such as the Cherokee "Trail of Tears" or under the inhospitable conditions they encountered in the newly established Indian Territory (present-day Oklahoma). In 1836, the government set up the

Bureau of Indian Affairs to manage relations and protect Indian rights, but within fifteen years, the inexorable spread of whites and their insatiable land hunger was again altering government policy and undermining government promises.

Manifest Destiny (1836–48)

By the 1830s, a renewed vitality characterized American optimism, pushing citizens toward brasher ventures that resulted in another territorial surge, the most momentous one of American history. Central to that experience was the enduring role of the frontier, which in the early nineteenth century was still performing the same function it had in colonial times. Mastering a wilderness bred a peculiar American spirit that would make revolution rather than bow to external power. It would do the same again in the advancing West where new settlements, tied to no particular state and owing no particular section any allegiance, were more nationalistic than other parts of the Union. Their inhabitants were also adventurous, continually striding beyond U.S. borders to entangle their country in quarrels that ultimately resulted in annexation.

The Texas Revolution

As Indian removal consolidated U.S. territory, American settlements continued to stretch westward. Settlers in the Southwest technically expatriated themselves to take up residence in the Mexican province of Texas where events produced an unexpected turn in American expansionism. It began with a ragtag revolt.

Although the United States surrendered all claims to Texas in the Transcontinental Treaty of 1819, Americans entered and settled the region throughout the period. After winning independence from Spain in 1821, Mexico encouraged American migration to boost Texas's meager population by awarding land grants to Americans under the stipulation that they would become Roman Catholics and adopt the Spanish language. Emigrants from the United States, however, remained adamantly American. In due course, they grew resentful of Mexico's efforts to govern them.

By the mid-1830s, about thirty thousand Americans of various and occasionally colorful backgrounds lived in Texas, including adventurers, such as Andrew Jackson's friend Sam Houston, who could find a fight with little provocation. To many Texans' thinking, however, Mexico had provided plenty of provocation. When the Mexican government abolished slavery in 1830 and tried to ban additional American settlement, resident Texans openly disobeyed the emancipation order. Undeterred, new arrivals blithely brought their slaves with them. Ignoring the signs of smoldering discontent, Mexican president Antonio López de Santa Anna in 1835 announced that he would henceforth govern the province from Mexico City, by force if necessary.

Force was necessary immediately in early 1836. Under the Lone Star flag, Sam Houston gathered a motley army as Santa Anna and his lieutenants marched six thousand soldiers into Texas to annihilate the small garrison at the Alamo in San Antonio and massacre Americans after they had surrendered at Goliad. By then, Texas had declared its independence. Santa Anna's "victories" were to prove costly by delaying his advance and by stirring Texans to stern vengeance. At San Jacinto on April 21, 1836, Sam Houston's small force destroyed a part of the Mexican Army and captured Santa Anna, compelling him to recognize Texas's independence and the Rio Grande as its boundary.

Lone Star Republic

The Mexican government refused to recognize Texas independence, setting the stage for bitter recriminations that the United States had violated its own neutrality laws by allowing Americans to abet Texas revolutionaries. It mattered little to President Andrew Jackson that such accusations were true—he regarded the Mexican government with contempt—but Jackson nonetheless moved cautiously in the matter of Texas independence. To extend formal recognition to Texas would revive the slavery issue just as the 1836 presidential election drew near. Only after Jackson's heir apparent Martin Van Buren won election did Jackson formally recognize Texas, doing so on the eve of Van Buren's inauguration in 1837.

Recognition was one thing, but annexation was quite another. When Texas officially requested annexation in 1837, the slavery issue refused to lie still. Northern abolitionists saw a southern plot to extend slavery, contending that even the earliest settlers in Texas had deliberately migrated from the South to achieve that end. Yet, the character of Texan settlement was simply another phase in a typical pattern of westward advance, carried out by southerners because of their proximity rather than their politics. This did not alter the fact, however, that admitting Texas to the Union would add another slave state to the American republic, tipping the balance achieved by the Missouri Compromise.

There the matter remained for almost a decade in which Texans, regarding Mexico as a sworn enemy, tried to find friends wherever they could, including Britain and France. When Texas negotiated treaties with Belgium, the United Provinces, and France at the end of the 1830s and finally with Britain in 1840, a potential British alliance with the Lone Star Republic became a major source of anxiety for the United States.

Oregon

British interests also posed a problem in the Pacific Northwest. The Oregon Country stretched from the Rocky Mountains to the Pacific and from California to 54°40', an expanse so colossal that few could imagine it being populated in less than a hundred years. Yet, the small American settlements south of the Columbia River in the Willamette Valley began a rapid increase in the early 1840s. "Oregon Fever" beckoned mounting numbers from the East, and by the mid-1840s, about five thousand Americans had reached the region by way of the 2,000-mile Oregon Trail. The men, women, and children who survived the journey were robust specimens who gave their approximately seven hundred British rivals north of the Columbia pause. The growing American presence clearly presented a situation that neither the British nor the U.S. governments could ignore.

In one respect, diplomacy surrounding the Oregon question had been simplified by the removal of other claimants such as Spain and Russia and by the narrowing of the dispute between the United States and Great Britain to the land between the Columbia River and the forty-ninth parallel. Domestically, however, the Oregon question was anything but simple when arguments over slavery and posturing over national honor turned it into a complicated muddle. Expansionists who wanted both to annex Texas and to expand claims to Oregon all the way to 54°40' found themselves opposed by impassioned abolitionists who wanted to bar slavery in Texas from the Union. On the other hand, abolitionists wanted to secure a large free Oregon. As the two regions became strangely linked in the minds of shifting and diversely oriented coalitions, the presidential election of 1844 became embroiled in both of these complicated problems.

American desires for Texas and Oregon revealed the serious problems that arose because of Manifest Destiny. Arguments over these two regions were grave warnings that the United States was entering the concluding phase of the quarrel over slavery. The question of whether the American empire would be free or slave would have to be answered.

James K. Polk, Cautious Expansionist

Expansionist Democrats nominated James K. Polk for the presidency in 1844, and Polk's slim victory over Whig opponent Henry Clay was deemed by President John Tyler as a mandate for Texas annexation. This questionable interpretation of an election that had featured disagreements over many matters that had nothing to do with Texas stirred considerable controversy. Nonetheless, three days before Tyler left office, a joint congressional resolution authorized Tyler to invite Texas to join the Union. He did so just one day before Polk's inauguration.

Lame-duck Tyler's last act saved incoming President Polk from a messy domestic annexation fight, but it left him with a degenerating diplomatic situation. Mexicans were furious that the U.S. government laid claim to what they still regarded as their territory. Furthermore, Tyler had done nothing to resolve the smoldering crisis in the Oregon Country, newly invigorated by abolitionists who were angry over Texas annexation.

After gaining Texas, Southern Democrats were no longer so enthusiastic about obtaining "All Oregon," despite the fact that their 1844 platform had called for American claims of the territory to 54°40'. When Polk offered Britain a settlement of the boundary on the forty-ninth parallel, he was accused of abandoning 54°40' because he was a southerner, but actually the long-standing American position had always embraced forty-nine degrees. In addition, Polk's luck saw him through. After a few tense turns, British opponents of imperial expansion—the so-called "Little Englanders"—made it possible for their government itself to propose forty-nine degrees as the boundary. Understandably, a settlement on that basis was not universally popular, but by the time it was under debate in the Senate, matters with Mexico had deteriorated into a shooting war, and the country was less prepared to heed abolitionist charges about a southern betrayal of "All Oregon." When queried about Polk's apparent hypocrisy in compromising over Oregon while rattling a saber over Texas, expansionist Thomas Hart Benton blithely noted, "Great Britain is powerful and Mexico is weak."[7]

Polk as Aggressive Expansionist

Polk, like other believers in Manifest Destiny, excitedly regarded California's harbors as a prime prize for the growing republic. Pacific ports at San Francisco and San Diego would provide access to lucrative trade with Asia. California itself featured a peculiar mixture of ethnic diversity of Spanish-Mexicans, Indians, and Americans. The Indians were much in the majority, constituting about nine-tenths of the population, but they were disorganized and disconsolate. The American transplants on the other hand were beginning to see themselves much as Texans had before their break from Mexico. Polk wanted to purchase California from Mexico, but Texas annexation had poisoned Mexican-American affairs, prompting the Mexican government to pull its minister from Washington and cut off all diplomatic relations.

Disagreements over the southwestern boundary of Texas also encouraged friction with Mexico. Tradition had established that border as the Nueces River, but Texans insisted that it was the Rio Grande farther to the south. Polk embraced the Rio Grande claim, but he did not press the matter while any possibility remained of negotiating California's purchase from Mexico.

Evolving events, or at least American perceptions about them, would not let the matter rest, however. Disturbing rumors—which were only that—reported that the British were on the verge of acquiring California, and Polk quickly dusted off the dormant Monroe Doctrine while sending a new envoy to Mexico City. Although Polk was prepared to pay $25 million for California and the arid territory to its east, the Mexican government could not risk the popular disapproval of negotiating with an American emissary. On the slightest technicality, it refused to receive Polk's representative. Using this diplomatic rebuff as a reason for confrontation, Polk sent four thousand men under General Zachary Taylor into the disputed area between the Nueces River and the Rio Grande in January 1846. Polk clearly meant the move to be provocative, and when the Mexicans did not take the bait, he grew impatient. In the second week of May, the president told his advisers that he wanted a congressional declaration of war based on Mexico's refusal to pay U.S. claims and its diplomatic misbehavior.

When a report arrived from the Rio Grande that on April 25, 1846, Mexican soldiers had finally attacked Taylor's army, Polk decided he had something worthy of a war message. Yet, his communication to Congress was a study in cautious half-truths. He described American behavior as devoted to avoiding conflict with Mexico and insisted that an unprovoked Mexican attack had resulted in the spilling of "American blood on . . . American soil."[8] Questions regarding that soil's ownership were for the moment immaterial to Congress, which voted for war. Volunteers rushed to the colors, and for a time even antislavery Whigs united with southern Democrats in supporting the push to punish Mexican miscreants.

Such cooperation would not last, however. An example of growing Whig rancor was freshman congressman Abraham Lincoln, who repeatedly presented resolutions that called for the House to obtain from Polk an indication of the precise "spot" on American soil where Mexicans had attacked Taylor. Lincoln's persistence soon subjected him to Democrats' ridicule. Nevertheless, his position avoided that of extreme antislavery members of his party who assailed Polk as a liar and fell closer to that of moderate Whigs who gradually came to oppose the war on principle.[9]

Polk really had not wanted war. He had posed as provocateur to persuade Mexico to sell California, and when war resulted, he tried to limit its objectives. Perhaps that was the reason he unwisely consented to Santa Anna's offer to betray his country. Recently overthrown and in exile in Cuba, Santa Anna pledged that if he were allowed to slither into Mexico, he would immediately end hostilities on American terms. Polk should have known better, for Santa Anna was as unreliable about treachery as he was about treason. No sooner had he returned to Mexico than he put himself at the head of his fellow citizens and took to the field to resist the American invasion.

New Mexico and California

Meanwhile, American campaigns proceeded apace against the Mexican provinces of New Mexico and California. General Stephen W. Kearny led seventeen hundred soldiers by way of the Santa Fe Trail from Fort Leavenworth to seize Santa Fe with little effort. He planned to proceed to California, but before his arrival, California fell to internal American intrigue led by Captain John C. Frémont, the so-called Pathfinder of the West. Frémont led a small assemblage in what purported to be a spontaneous rebellion but was actually a collaborative effort including the U.S. Navy and local American residents. Together these Americans overwhelmed the nominal Mexican authority and, emulating their Texan brothers, raised the standard of the Bear flag signifying the Republic of California, and with a great deal less trouble for their efforts.

Campaigns in Mexico

As these events occurred, General Zachary Taylor invaded Mexico from across the Rio Grande and fought several successful battles before arriving at Buena Vista where, on February 22–23, 1847, a force of fifteen thousand Mexican soldiers under Santa Anna fell upon his relatively small army of about five thousand men. Taylor barely managed to hold off the formidable Mexican onslaught, but his performance nonetheless gained him a reputation as a bona fide military hero. Just as political observers had talked about Andrew Jackson after the Battle of New Orleans, they now began to discuss "Old Rough and Ready," as his troops called him, as a presidential candidate.

Two factors diminished Taylor's future effectiveness, however. Such talk about him as a political entity alarmed the ever-vigilant James K. Polk, who had no desire to create a future president in a successful military commander. Secondly, Taylor was a talented leader, but his force was not sizable, and the terrain he had to traverse to capture Mexico City was discouraging. Consequently, the main thrust of American strategy shifted to an expedition mounted from Vera Cruz. In late 1846, Polk appointed General Winfield Scott to lead this campaign across the steep mountains and trackless wastes of central Mexico.

In contrast to the casual Taylor, Scott's reliance on military ceremony and fastidious attention to detail had earned him the uncomplimentary nickname "Old Fuss and Feathers." His eccentricities aside, he possessed undistracted focus and an incisive military mind, and in the coming campaign he overcame insufficient troop strength, difficult terrain, chronic sickness in his army, infighting among his officers, and fickleness in Washington to fight his way to Mexico City. The march to the Mexican capital still ranks as one of the most spectacular achievements in modern military history.

The collapse of the Mexican government, however, complicated the war's conclusion. With no other authority available to treat for peace and eager to conclude the war, Scott approved an armistice with Santa Anna, whose cooperation was purchased with a $10,000 bribe. Santa Anna, however, proved just as faithless here as he had at the outset of the war. He took the bribe but merely used the cease-fire to prepare for resuming the fight. Scott finally canceled the armistice and captured the city in September 1847.

Santa Anna's deceit was one thing, but Polk, as distrustful of Scott as he was of Taylor, had dispatched the State Department's chief clerk Nicholas P. Trist to accompany the Scott expedition. Trist had two tasks: negotiate a peace treaty and keep an eye on Scott's possible political ambitions. Initially detesting one another, Scott and Trist unexpectedly became friends. When Polk learned that his target had apparently mesmerized his spy, he recalled Trist. By then, however, Scott had ended his unwise truce to threaten additional military action, and Trist signed the Treaty of Guadalupe Hidalgo on February 2, 1848. He promptly forwarded it to an enraged Polk. The president never forgave Trist, but he calmed down once he had reviewed the treaty's terms.

Manifest Destiny Realized

The Treaty of Guadalupe Hidalgo satisfied all of Polk's demands. It validated U.S. ownership of Texas and surrendered the Southwest to the Pacific Coast, thus ceding about half of Mexican territory to the American government. In exchange, the United States agreed to assume all claims against Mexico (which totaled $3,250,000) and pay to Mexico an additional $15 million for the territory. The arrangement was peculiar in that the United States won the war but nonetheless bore all of its expenses and disbursed additional money to its defeated foe. Polk doubtless calculated the terms a bargain, though, because he had planned to pay $25 million before the war. In any case, tangible domestic opposition to the war and its outcome, along with an unstable Mexican government, required that he not quibble over these awkward arrangements.

Swallowing his anger over Trist's disobedience, Polk sent the treaty to the Senate. Antislavery elements in Congress, especially Whigs in the House, had opposed the war from the start, and they were no happier about its conclusion. These "Conscience Whigs"—called such because of their opposition to slavery—also had sufficient numbers in the Senate to imperil a treaty vote there. Meanwhile, proponents of Manifest Destiny had gravitated to demanding the annexation of all Mexico, a prospect that alarmed both racists fearful of assimilating the Spanish-American-Indian population and those merely apprehensive about controlling such an expansive, alien land. During the ensuing debate, those who wanted all of Mexico and those who wanted none of it became odd allies in opposing the treaty. In the end, however, their combined numbers were not enough, and the Senate ratified the treaty by 38–14.

Legacy

The Oregon settlement and the Mexican-American War marked the end of an impressive journey of rapid expansion for the United States. As the nation approached the presidential election of 1848, it had stretched its dominion from the Atlantic to the Pacific and from the forty-ninth parallel to the Rio Grande. Yet, even as James K. Polk effectively concluded one phase of the American journey, his legacy irreversibly embarked the country on another. Even before the campaigns in Mexico were underway, Manifest Destiny was again casting long shadows as Congress and country renewed with greater fervor the argument over freedom and slavery.

Just months after the declaration of war in 1846, Pennsylvania congressman David Wilmot introduced a measure that would have forever banned slavery in any territory acquired from Mexico. Southerners reacted as violently as they had over the Missouri debates a quarter century earlier, and although their numbers in the Senate stopped the Wilmot Proviso, it came to embody a growing sentiment in the North. Antislavery attitudes became so unyielding, in fact, that subsequent expansionist efforts, especially focusing on Cuba, became impossible. As the country tried to assimilate and organize a territorial addition comparable in scope to the Louisiana Purchase, arguments over slavery spiraled out of control and finally resulted in southern secession and the Civil War. Realizing the destiny that had stretched the country from one coast to the other came at an awful price.

Meanings

The very label "Manifest Destiny" has inspired considerable debate among historians, both as to its origins and its meaning. The

phrase almost certainly first appeared in 1845 in the writings of journalist and lawyer John L. O'Sullivan as he argued for Texas annexation
and a hard line with Britain over Oregon.[10] Yet, the question persists
about why both the phrase and the sentiment it represented appeared at
just that moment.

One of most enduring explanations of U.S. history is the Turner thesis, proposed in 1893 by historian Frederick Jackson Turner in his essay,
"The Significance of the Frontier in American History." Turner believed
that the rigors of the westward movement and the frontier it consumed
forged the unique American character. As trailblazers strode into the
western wilderness, the frontier changed them into rugged and resource-
ful Americans. From that perspective, Manifest Destiny was a natural off-
shoot of the singular American habit of taming and populating frontiers.
Yet, New Western historians have pointedly disputed the Turner thesis,
especially its claim that Americans tamed the western wilderness and
were transformed by the experience. Instead, they underscore how American pioneers, the U.S. government, and powerful economic interests
conquered the West by overpowering native peoples and Hispanic fore-
runners.[11] These historians also argue that the Turner thesis overempha-
sizes the West's role in creating American national identity and ignores
how the interaction of cultures, rather than the environment, worked to
produce a unique regional character of broad diversity.

Nobody can argue, however, that westward expansion is not key
to a proper understanding of U.S. history, and because arguments over
slavery became such an obvious consequence of Manifest Destiny, it
was easy to deduce that slavery had caused it. Contemporary antislavery opponents of expansion saw a dark conspiracy of slaveholders
behind the high-flown rhetoric of expansion.[12] At the close of the nineteenth century, historian James Ford Rhodes embraced this view in his
seven-volume history of the United States.[13] Yet, subsequent students of
the period would rightly challenge the notion of a southern proslavery
conspiracy. As evidence, they pointed to the South's lack of unity for
expansion or underscored the West's hunger for land and New
England's desire for commercial opportunities.[14]

Was Manifest Destiny, then, a genuine ideological movement?
Albert K. Weinberg took expansionists at their word and concluded
that it was. Expansionists were not only motivated by a desire to spread
democracy and liberty, they also believed that their ideals were the

exclusive property of Anglo-Saxon Protestants.[15] Yet, some interpretations say the great torrent of words promoting Manifest Destiny was just that—a great torrent of words. In this view, expansionist writers and politicians did little to influence or direct the hardheaded and resolute government policies that strove to acquire Oregon with diplomacy and California with war.[16]

From another perspective, evolving concepts of racial uniqueness clearly figured into the rhetoric and meaning of Manifest Destiny. Reginald Horsman has shown that assigning hierarchies according to racial identity existed as early as the eighteenth century. By the mid-1800s, both science and philosophy categorized the different races almost as different species. Americans were adhering to historical trends when they justified expansion with claims of Anglo-Saxon racial superiority. Believing that indigenous people (Indians or blacks) or inhabitants of neighboring countries (Mexicans) were fated by the natural order for subjugation, Americans without guilt could justify perpetuating slavery, acquiring land for agricultural increase, and securing markets for commercial growth. Manifest Destiny could thus validate the interests of empire without acknowledging the corruption of imperialism.[17]

Such diversity of interpretation attests to the vague and changing contours of our understanding of Manifest Destiny when we view it from a single perspective and then a variety of perspectives. In the simplest assessment, Manifest Destiny was conceivably an American version of an age-old chronicle, another chapter in the human story of migrations and conquests spurred by natural urges for change and acquisition, "a repetition . . . of the old frontier process of state making . . . through migration and compact."[18] As one historian has recently mused, "Perhaps it had to happen the way it did."[19]

Notes

1. Jill Lepore has persuasively argued that American perceptions of King Philip's War set the pattern for hostility between white and Indian cultures and contributed to the drive for Indian removal more than two centuries later. See Lepore, *The Name of War: King Philip's War and the Origins of American Identity* (New York: Knopf, 1998).

2. Lawrence Henry Gipson, *The Great War for the Empire: The Years of Defeat, 1754–1757* (New York: Knopf, 1956); *The Great War for the Empire: The Culmination, 1760–1763* (New York: Knopf, 1966). The most recent analysis of

the conflict that focuses on the American setting is Fred Anderson's superb study, *Crucible of War: The Seven Years' War and the Fate of Empire in British North America, 1754–1766* (New York: Knopf, 2000).

3. See glossary for the technical definition of "range" in surveying.

4. Quoted in Dumas Malone, *Jefferson the President, First Term, 1801–1805*, vol. 4 of *Jefferson and His Time*, 6 vols. (Boston: Little, Brown and Company, 1970), 256.

5. Quoted in Malone, *The Sage of Monticello*, vol. 6 of *Jefferson and His Time*, 6 vols. (Boston: Little, Brown and Company, 1981), 109.

6. When Mexico gained its independence from Spain in 1821, American concessions became meaningless for Madrid but increasingly important for Mexico City.

7. Thomas Hart Benton, *Thirty Years' View*, 2 vols. (New York: Appleton, 1854–1856), 2:610.

8. James D. Richardson, comp., *A Compilation of the Messages and Papers of the Presidents, 1789–1908*, 20 vols. (Washington: Bureau of National Literature and Art, 1908), 4:442.

9. See David Herbert Donald, *Lincoln,* (New York: Simon & Schuster, 1995), 123–26.

10. Julius W. Pratt, "The Origin of 'Manifest Destiny'," *American Historical Review* 32 (July 1927): 795–98; and "John L. O'Sullivan and Manifest Destiny," *New York History* 14 (July 1933): 213–34.

11. Patricia Nelson Limerick, Donald Worster, and Richard White are typical representatives of the New Western history.

12. See abolitionist Theodore Parker's *The Slave Power* (Boston: American Unitary Association, 1916).

13. Rhodes, *History of the United States from the Compromise of 1850*, vol. 1 (New York: Harper & Row, 1892–1922).

14. Chauncey W. Boucher, "In Re That Aggressive Slavocracy," *The Mississippi Valley History Review* 8 (June–September 1921): 13–17; Frederick Merk, *Manifest Destiny and Mission in American History* (New York: Knopf, 1963); Norman Graebner, *Empire on the Pacific* (1955; reprint, Claremont, CA: Regina, 1989).

15. Weinberg, *Manifest Destiny: A Study of Nationalist Expansion in American History* (Baltimore: Johns Hopkins University Press, 1955).

16. See Merk, *Manifest Destiny*, and Graebner, *Empire on the Pacific*.

17. Horsman, *Race and Manifest Destiny: The Origins of American Racial Anglo-Saxonism* (Cambridge, MA, and London: Harvard University Press, 1981). Also see Anders Stephanson, *Manifest Destiny: American Expansion and the Empire of Right* (New York: Hill and Wang, 1995).

18. Merk, *Manifest Destiny*, 22.

19. Stephanson, *Manifest Destiny*, xiv.

CHAPTER 2

PEOPLE ON THE LAND:
POLICY, WAR, AND THE GREAT MIGRATIONS, 1784–1841

The large western land cessions of the seven states during the closing years of the American Revolution became the public domain, the most valuable, tangible asset the new and frail U.S. government possessed. Pioneers who trekked into this American wilderness were settling on public lands that belonged to the federal government and, by extension, to all the states of the Union in common. While policy was dedicated to promoting rapid and orderly settlement, it also was balanced against the government's need to sell lands to raise revenue. Thus from the outset, the process of transferring ownership of public lands to individuals while not sacrificing the nation's bounty required considerable ingenuity. Understandably, any policy would be at best a sequence of experiments aimed at correcting errors as they appeared.

The Evolution of U.S. Land Policy

The Ordinances of the 1780s

The first serious steps in formulating a land policy were undertaken at the close of the American Revolution. In 1784, Congress, then operating under the Articles of Confederation, enacted an ordinance drafted by Thomas Jefferson that called for the division of western lands into surveyed districts. These districts could apply for statehood upon reaching a population of 20,000. The ordinance of 1784 never took effect because its application was delayed until it was supplanted by other legislation, but it established the important principle of promoting systematic settlement and providing for self-government that could evolve into statehood.

Congress adopted a more permanent arrangement the following year in an ordinance "for ascertaining the mode of disposing of lands in the Western territory."[1] Passed on May 20, the Ordinance of 1785 set out a more elaborate and detailed method for organizing the western territories. As with Jefferson's plan, the process abandoned the age-old method of determining boundaries along characteristics of the terrain. Instead of relying on clumps of trees or shifting watercourses, the ordinance called for a methodical survey of the land to subdivide it into uniform squares starting with a six-square-mile township. Townships would be situated along parallels of latitude and meridians of longitude at right angles north, east, south, and west of a starting point called the baseline. Townships would be further subdivided into numbered 640-acre sections that, once registered with the Treasury Department, would be sold at public auction at a minimum price of one dollar per acre.

It was an appealing plan on paper. Public auctions were meant to assure the cash-strapped national government the highest land-sales revenue, and sales were to commence after the first seven ranges of townships had been surveyed. Problems, however, soon appeared; surveyors who plunged into the wilderness found the work slow and hazardous. In two years only four ranges of townships were surveyed, and the debt-ridden government was eager to reap the benefits of its only material asset. Consequently, four ranges (rather than the stipulated seven) went on sale immediately. Disappointing proceeds soon forced Congress to revise land policy with another ordinance.

The impetus for and substance of this change came from a group of New England investors who had established the Ohio Company of Associates. The sluggish land business made the idea of selling a sizable tract of the Northwest appealing to Congress, so members not only consented to sell a million acres to the company, they also adopted a measure that the Ohio Company had in large part drafted. Adopted on July 13, 1787, the Northwest Ordinance laid out a process for establishing local government north of the Ohio River. A governor, secretary, and three judges appointed by Congress would administer the territory until five thousand adult free males inhabited the area, when a representative assembly would convene to cooperate in conducting the territory's affairs and would send a delegate to Congress as a nonvoting member. When the population reached sixty thousand, the territory could apply for statehood. Because of the Northwest Territory's large area, the Ordinance of 1787 also provided for it eventually to form into at least three but not more than five states. The ordinance also reflected the moral sensibilities of its New England authors as well as the Revolutionary generation by establishing religious liberty and prohibiting slavery in the Northwest Territory, features that Jefferson had included in his 1784 draft.

The two ordinances had much to admire, for they outlined a fundamental and sound system to advance orderly settlement and reduce political disaffection. Yet, flaws remained in the details. Surveying was slow, expensive, and dangerous. Public auctions required a minimum of $640 to purchase the smallest plot of land, and sometimes more for valuable tracts. Payment was due immediately upon transaction, and the high prices under such terms dampened sales. The result was continuing concessions to land companies such as the Ohio Company and others, with distressing results for the federal treasury. Land companies could arrange purchases with complicated financing schemes, some of questionable legality. The Ohio Company's million-acre acquisition, for instance, was arranged so that the land went to the company for about eight cents an acre. Through the crafty manipulations of William Duer, secretary of the Board of the Treasury that oversaw land sales, the Scioto Company obtained five million acres with no intention of promoting settlement, but for the speculative purpose of profitable resale.

Land companies could bring about positive measures such as the Northwest Ordinance, and they wielded considerable political power— the Scioto Company included members of Congress—but they were frequently nests of special interest and corruption. In one respect, the Northwest Ordinance was a way for the East to exert extended control over the economic fortunes and political standing of the West, something that eventually was not lost on resentful frontier settlements. In the near term, the Northwest Ordinance's encouragement of speculation in huge amounts of acreage completely overthrew the aims of the Ordinance of 1785, which had been designed to encourage small farms and communities in a tidy process of advancing settlement. Land company purchases also cut into the government's anticipated revenues because they procured land at considerable discounts, sold it well below the government's minimum dollar-per-acre charge, and still realized significant profits. Finally, the speculative and sometimes shady dealings of the land companies made them risky and fragile. The Scioto

Company failed without making a single payment on its five-million-acre tract.

The Land Act of 1796

The new government established under the Constitution in 1789 inherited an increasingly muddled situation on the western frontier. Not only were public lands not performing as the cash cow everyone had expected, they were increasingly inhabited by squatters—settlers who simply cut clearings and built cabins on land they had no intention of purchasing. Part of the problem lay in the slow progress of surveying and registering land to bring it to auction, but squatters were not always the victims of a sluggish government bureaucracy. Many were simply following a tradition dating from colonial times that viewed land as belonging to the first person who claimed it and with no more formality than physically inhabiting it. Repeated efforts by the army to clear squatters off the land proved as effective as damming the ocean: once the soldiers disappeared, the squatters reappeared.

While this problem persisted throughout the period, the issues surrounding revenue were the pressing concern for the new government as it wrestled with a crippling national debt and impaired credit abroad. President George Washington's administration set itself to putting the nation's finances in order, including a revision of land policy. Several attempts to revise the system finally resulted in the passage of a new land law in 1796. Officially titled a law "for the Sale of Lands of the United States, in the territory northwest of the river Ohio, and above the mouth of the Kentucky river," the Land Act of 1796 revived the spirit of the Ordinance of 1785.[2] It again established the system of townships spanning an area of six square miles and divided into 640-acre sections, the smallest tract available for purchase. Public auctions would sell tracts to the highest bidder, starting at two dollars per acre. A 10 percent discount encouraged immediate payment of the entire sum, but purchasers had a year to pay. A surveyor general, appointed by the president, would organize teams to speed the work of mapping townships and bringing them to sale, both at a central land office and at local offices on the frontier.

The good intentions of this legislation, however, fell victim to the $1,280 necessary to buy the smallest tract, a sum beyond the means of most settlers. Rather than helping small farmers, the 1796 reform again promoted speculation by investors able to raise large quantities of cash.

As the nation's political structure reflected growing divisions over domestic and foreign policy by forming into opposing Federalist and Republican parties, the West increasingly caviled over the ruling Federalist policies and gravitated to the opposition Republicans. Both the intended results and the unintended consequences of the Land Act of 1796 increased Republican loyalty in the West.

The frontier finally lost patience with what it saw as persistent attempts by eastern Federalists to control western destiny under the guise of reform. In only four years, this western discontent compelled another revision of the land policy.

The Harrison Act of 1800

Under the provisions of the Ordinance of 1787, a census conducted in 1798 revealed that the population north of the Ohio River was more than sufficient to qualify the Northwest Territory for a territorial legislature. Although Federalist governor Arthur St. Clair administered the territory, the legislature that convened in December 1798 reflected the Republican leanings of the pioneer population and accordingly appointed one of their own, young William Henry Harrison, as the territory's delegate to the U.S. Congress. This contentious move, accomplished only by a close vote, placed Harrison in a position to help modify federal land policy from a purely western perspective.

Shortly after his arrival in the new national capital of Washington, D.C., Harrison began a campaign to liberalize the land laws governing the sale of public lands in the West. Under his plan, the government granted individuals generous credit to purchase small tracts at easily accessible federal land offices on the frontier. Harrison's advocacy coincided with the Republican campaign of 1800 that later delivered the presidency to Thomas Jefferson and a healthy congressional majority to the Republican Party. An immediate consequence was the passage on May 10, 1800, of a law that embodied many of the reforms that the West desired. Although the relatively high price of two dollars an acre was preserved from the Land Act of 1796, the 1800 act halved the minimum tract size to 320 acres and required the purchaser to place only one quarter of the price as a down payment.[3] The balance could be spread over the next four years. District land offices at Chillicothe, Cincinnati, Marietta, and Steubenville, Ohio, soon were doing a brisk business.

Under such provisions, the pioneer desirous of becoming a small farmer quickly replaced the speculator as the government's primary land purchaser in the Old Northwest. In 1804, Congress provided additional incentives to small farmers by further reducing the minimum plot for purchase to 160 acres.

The Jeffersonian Era

President Thomas Jefferson's Treasury Department, under Secretary Albert Gallatin, worked tirelessly to improve and streamline the process of land sales. For a dozen years, during Jefferson's two terms and James Madison's first term, Gallatin ran a complicated and growing enterprise that saw Congress passing additional laws and pioneer settlement accelerating, especially in the Northwest. When the Jefferson administration doubled the national expanse with the Louisiana Purchase in 1803, another set of complications arose. Aside from the sheer size of the Purchase, French and Spanish systems of property grants based on landmarks frustrated efforts to impose the orderly grid system in Louisiana, and land offices struggled for years to straighten these matters out. Nonetheless, the creation of district land offices and steady oversight by the Treasury sped surveys, leading to the creation of new territories, the admission of new states, and a marked increase in revenues. Money from land sales reached a record level in 1811 of $1.2 million. Before that year, Gallatin and his meager staff could barely keep pace with the workload, and the volume in 1811 became unmanageable. Finally, on April 25, 1812, Congress abandoned efforts to correct the problem by gradual increases in Gallatin's staff and instead established a General Land Office under a separately staffed bureau within the Treasury Department.

It was good for the country's economic health that land revenues increased so dramatically, because by 1807 foreign tensions were severely disrupting the American economy. The Embargo Act of that year virtually eliminated revenues from tariffs, and the Republican desire to work under balanced budgets and retire the debt suffered accordingly. President Madison inherited the unresolved problems of how to protect American trade in the face of the great clash between Britain and Napoleon's France, and finally in June 1812, he asked Congress to declare war against Britain. In spite of the considerable British provocations that led to this move, some Americans nevertheless raised questions about their country's motives for going to war. Many would insist, in fact, that the war had more to do with acquiring land than with protecting principles.

The War of 1812

The question of why the United States went to war with Britain in 1812 has stimulated an ongoing debate. As the Napoleonic Wars entered their final phase, American neutral trade suffered serious damage at the hands of French privateers and British warships. The British compounded their obnoxious activities with the policy of impressment, the forcible abduction of alleged Royal Navy deserters from American merchant ships. After years of trying to cope with this intolerable situation through diplomacy and economic sanctions, the United States declared war on Britain in June 1812. The strongest supporters of the war were the War Hawks, a congressional faction that had literally forced the issue of war on James Madison's administration. Conversely, the War Hawks were mainly westerners and southerners.

The averred issues of protecting free trade and sailors' rights would seem of little importance to citizens far removed from the consequences of England's brawl with Napoleon. Consequently, the question arose as to why it was almost exclusively westerners and southerners who clamored for war. The conclusion reached by some was that the war was not about protecting American trade and vindicating national honor at all. Instead, it afforded opportunities to extend U.S. territory at the expense of America's neighbors. The West wanted Canada. The South wanted Florida.

On the face of it, this assumption seems valid. Most historians, however, have concluded that support for the war derived from more complicated motives. We need to understand those motives and their consequences if we are to comprehend the complex reasons that stimulated the surge of American expansion dubbed Manifest Destiny for thirty-five years after the War of 1812.

Honor and Economics

Most historians agree that the United States went to war to avenge American honor injured by British violations of neutral rights and the practice of impressment. Behind this reflexive response to British effrontery, however, lay a multifaceted desire to prove that the American experiment in republican government could thrive in politically as well as commercially competitive settings.

Aside from engaging in a cutthroat rivalry with Canadian trappers over the fur trade and enduring increasingly violent Indian attacks on remote settlements, the regions west of the Allegheny Mountains experienced an acute economic downturn in the years before the war. Most frontiersmen blamed all of this on the British, concluding that only war against them could bring relief. In the western view, seizing Canada would eliminate fur trade competitors, stop Indian attacks, and provide the United States with a significant bargaining chip to compel the British to respect American neutral trade. This last—the desire to secure neutral rights—was not an empty objective: the economic sanctions that preceded the war, including the British blockade, were blamed for the West's severe economic depression because western produce could not reach European markets. Conquering Canada was a military means to an economic end.

Southerners too had economic reasons for wanting war. War with England would make Britain's European ally, Spain, open to attack in Florida. The border with Spanish Florida had become a scene of violent confrontation as American planters fumed over runaway slaves escaping to Spanish territory. When Americans conducted raids into Florida to capture these fugitives, they provoked Indian reprisals on the Georgia and Alabama frontier. Ejecting Spain from Florida would calm the border and make the rivers that cut through the Florida panhandle available for transporting goods to the Gulf of Mexico and beyond. Before the War of 1812, such a possibility made Florida an object of both official U.S. negotiations and unofficial American filibustering expeditions.

Consequences of the War of 1812

When Congress declared war on Great Britain on June 18, 1812, the nation was woefully unprepared to wage a major struggle against the most powerful empire on earth. Only a handful of U.S. warships roamed the seas, and the army consisted of about 6,700 poorly trained soldiers led mainly by incompetent officers. James Madison proved a clumsy war president, and most people were apathetic to the fight. Many New Englanders openly opposed it. Forced by both circumstances and temperament to rely on state militia, the government waged a series of campaigns against the British in Canada that were at best ineffectual and occasionally disastrous.

By the latter stages of the war, the army's size gradually increased and the competence of its officers steadily improved, but the grand design of conquering Canada simply never panned out. In the final year of the war, when Britain defeated Napoleon and turned its full attention to the American conflict, the United States was hard-pressed to stave off serious invasion attempts in upstate New York and on the Gulf Coast at New Orleans. The war ended with U.S. borders unchanged, except for the minor addition of the city of Mobile, a testament to the fatigue of Britain coming off a quarter century of almost ceaseless European conflict. Although they had failed to secure formal British recognition of neutral rights, Americans were relieved at not having lost any territory.

The war resolved for the United States none of the stated problems that prompted it, but the episode did mark a significant turning point in the American story. In the first place, the republic emerged from the conflict with more national unity than at any time since its formation. Because New England had so vehemently opposed the war for seemingly selfish reasons, sectionalism was discredited, at least for the time being. The Federalist Party's behavior was so controversial that many called into question its patriotism. Chiefly centered in New England, the Federalists were branded as both stupid and treacherous and did not long survive as a viable political entity after the war. In the absence of a coherent Federalist opposition, their opponents, the Republicans, held sway in an atmosphere of such seeming harmony that the years after the war would be dubbed "The Era of Good Feelings."

As for U.S. expansion, the War of 1812 boosted the chances for increasing American settlement by quashing Indian threats in the Northwest and the South. Before the war, Indian raids had so enflamed the Northwest frontier that in 1811 Indiana territorial governor William Henry Harrison tried to eliminate the threat by destroying forces assembled by the Shawnee prophet Tenskwatawa and his brother, the charismatic Tecumseh. The result was the Battle of Tippecanoe, a mixed affair that made Harrison famous while also making the northwestern tribes British allies when the United States went to war with England the following year. The war allowed Harrison to finish the work he had begun at Tippecanoe. On October 5, 1813, American forces defeated the British and their Indian allies at the Battle of the Thames. Tecumseh was reportedly killed during the fight, and with his death, the Indian unity he and his brother had envisioned died as well.

Likewise, American forces cleared Indians as an impediment to expansion in the South during the War of 1812. In the Mississippi Territory (present-day Alabama and Mississippi), Indian nativists had already embraced a return to spiritual traditions as a way to defend against white encroachment when they heard Tecumseh's message. A sharp division in the Creek Confederation between these nativists (called Red Sticks) and those wishing to adopt white customs erupted into a fierce civil war coincidental to the War of 1812. This internal Creek clash soon spilled over into the white community and provoked surrounding state militias to wage the Creek War. Andrew Jackson led the Tennessee militia in a victorious campaign that concluded with the despoliation not only of defeated Red Sticks but also of those Creeks who had allied with Jackson to defeat their brethren. The Treaty of Fort Jackson forcibly obtained 23 million acres of land from the Creeks and set the stage for a surge of white settlement in the region that was so rapid it became known as "Alabama Fever."

Finally, the Treaty of Ghent that ended the war between the United States and Britain also ended Britain's promise of assistance to Indians who had been resisting U.S. expansion into their lands. Never again would northwestern tribes receive support from Canadian fur traders or British officers; southeastern Indians, similarly forsaken by their redcoat allies and ignored by enfeebled Spaniards, were dealt a deep blow by Jackson's terms and would subsequently feel only increased pressure from a growing white presence. Thus the war began the process of clearing the way for a new age of American expansion whose political, economic, social, and technological implications would shape U.S. policy for the next thirty years.

The American Hemisphere

In 1820, the U.S. government heard that reactionary European monarchies intended to quash South American rebellions to restore Spain's colonial empire. Rumors filtering through an imperfect network of diplomatic operatives told of plans by Russia, Austria, Prussia, and France to dispatch fleets and armies to Spanish America, a prospect doubly disturbing to the United States. Not only did Americans naturally identify with the idea of colonial revolution, they also feared that Old World monarchies that reestablished themselves in the western hemisphere might imperil U.S. national security. Already, Secretary Adams had apprehensively watched as the Russian tsar issued a ukase (a decree) that defined Russian jurisdiction in Alaska as stretching to the fifty-first parallel; Russian traders and fishermen were already working the Pacific Coast south toward San Francisco Bay. When Adams resolutely protested that Russia was violating American property rights in the Pacific Northwest, the tsar chose to back away. In the Russo-American Treaty of 1824, Russia's southern border in the region was drawn at 54°40', leaving only Britain and the United States as rival claimants to the Oregon Country.

The Monroe Doctrine

Great Britain opposed European plans to crush Spanish American rebellions, especially after Latin American revolutionaries abolished Spain's trade monopoly to the lucrative benefit of British commercial shipping. In fact, British foreign secretary George Canning proposed in 1823 that the United States and Britain issue a joint statement condemning before the fact any European attempt to quash the rebellions. Although the offer was attractive and Britain's Royal Navy would certainly make the policy enforceable, John Quincy Adams disapproved of an Anglo-American arrangement that made the United States seem a "cockboat in the wake of the British man-of-war."[4] In addition, an alliance with Britain would likely obstruct future American expansion. Calculating that British policy to protect Latin American markets would prevent European intervention anyway, Adams confidently advised James Monroe to issue a unilateral pronouncement that became known as the Monroe Doctrine. The president in his regular annual message to Congress on December 2, 1823, firmly told the European monarchies that the United States would permit neither additional colonization nor intervention in the Western Hemisphere. In exchange, the United States pledged not to interfere in the affairs of Europe.

The Monroe Doctrine was remarkable for several reasons. With its modest army and puny navy, the United States could not possibly challenge the great European powers, but the sheer audacity of the pronouncement delighted Americans, and its timing protected it from immediate European challenges. The British government was annoyed that Monroe's warning also technically applied to Britain's imperial ambitions, especially because Canning believed he had come up with the idea in the first place, but he could not object to a policy with which he fundamentally agreed. Other European governments grumbled about the pushy Yankees they had never liked anyway, but wary of the Royal Navy, those governments could do little but grumble. For their part, Latin American republics generally understood that the British navy offered them more protection than James Monroe's words did, while in the United States, Americans finished congratulating each other for staring down the Old World and returned to more immediate concerns of clearing the wilderness of trees and Indians. But the policy defined by the Monroe Doctrine established the principle that the Western Hemisphere was an American hemisphere, even though that principle lay dormant until 1845 when President James K. Polk revived it on the eve of another American expansionist surge.

The Great Migrations

At the close of the War of 1812, the American people most densely inhabited a relatively thin strip along the Atlantic Coast. A traveler could journey as little as two hundred miles away from the seaboard and find himself in wild and unpopulated territory. Yet, that rapidly changed in the next quarter century. A torrent of migration occurred that not only settled the eastern portion of the continent to the Mississippi but also began to send tendrils of travelers into the vast expanses of the plains and beyond.

Forts and Force

After the War of 1812, the U.S. government fretted over the possibility that native uprisings would seek to avenge losses experienced in the war. In the summer of 1815, the Madison administration tried to soothe unrest by negotiating a series of treaties with northwestern Indians, but the effort was only partly successful. To protect advancing settlement, the government began a fort-building program on the frontier, beginning with the renovation of forts in Indiana and the revival of posts in Detroit, eastern Michigan, and Illinois. In addition, new garrisons were established in Wisconsin, western Illinois, and by 1822 in the upper Mississippi Valley.

The forts were illustrative of U.S. Indian policy after the War of 1812. The guiding principle concentrated on establishing dominion over the tribes so that their land could be opened to white settlement. In addition, new American techniques of dealing with Indians marked a bold departure from methods applied before the war. Rather than resorting to bribes and blandishments, U.S. officials routinely emulated Andrew Jackson's blunt behavior with the Treaty of Fort Jackson. They candidly advised northwestern Indians that they had no choice but to cede their lands for annual payments and gifts. Likewise, in the South, Jackson continued as the principal government agent in extracting increasing land cessions from that region's tribes. In 1818, he would lead troops into Spanish Florida to conduct the First Seminole War.[5]

As settlers flooded both the northern and southern regions east of the Mississippi, the U.S. government felt increasing pressure to gain title to additional Indian lands. The result was a significant shift in Indian policy that abandoned acculturation and the setting aside of reservations within regions of rising white settlement. As it became apparent that whites would resent their exclusion from even the tiniest of Indian enclaves, the government resolved to eliminate the enclaves by relocating the Indians. By 1825, Indian removal ceased as a theoretical plan and became policy.[6]

Toward the Great Missouri

Early in the nineteenth century, most Americans were farmers, and their search for better lands became an all-consuming passion. The region south of the Great Lakes was more than alluring to settlers coming from northern Tennessee and the western parts of the Carolinas and Virginia. Once covered by an ocean and then gouged by glaciers, the northern areas of Illinois, Indiana, and Ohio resembled the coastal plains of the Upper South and featured some of the most fertile soil in the world. The southern parts of Illinois and Indiana included dense stands of hardwood trees—a sign of fruitfulness to people in that day. To the west, a wide plain ran some forty miles along the yellow-brown waters of the Mississippi to its tributary, the Kaskaskia. In the middle, a landscape of extensive grasslands mottled by spacious, towering forests stretched through Indiana and Illinois into the southern part of Michigan. The central Illinois plain, aptly named the Grand Prairie, was covered with waving grasses higher than a man's head and was so extensive that settlers found it both dazzling and daunting. Only after other lands filled up would settlement eventually spread into this region. After that, even the less desirable piney woods that thrived in the sandy soil of northern Michigan and Wisconsin attracted homesteads.

The first wave of homesteaders was composed of small farmers from Kentucky, eastern Tennessee, and the western parts of Georgia and the Carolinas. Displaced by the rapidly advancing plantation culture, they disliked either slavery or the antidemocratic social distinctions it created and thus traveled north of the Ohio to settle rich river lands. Immigrants began to appear as well, floating down the Ohio on flatboats to fan out on lush riverbanks in such numbers that later arrivals had to move to higher ground and trek farther westward. Migration from the South continued for fifteen years after the War of 1812 before tapering off after 1830.

The second wave of migration into the region spanned twenty years after 1830 and included hardy New Englanders escaping an economy that was rapidly transforming their communities. Many were farmers displaced by New England's burgeoning textile industry. Those who early on shifted from growing crops to raising sheep became rich in the process and expanded their operations by absorbing the farms of their less prosperous neighbors. As rising numbers of woolly sheep dotted the landscape, rising numbers of newly landless farmers headed out for a fresh start in the Old Northwest.

Farmworkers of the Middle Atlantic states, similarly displaced by that region's economic transformation, joined them. Unable to compete with the West's high grain productivity, farmers in New York and Pennsylvania set aside their depleted soils for large herds of milk cows. Consequently, the trickle of landless and unemployed workers became a flood of families heading for Michigan, Indiana, and Wisconsin.

New and newer farms in the Great Lakes region and the Ohio River Valley produced even higher yields that further lowered grain prices. The process hastened as well as deepened the agricultural transformation in the East, compelling continued migrations to what was being touted as a "Promised Land." Even New England woolgrowers eventually joined the tide when it became apparent that sheep could be raised less expensively on verdant western meadows. The population surge quickly fulfilled requirements for territorial government and statehood, almost immediately for Indiana (1816) and Illinois (1818) in the first wave of migration, and relatively quickly for Michigan (1837) and Wisconsin (1848) during the second.

Meanwhile, the region reflected the sectional concerns of settlers that ranged from New Englanders to southerners, yet it also developed a distinct western identity that evinced an elevated sense of nationalism, unqualified allegiance to the federal government, and an unfettered belief in the inevitability of the continuing westward march.

The Cotton Kingdom

The Mississippi Territory, consisting of the present-day states of Alabama and Mississippi, was established twelve years before the War of 1812, but not until after the war did migration into the region begin in earnest. The principal motivation was a rising demand for cotton that encouraged the abandonment of exhausted eastern soil, especially after the war had cleared Indians from much of the western wilderness and had opened access to the gulf by way of the American occupation of Mobile and later of Spanish Florida. High cotton prices promised such prosperity that planters rushed into the Mississippi Territory as further Indian cessions opened increasingly larger sections of formerly closed lands.

Cotton was as demanding as it was profitable. It required a lengthy growing season of at least six and a half months and highly fertile soil to achieve significant yields. The need for such conditions necessarily restricted cotton's cultivation to the lower elevations that lay within a long crescent from North Carolina to western Tennessee. Most notably, the Black Belt of central Alabama extending into Mississippi and the fabulously fertile flood plains produced a spectacular prosperity visible in sprawling plantations and stately homes.

Alabama Fever

For five years after the War of 1812, pioneers bought their homesteads from government land offices that granted liberal credit. Such easy terms and low prices dissuaded land speculators, who instead directed their energy to selling lots in future town sites, many of which remained wilderness or were stillborn and became farms. Speculation north of the Ohio, though, had far less scope and impact than that which fueled the land frenzy to the south, especially in Alabama.

In Alabama, eager settlers crowded into land offices at Huntsville, St. Stephens, and Catawba to purchase six hundred thousand acres in 1816 alone. Influenced by the postwar boom, sales rapidly increased and prices accordingly rose, especially when speculators from all over the country began bidding against prospective settlers. Desirable tracts were going for as high as fifty dollars an acre in the peak year of 1817. Rather than discouraging settlement, the skyrocketing prices sparked increasing interest. The result was a flood of migrants. Some easterners actually began to fear their states would be depopulated. A North Carolina planter noted, "Some of our oldest and wealthy men are offering their possessions for sale and [are] desirous of removing to this new country."[7]

The fervor filled up not only Alabama but also spilled a growing torrent of settlers onto the appealing soils of the Tennessee Valley and westward toward Natchez. Receding frontiers in the South brought statehood there as in the North. Mississippi was admitted to the Union in 1817, and Alabama in 1819, their rapid peopling reflecting a frontier habit of erecting fairly liberal state governments where all white males could vote regardless of their status or property holdings. Yet, the stipulations of government outlined in state constitutions told only part of the Old South's story.

Spurs to Continuing Migration

As noted, many small farmers resisted being relegated to marginal lands and migrated northward across the Ohio River. Nonslaveholding whites who remained accounted for almost three quarters of the southern white population, but they inhabited inferior farmlands. The gap between upper-class planters and lower-class farmers steadily widened over the years to create an oligarchic pyramid fraught with fears at its top and resentments at its bottom. Smaller planters far outnumbered the large grandees of white-columned mansions, but they performed a strange function of bolstering the maintenance of the slave culture while making its trappings less ostentatious to the lower classes. The lowest class of whites was composed of "crackers," a miserable lot beset by debilitating intestinal parasites and consigned to lands that produced only a scanty subsistence in the best of years.

For white planters, large and small alike, and all classes of poorer whites, slavery became economically and socially embedded in southern culture, the one because the labor intensive process of planting and harvesting cotton required its preservation, and the other because slavery itself was a way of socially controlling the large black population the plantation system required. Although the impoverished cracker might nurture a host of resentments over his low place in the southern social scheme, he took comfort and pride in not being as low as the slave. Slaves in the main led a wretched existence, and their brooding bitterness over their lot carried an incipient threat of revolt. Vigilance against that prospect united whites regardless of caste or custom.

Ironically, the slaves' desolate condition served to bond poor whites and wealthy planters in an unhealthy partnership of economic and psychological dependence. It was an attitude that persistently set the South apart from the rest of the growing American republic, the other parts of which became progressively more uncomfortable with the presence of human slavery in the land of liberty.

And it was a circumstance that had a profound impact on American expansion. As the decreasing availability of suitable land dimmed a poor white's hopes of becoming a slave-owning planter, it correspondingly encouraged him to pull up stakes and move west. Much of the spreading American influence west of the Mississippi thus carried with it a distinctly proslavery inclination. It would have unsettling implications for the regions that awaited his arrival as well as the country he left behind him.

Roads and Rivers

Rapid migration after the War of 1812 into the Old Northwest and the Mississippi Territory would not have been possible without the construction of a new transportation network. Most important were the major roads that the federal government systematically cut through the wilderness. Subsidiary routes soon stemmed from these main trunks. The Cumberland Road (also called the National Road) by 1818 extended from Maryland through Virginia to Wheeling where the Ohio River could float large barges and rafts into the interior. Fifteen years later, the Cumberland Road arrived at Columbus, Ohio. Meanwhile, primitive paths opened the way for southern pioneers heading toward

the Ohio. More a trail cut through the backwoods than an actual highway, the Wilderness Road ran across Kentucky toward Louisville. From
there and from Cincinnati just across the Ohio, a steady stream of travelers trekked on raw local trails into Indiana and Missouri, encouraged
by the sound of ringing axes and the aroma of burning scrub along the
way, the marks of earlier arrivals turning forests into farms. "Labor,
labor, labor, hard, heavy, incessant labor," remarked one observer, "is
the lot of him who proclaims war against the forest." Yet, he added that
"the victory is certain, and the conqueror's reward is rich and simple."[8]

The second wave of migration into the Old Northwest, especially
from New England, used the relatively rapid transportation provided by
the new Erie Canal, which began carrying travelers from the Hudson
River to Buffalo in 1825. Travel on packed canal boats was not without its
difficulties, but it was safe and affordable. Thousands of horses trudged
along each side of the big ditch, pulling the boats that ferried thousands
of migrants toward the Great Lakes region. By the 1830s, the advent of
steamboats allowed Erie Canal travelers to embark at Buffalo and traverse
Lake Erie to Detroit for as little as three dollars a person. Just as the railroad later sped the peopling of the plains beyond the Mississippi, these
transportation improvements so diminished the age-old difficulty of
getting from one place to another that they were largely responsible for
the rapid pace of the epic migration into the Old Northwest.

In the South, new roads laid out by the federal government and
the states also made pioneer journeys into the wilderness more feasible.
The Fall Line Road and Upper Road met at Columbus, Georgia, and
became the Federal Road, an artery under construction before the War
of 1812 and eventually extending to Mobile and beyond to Natchez.
Another road traversed the hollow of the Appalachian Mountains to
split at Knoxville, Tennessee, heading toward Memphis along its northern stem and toward the rich Tennessee Valley along its southern one.
From Huntsville, Alabama, travelers could fan out on trails that took
them farther into the interior. The Military Road, opened in 1820 under
army auspices and hence its name, allowed travel from western
Alabama toward New Orleans. In the 1830s and farther north, engineers hacked another route through the Alabama wilds that would be
unimaginatively called the Upper Federal Road. By then, steamboats
regularly chugged and churned along yellow rivers with melodic names
like Oconee and Chattahoochee and Tombigbee, carrying settlers to

new villages aspiring to be towns and uncleared lands waiting for the ax and plow. Meanwhile, both roads and rivers moved through forests retreating before the steady and relentless march of cotton and slavery.

The Missouri Fire Bell

A warning about the reckoning over slavery came in 1819 when a serious sectional dispute emerged. The territory of Missouri requested admission to the Union as a slave state, opening a controversy that exploded into a major congressional debate. The House of Representatives blocked Missouri's application by adopting New York congressman James Tallmadge's amendment that sought Missouri's gradual elimination of slavery as a condition of its statehood. Southerners violently opposed to Tallmadge's provision reacted reflexively, but a troubling reality also motivated them.

In 1819, the United States comprised eleven free and eleven slave states. The North's burgeoning population, however, had so outstripped the South's that its free-state majority in the House of Representatives could successfully assail slavery. It seemed to be doing just that with the Tallmadge Amendment. In the Senate, equal representation empowered southerners to frustrate any such northern effort, and the Senate indeed defeated the amendment. Because the terms of Missouri's admission would tip that senatorial balance either to the North or to the South, congressional debate descended into ever angrier denunciations and legislative business stalled into a confused paralysis.

The Missouri Compromise

Finally in 1820, one of the most famous compromises in American history broke the impasse by admitting Missouri as a slave state while balancing it with the admission of Maine, a free state formerly recognized as the "District of Maine" on Massachusetts' northeastern frontier. In addition, Congress agreed that Missouri would be the last part of the Louisiana Purchase north of 36°30' to allow slavery. In the truest sense of successful compromise, the bargain over Missouri pleased no one entirely, but it had the advantage of intensely displeasing only abolitionists and extreme proslavery advocates.

Although most southern congressmen voted against the Missouri Compromise, it was nevertheless enacted and endured for almost three and a half decades. Moralists who rightly condemn slavery, however, have always been uneasy about the deeper implications of the arrangement. By spinning the nation's moral compass from its stated doctrines of liberty and equality, the compromise plainly set a course for political accord and away from human freedom. Two founders from different sections of the country ruminated over the Missouri controversy's troubling conclusion. In Virginia, Thomas Jefferson remarked that the disagreement had awakened him "like a firebell in the night," and John Adams in Massachusetts "shudder[ed] when I think of the calamities which slavery is likely to produce in this country."[9] As usual, in their unique ways, both men were perceptive. During the seminal years to come, the arguments over slavery would be muffled, but as fires only partly extinguished, they continued to smolder. In the end, the nation in another twenty-five years returned to the issue of slavery in territories many miles west of Missouri.

Land Policy, 1820–41

The rapid pace of settlement after the War of 1812 occurred in conjunction with a postwar economic boom that inflated commodity and manufacturing prices, drove up land revenues, and encouraged risky speculative investment. For three years, the financial picture seemed so endlessly promising that reckless lending and extravagant borrowing became routine, and what ordinarily would have been obvious warnings of overheated growth went unheeded. When the wobbly credit structure finally collapsed in 1819, it destroyed the fortunes of countless numbers, forcing many into bankruptcy and severely depressing wheat and cotton prices that heavily indebted western farmers and southern planters relied on to meet their obligations. The Panic of 1819 especially menaced small farmers on the frontier with the frightening prospect of foreclosure. Such a possibility was particularly dire. Not only might they lose their homes but also fields they had cleared and tilled with backbreaking labor.

Under pressure from the frontier, Congress again modified the government's fundamental land policy, the first time in sixteen years. Seeking to prevent the kind of debt disaster that had engulfed western farmers, the Land Act of 1820 eliminated the Harrison Act's extensive credit provisions, but it also lowered the per-acre price to $1.25 and halved the minimum size of a land parcel from 160 to 80 acres. Additional relief legislation eased the terrors facing bankrupt farmers by allowing them to trim their land holdings to reduce their obligations, take up the payments of their balances owed at the new $1.25 per acre price, or extend the schedule for their remaining payments.

Although the situation eased in time, the hardships caused by the economic crash remained in the frontier's memory. Inhabitants of the region believed that the principal author of their misery had been the credit policies of the Second Bank of the United States (known as the BUS). It was an attitude that formed the foundation for Jacksonian Democracy, a political movement that arose in the 1820s embracing widened voting rights, lower tariffs, decentralized government, and the elimination of the BUS.

In the wake of the Panic of 1819, the BUS performed well during the 1820s to control credit and help nurture a new economic boom, but Jacksonians in the West remained inflexibly anti-bank. The region's growing political influence played a key role in elevating Andrew Jackson to the presidency. In what came to be called the "Bank War," Jackson successfully destroyed the BUS in 1832 by vetoing its recharter and removing from it all government deposits. Without the BUS's restraint, another dangerous credit spiral ensued and, like its predecessor in 1819, collapsed in 1837 to cause another panic.

Hard times again engulfed the country and rippled out to settlements on the frontier, and the government accordingly contemplated revising its land policy. This time, new and innovative ways to modify the way the public domain passed into private hands would animate a debate that increasingly reflected how sectional discord and Jacksonian Democracy were shaping political discussion.

Preemption

In spite of the pejorative sound of the label, squatters were not always wastrels. Many were hardworking pioneers whose intrepid spirit was tested and proved by their roaming beyond civilization's authority and protection. Yet, they created a peculiar set of problems for themselves and the United States. Their presence beyond the frontier often provoked local Indian tribes, requiring the intervention of the U.S. Army, a costly exercise that also disrupted U.S.-Indian relations. The squatter also lived with the daily threat that later arrivals might exploit the absence of a legitimate title to grab parcels of the land he claimed.

Where each man was a law unto himself, claim jumping usually ended in violence and reprisal.

As noted, the army occasionally swept both surveyed and unsurveyed regions clear of squatters, but as soon as the soldiers disappeared, the squatters returned. For all the squatter's efforts to survive hostile Indians and stave off rival claimants, government surveyors would finally arrive to create a final and inescapable problem. Once charted into a township, squatter lands sold to the highest bidder at public auction. The squatter thus faced the prospect of having his farm and all its improvements literally sold out from under him.

To pioneer thinking, the solution was preemption, which meant that the claims of the land's occupants would take precedence over any rival bids, especially those by speculators. Squatters under preemption would have first chance to purchase the land at its minimum price. From the War of 1812 to 1840, Congress conferred preemption on groups of squatters no fewer than twenty-one times. In each case, though, preemption was an *ad hoc* arrangement that applied only to specific squatters on surveyed lands. Those who continued to move and settle beyond the charted ranges could not be certain that their lands would come under a subsequent preemption grant. The federal government's reliance on land sales for revenue contributed to that uncertainty.

Tariffs and Sectionalism

Other than land revenues, tariffs were the only other significant source of money for the government. By the mid-1830s, land policy and the tariff became paired in a complicated balancing act. Those wishing to lower the tariff had to advocate high land prices to balance the government's books.

Those books, however, became an embarrassing chronicle of government riches during the 1830s. The remarkable boom years of 1830–37 netted the Treasury sizable surpluses from both tariff proceeds and land revenues. Citizens embracing Jacksonian precepts of limited government called either for tariff reductions or for lower land prices, depending on what sectional interests motivated them. The West naturally wanted lower land prices, but some advocated that the federal government cede the public domain to the states while others wanted it given outright to settlers through homesteading provisions. The agricultural South, which purchased most of its manufactured goods from outside its region, wanted to lower the tariff and thus make manufactured goods less expensive. Factory owners in the Northeast wanted to keep a high tariff, but they resisted generous land policies that would continue to drain off people and political influence from the East.

This complicated mix of conflicting sectional aims stalled meaningful revisions of land policy. It also made the political system vulnerable to significant discord. In 1830, Southerners led by John C. Calhoun and his mouthpiece in the Senate, South Carolina's Robert Y. Hayne, tried to forge an alliance with westerners to oppose northern resistance to generous land policies and lower tariffs. The occasion spurred the famous debate between Hayne and Massachusetts senator Daniel Webster in 1830, and the episode ended with the Nullification crisis, South Carolina's 1832 attempt to invalidate federal tariff law. South Carolina's actions, unsupported by the South as well as the West, nearly brought the country to civil war.[10]

Distribution

By the mid-1830s, the political system had again formed opposing factions to create the second American party system. Jacksonian Democrats faced off against Whigs, so named because they opposed both the policies and the cult of personality around Andrew Jackson, whom they caricatured as "King Andrew." Led by Kentuckian Henry Clay, the Whigs promoted what they styled the American System, an integrated program of internal improvements, protective tariffs, and the national bank. The Whig program in its purest form directly contradicted Jacksonians' anti-bank and limited government ideas, and the contest between the two agendas was to dominate political debate during the remainder of the period.

The Whig program was an expensive one, so Clay opposed sacrificing the substantial land-sales revenues. A foe of preemption, he looked upon squatters as "lawless rabble."[11] He preferred to distribute a portion of the land-sales proceeds to the states, an idea that appealed to northeastern manufacturing interests as well. He first introduced the idea in 1832 under a plan to pay 10 percent of net land revenues to the states where the lands were situated, distributing the remaining 90 percent to all states and territories in proportion to their population.

Opponents repeatedly defeated the measure until 1841 when Clay successfully courted western support by including preemption for squatters on surveyed lands in a distribution bill. The resulting marriage of the two ideas attracted enough votes to secure its passage, although with a stipulation that also tied distribution to the tariff. If tariffs subsequently exceeded the 20 percent level where they stood in 1841, distribution would cease. In less than a year, tariffs were raised and distribution became a dead letter. Preemption, however, remained in force until 1891.

Meanwhile, the homestead movement—the outright gift of public lands to those who took up extended residence on them—was gaining momentum. In his 1832 annual message, Andrew Jackson endorsed the idea of removing the public domain as a revenue source for the government. Early labor movements lent their advocacy as well. Like much else during the 1840s, however, the homestead movement became embroiled in the slavery controversy, especially after the antislavery Free Soil Party endorsed the idea. Not until southern secession in 1860–61 removed stiff opposition to the measure did homestead legislation pass Congress. On May 20, 1862, seventy-seven years to the day after the Ordinance of 1785 had passed Congress, Abraham Lincoln signed the homestead bill into law.

Conclusion

The great westward migration of almost five million Americans during the period stretching from the 1780s to the 1840s was nothing short of epic. Jefferson had reckoned that it would take centuries and a hundred generations for the American people to populate the vast area of his Louisiana Purchase. Yet, in only fifty years the children of the first pioneers pushed to the Mississippi and Missouri, and then their children began spilling toward the Rocky Mountains and beyond to the Columbia River basin of the Oregon Country.

During it all, the government continually tinkered with land law through numerous revisions, worked to eliminate the Indian presence with negotiation and force, asserted U.S. hegemony in the Western Hemisphere, wrestled with the implications of the growing slavery controversy, and finally in the fifth decade of the nineteenth century came to a crucial decision. Should the country proceed with further acquisitions, risking the perils of empire and sectional eruptions over human freedom? Or should it look upon the Rockies and the Red River as the natural boundaries of the American experiment?

We know the decision that those Americans made, and in truth, they likely had little choice but to accept continental expansion as fore-ordained. Perhaps the only point of dispute was whether, as John L. O'Sullivan proclaimed, God had so ordained it.

Before turning to those culminating episodes of Manifest Destiny in the West, however, we must first examine in detail two additional and important tiles of this complex story's mosaic: the acquisition of Florida from Spain and the extension of the American boundary to the Pacific Northwest; and the manner and methods employed by the government toward Indians in its removal policy.

Notes

1. Worthington C. Ford et al., ed. *Journals of the Continental Congress, 1774–1789.* (Washington: Library of Congress, 1904–37), 28: 375–81.

2. *House Journal,* 4th Cong., 1st sess., 18 May 1796, 562.

3. *Statutes at Large of the United States, 1789–1873,* 17 vols. (Boston: Charles C. Little, and James Brown, 1845), 2:73–78.

4. Charles Francis Adams, ed. *Memoirs of John Quincy Adams, Comprising Portions of His Diary From 1795 To 1848,* 12 vols. (Philadelphia: Lippincott, 1874–1877), 6:179.

5. U.S. diplomatic and military policy toward Spanish Florida is discussed in Chapter 3.

6. Indian removal policy is discussed in Chapter 4.

7. James Graham to Thomas Ruffin, 9 November 1817, James G. de Roulhac Hamilton, ed., *The Papers of Thomas Ruffin,* 4 vols. (Raleigh: Edwards & Broughton, 1918–1920), 1:198.

8. James Hall, *Letters from the West, Containing Sketches of Scenery, Manners, and Customs, and Anecdotes Connected with the First Settlements of the Western Sections of the United States* (London: Colburn, Shackell and Baylis, 1828), 345.

9. Thomas Jefferson to John Holmes, 22 April 1820, Thomas Jefferson Randolph, ed., *Papers of Thomas Jefferson,* 4 vols. (London: Colburn and R. Bentley, 1829), 4:323; Adams is quoted in Page Smith, *John Adams,* 2 vols. (Garden City, NY: Doubleday, 1962), 2:1126.

10. South Carolina led the tariff fight because states' rights proponents feared unchecked federal authority. If the national government possessed the power to enact such sweeping tariff legislation, they presumed it might one day exercise this power to abolish slavery.

11. Quoted in Ray Allen Billington, *Westward Expansion: A History of the American Frontier,* 2nd ed. (New York: Macmillan, 1960), 374.

CHAPTER 3

FINISHING OFF FLORIDA

Three centuries before the birth of Christ, the Roman Republic began conquering its fierce neighbors and taming the provinces on its borders. Over the years, the Romans steadily expanded and built an empire. Twenty centuries later, the American Republic followed suit for its own reasons, in its own way, and in its own time, beginning with the wilderness to its south, a land of tangled mangrove forests and malodorous swamps called Florida. For almost four hundred years, with only a twenty-year interruption in the late eighteenth century, Spain had owned Florida. In 1816, Spain still owned it, but only just barely.

Because the United States had seized part of Spanish West Florida and had tried to take the remainder of it during the War of 1812, Spain remained apprehensive after the war about American designs on the entire peninsula. Spain had reason to be nervous. Florida's small garrisons could offer little challenge to an invasion that many believed was only a matter of time in coming. Protecting Spain for the time being, however, were the domestic and diplomatic repercussions that would likely condemn blatant American aggression. Many Americans doubtless regarded an unprovoked invasion of Florida as immoral, and Europe might side with Spain to force the United States to stand down.

Such factors gave President James Madison and his successor James Monroe pause enough to presume that Florida would best be acquired through negotiation. Force in response to overt aggression against American citizens and territory nonetheless remained an option. Florida had become a sanctuary for many disgruntled Creek Indians displaced by the Treaty of Fort Jackson, and the region's native Seminoles still brooded over American invasions of their territory before the War of 1812. The situation promised to unsettle an already troubled border that stretched from the Atlantic Ocean to the Perdido River, too long for Spain to police and too permeable for American frontiersmen to resist.

A Violent Frontier

Immediately after the War of 1812, American officials suspected that the British would try to help their Creek allies in Florida reclaim the land they had lost in the Treaty of Fort Jackson. Actually, American fears were unfounded, for the British government had no such plans. British forces in Florida, however, did not depart until the middle of 1815, and Americans understandably remained nervous. Even after the British left, Americans anxiously took into account the residue of British activity that remained in Florida: assorted small arms, artillery, and a fortification at Prospect Bluff on the Apalachicola River. The fort became a magnet for runaway slaves from both the American Southeast and Spanish Pensacola. In addition, some Creeks who had fled to Florida during and after the Creek War settled nearby. Both groups were hostile to the United States. A sizable number of them sported cast-off British arms and ammunition.

Meanwhile, American survey teams stumbled through the brush to plat the Treaty of Fort Jackson cession, worsening tensions on the border and further agitating a seething Creek population. The U.S. Army came to protect the surveyors, and squatters wanting free land poured into the ceded territory intensifying an already explosive situation. The army, in fact, had the exasperating task of guarding survey crews while rousting squatters and fending off Indian raids. Squatters regularly slunk into Florida to steal Creek and Seminole livestock, and the Indians countered with their own retaliatory forays into Georgia and Alabama. Thus did the frontier edge toward full-scale war.

Negro Fort

Frontier Georgians dubbed the abandoned British works on the Apalachicola River "Negro Fort" because its garrison included runaway slaves, but Indians also resided there. The distinction was immaterial to edgy American planters. As slaves fleeing to Florida found refuge in Negro Fort, southerners became both angry and alarmed, demanding that the government either destroy or bring about the destruction of this tempting sanctuary. Southern political pressure was strident, but not until the fort began firing at American supply transports on the Apalachicola did the army have a pretext to reduce it.

It happened this way. To calm Southerners, the army began moving troops into southern Georgia in early 1816. The soldiers built forts, and to supply them they planned to use the Apalachicola River into Georgia where it became the Chattahoochee. Any obstruction of this supply line would give the commander in the region, Brigadier General Edmund Pendleton Gaines, a reason to invade Florida and attack Negro Fort. Some Americans, Major General Andrew Jackson among them, pondered an even more ambitious response. Negro Fort's threat and Spain's failure to control it and the Indians, they said, justified seizing Florida.

Madison was not so sure and urged caution. So soon after the war with Great Britain, the Madison administration was especially keen to avoid one with Spain. Nonetheless, from his headquarters at his home in Nashville, Tennessee, Jackson sent a message to the Spanish governor of West Florida asking him to do something about Negro Fort. Jackson bluntly advised the governor that if Spain did nothing, it "will compel us . . . to destroy them."[1]

The letter to the Spanish governor appears to have been nothing more than an empty ritual because Jackson also ordered Gaines to prepare an expedition into Florida aimed at Negro Fort. Violent border incidents further encouraged Gaines to advance plans for an invasion. He ordered Lieutenant Colonel Duncan Clinch to lead it.

A combined operation of the army and navy conducted the assault, Clinch's infantry moving down from Georgia and gunboats under Sailing Master Jarius Loomis coming up the Apalachicola from the Gulf of Mexico. Loomis arrived at the mouth of the Apalachicola on 10 July 1816 and while waiting for word from Clinch, sent five men ashore for fresh water. Indians and black men ambushed the sailors, killing three and dragging off another to die by torture. Only one man escaped, running into the water and thrashing about until rescued by the gunboats. For the Americans, it was not a good start.

Two weeks and several miscommunications between the navy and army later, the two groups finally rendezvoused south of Negro Fort and commenced the attack on July 27. Despite the army's initiation of the project, it was mainly a naval operation. Pulling abreast of the fort, the gunboats lofted hotshot into it, and when one struck the fort's powder magazine, a shocking explosion virtually obliterated the bastion and most of its inhabitants.

Spain did not object to the invasion. In fact, the governor in Pensacola was secretly pleased to be rid of Negro Fort, as much a haven for Spain's fugitive slaves as it had been for America's. For its part, the Madison administration, careful to avoid offending the popular Andrew Jackson, did not make an issue over the unauthorized expedition either. Instead, the administration issued instructions that henceforth invasions of Florida would require unambiguous permission from Washington. The government hoped the directive would prevent future incidents that Spain might not find so agreeable.

Britons, Spaniards, and Freebooters

Despite the destruction of Negro Fort, raids across the Florida border continued, and the province remained an asylum for runaway slaves. Although nothing much had changed, many landless poor concluded that the frontier was now safe and poured into the Fort Jackson cession, incensing Creek inhabitants as they displaced them. To avoid another U.S. invasion of their territory, the Seminoles for a time ignored these new interlopers, but by early 1817 that changed.

Former British marine lieutenant George Woodbine arrived in Florida accompanied by Alexander Arbuthnot, an elderly Scottish trader. Woodbine lied to the Seminoles that the British government was considering offering them aid. On top of that, supplies traded by Arbuthnot in exchange for animal pelts convinced the Indians that possibly they could resist future American incursions. No longer restrained by caution, a party of Seminoles in February 1817 trekked to southern Georgia and killed a woman and her two children at their isolated homestead.

Initially gauged an isolated incident, the murder prompted no extra protection on the frontier. By that summer, though, violence along the Georgia-Florida border had become a regular occurrence. The U.S. government was far more interested in growing Latin American unrest in Spanish colonies and what that portended for Florida. Spain might decide to cut its colonial losses by selling Florida to the United States rather than risk losing it outright through military intervention.

During the spring of 1817, all appearances indicated that army commanders were planning something new for the Spanish in Florida. Gaines began a military buildup in the southern part of the Alabama Territory and then tried to provoke a controversy with Spanish officials by insisting that he be allowed to move supplies through Pensacola on the Escambia River without paying Spanish customs duties.

While Gaines quarreled with West Florida's governor, old Arbuthnot began writing letters to the American government protesting its behavior toward the Creeks and Seminoles. He also wrote to the British minister in Washington asking for help in redressing Indian grievances. The efforts yielded no material result. In fact, everybody ignored Arbuthnot except his new Indian friends. The Seminoles came to believe that the letters would bear fruit, that help from the redcoats was again on the way, and thus emboldened increased their attacks into Georgia.

As if all this were not enough, another complication arose on the eastern edge of the Florida frontier. In June 1817, a soldier of fortune named Gregor McGregor landed 150 mercenaries on Amelia Island off the north coast of Florida. McGregor apparently planned to conduct operations against Spain's authority in Latin America, but both Americans in Georgia and Spaniards in St. Augustine saw him as a threat to their security. The government's concern over these developments was finally palpable as well, but by the time the Monroe administration moved to mobilize the southern army to deal with McGregor's mercenaries, Gaines had already made a decision of his own. He was going to move against the Florida Indians.

The Village and the Island

Gaines spent the summer of 1817 reestablishing a military presence in southwestern Georgia and garrisoning an abandoned fortification named Fort Scott. He again established a supply route from the Gulf of Mexico up the Apalachicola River and entertained hopes that he would be allowed to invade Spanish Florida. Perhaps Seminole attacks on American vessels would provide the excuse for an invasion just as Negro Fort's behavior had justified an earlier one. Gaines made no secret of the real object, however. "Shall we be permitted to visit the Spaniards?" he asked a Tennessee senator.[2]

In July 1817, a detachment of the 7th United States Infantry commanded by Major David E. Twiggs took up positions at Fort Scott.

Twiggs immediately contacted nearby Creek and Seminole towns to arrange meetings, but the situation had badly deteriorated. Most Indian headmen wanted peace, but white squatters had continued to steal their cattle and randomly kill their people. Gaines had the authority to remove these offending squatters, but the army had proved surprisingly unfocused in doing so. In fact, Gaines, apparently hoping for permission to invade Florida, stubbornly blamed the Indians for all the latest violence. Seminole protests were ignored.

Near Fort Scott lay the Indian village of Fowltown whose inhabitants were especially angry over disregarded grievances. When Fowltown warned Fort Scott's garrison not to enter land claimed by the village, Gaines responded by shifting more troops to the fort. He had the War Department's blessing in doing so—interim Secretary of War George Graham told the general he could punish hostile Indians north of the Florida line—but Gaines's orders still forbade him from crossing into Florida.

Of more concern to the Monroe administration was the nest of international outlaws parked on Amelia Island. Whether they styled themselves freebooters, pirates, or true friends of Latin American revolutionaries, their obvious intention was to assail merchant shipping off the American coast. They also began to smuggle African slaves into the United States through the vulnerable eastern end of the Florida border, a barefaced violation of American law banning the foreign slave trade. St. Augustine had neither the will nor the way to deal with brigands on Amelia Island, so the Monroe administration at last moved to smash them and their operation. In late October 1817, the administration authorized the army and navy to undertake the task.

Even as the administration was arranging the assault on Amelia Island, Gaines continued his plans to provoke a conflict with the Florida Indians. He directed supplies and reinforcements to move up the Apalachicola River through Florida to Fort Scott. He further strengthened Fort Scott and fattened his rosters for a possible campaign against the Seminoles, requesting Georgia militia from Governor William Rabun. From Fort Scott, he warned Fowltown about making threats against his army and emphasized the point by sending 250 soldiers under David Twiggs to bring in the village's headmen. On November 20, the soldiers were approaching Fowltown when they exchanged fire with Indians who fled into nearby swamps, leaving a few dead in the brush, silent inhabitants of the soon deserted village. A few days later Gaines sent another detachment of soldiers to burn the empty town.

The First Seminole War

Though they lived in Georgia, the Fowltown Indians had closer kinship ties and trade alliances to nearby Florida Seminoles than to distant Creeks. Seminoles thus viewed the attack on Fowltown as an attack on their kinsmen and by extension an attack on them, placing them at war with the United States. Gaines, by attacking Fowltown, had finally gotten what he wanted, a conflict eventually known as the First Seminole War. Although at the time nobody knew this fight would have successors, many were well aware that it could lead to acquisition of Spanish Florida.

The Massacre

Fowltown's warriors and their Seminole kinsmen, eager for revenge, began congregating at the confluence of the Flint and Chattahoochee rivers. The Indians likely knew about an American supply convoy moving up the river guarded by soldiers under Lieutenant R. W. Scott. Scott himself had taken several vessels ahead of the other boats carrying families of the Fort Scott garrison and ailing soldiers.

That December, President James Monroe sent his annual message to Congress in part assuring the legislature and the country that the frontier was calm. He had no way of knowing that a few days before and a thousand miles to his south, one mile below Fort Scott on the Chattahoochee River, a large party of Indians had attacked Lieutenant Scott's boats as the current drove them close to shore. All but one of the forty men, seven women, and several children were killed. The Indians took a woman captive and disappeared into the forest. Just that quickly, Fowltown was avenged, yet so was the Seminoles' future decided and Florida's fate sealed. Andrew Jackson saw to that.

The Orders

It took James Monroe nine months from his inauguration to find a permanent secretary of war. The third man offered the job, and the first to accept it, young South Carolina congressman John C. Calhoun had to deal with the war on the Florida border. Gaines's orders had barred him from pursuing Indians into Florida, but with the president's agreement, Calhoun modified the instructions to allow pursuit into Florida as long as the army carefully avoided Spaniards.

Looking back on the closing months of 1817, we can see that the United States War Department was trying to do too many things at once from too great a distance. Earlier, interim secretary Graham had issued orders to Gaines, the general officer nearest to Florida, to proceed to the Georgia coast and prepare the Amelia Island expedition. The attack on Lieutenant Scott's party theoretically changed all priorities, but Gaines nonetheless set out for his new assignment, unnecessarily as it happened. Before Gaines arrived at Amelia, American army and navy forces quickly subdued the island without firing a shot. The general quickly turned around and headed back to the impending action on the West Florida border. By then, however, the War Department had made a fateful decision.

Calhoun did not know about Gaines's availability when he sent the order to Andrew Jackson to assume command of the operation to chastise the Seminoles. Jackson, major general of the United States Army and overall commander of the nation's Southern Department, sallied forth from his home in Nashville heading toward south Georgia in early 1818, just as his subordinate Gaines headed back from the east. The operation would have plenty of commanders, especially considering that Andrew Jackson was more than enough.

Whether there would be plenty of men was another question. The militias of Georgia and neighboring states and territories were mustered, and allied Creeks as well as Cherokees were enjoined to augment the U.S. regulars and militia. The business of gathering, supplying, and moving these men, as well as feeding them along the way, strained the War Department's administrative capacity beyond its limits. In the coming war, hunger would be the greatest and most persistent enemy.

What this army was actually supposed to do and, more importantly, what it was not supposed to do once it entered Florida remained unclear. Calhoun no doubt expected his modified orders to unleash the American military to find and punish Indians and likewise constrain it to prevent an international incident with Spain. A few days after instructing Jackson to take command, Calhoun sent copies of all orders previously sent to Gaines specifically directing him to avoid Spaniards. Although Jackson had always received copies of such orders, Calhoun took the extra precaution of reiterating them, apparently to make sure that Jackson understood what the government did not want him to do.

Caution and prudence guided the government. Monroe wanted Florida just as his predecessors had beginning with Thomas Jefferson, but he did not want a war over it. By 1818, most perceptive observers, including important Spanish officials, believed that American ownership of Florida was inevitable. For Spain, it was a matter of saving face. For the United States, only three years removed from the costly War of 1812, it was a matter of cost and risk. America could not afford a war with Spain, no matter how weak that rupturing empire was, nor could America chance the possible international consequences of seizing foreign territory through military force.

The Letter

Caution and prudence did not guide Andrew Jackson, however. He intended to seize Florida. Before he received Calhoun's modified orders and the ones previously conveyed to Gaines, Jackson sent a letter to President Monroe proposing the conquest of Florida and suggesting that if Monroe agreed, the president should send his approval through Tennessee senator John Rhea. We should remind ourselves that caution and prudence, rather than a scrupulous regard for Spanish territory, guided Monroe. Yet, that does not diminish the fact that a real concern about starting a war and possibly prompting British intervention stayed his hand.

Simply put, Spain had done nothing to justify war. The administration could defend seizing Amelia Island because its mercenaries and pirates were a threat to American national and economic security. The administration could support chastising Seminoles because they had attacked Americans. Taking Spanish towns, however, was quite another matter. Monroe could not agree to Jackson's plan.

Therefore he said nothing, either to Rhea or Jackson, and he later claimed that when Jackson's letter arrived he had been ill and had not seen it. Jackson, on the other hand, later asserted that he had received the requested authorization from Rhea but had burned the letter after reading it. As for John Rhea, during the decade that followed he would support Monroe's version of events by stating that no such permission ever came from Monroe nor had he ever delivered any such authorization to Jackson.

Map 3.1
The Florida Invasion, 1818

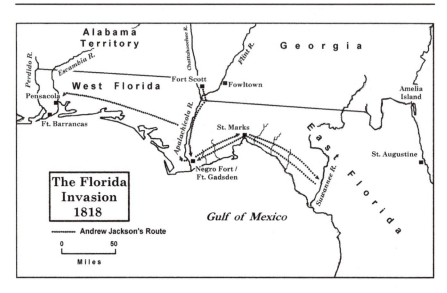

The controversy and contention over the so-called Rhea Letter remains one of the great storms clouding the origins of Jackson's behavior in Florida. Scholars still argue over whether Jackson's plans for his campaign had at least the tacit sanction of the President of the United States. Even so, those who insist that Monroe had to know what Jackson would do in Florida miss the point. Absolutely no evidence indicates that Jackson had either official or unofficial approval of the president. Moreover, Jackson never had the endorsement of Congress, the only branch of the government constitutionally empowered to declare war on a foreign power. A thousand Rhea Letters would not have made right that constitutional impropriety.[3]

The Preparations

Calhoun in the War Department continued to labor under the constraints of time and distance. Assuming that Gaines was still at Amelia Island, he ordered him to return to Fort Scott in southwestern Georgia after finishing off the pirates, taking what troops he had along the length of the Florida border to punish Seminoles along the way.

Of course, Gaines had already returned to Fort Scott, but he was no less misinformed than Secretary Calhoun. He did not, for instance, know that Jackson was to take command and would be bringing more troops. Nonetheless, once they had caught up to him or he to them, Calhoun's orders greatly encouraged him. At last, here was the authorization to invade Florida. For the moment, it did not matter that the Georgia frontier remained isolated from supplies and that food was becoming increasingly scarce—Fort Scott near the Florida line was nearing a provisioning crisis—at last, the army could put Florida in its sights. Gaines set about the business of mounting a campaign.

His first chore was to find enough men. The terms of the first muster of Georgia militiamen were about to expire, so Gaines had to wait for a new levy. Even after such men came into the ranks, their value was mixed at best. Usually they were poorly trained, difficult to control, and unreliable, with little motivation for service except the chance to plunder Indian villages. Jackson knew all of this too, but he had less cause to worry about manpower. Before heading south, he raised a throng of volunteers in Tennessee. Many had served under him in the War of 1812 and thus were likely to be more steadfast out of personal loyalty to him. Jackson's expectation that Creek and possibly Cherokee warriors, also veterans of his 1812 campaigns, would join him in this war would not be disappointed. Creeks under William McIntosh would be waiting on him when he arrived in Georgia.

The force had plenty of men but almost no food. The army's contract system relied on civilian provisioners who won their agreements through a bidding process. To enlarge profits, contractors provided cheap, inferior provisions when they provided anything at all. In short, the system was both prone to corruption and remarkably inefficient, especially when the lack of roads on the frontier made transporting rations to the forts difficult. Jackson knew all of this too, so he arranged before leaving Nashville to purchase supplies for the expedition. Their adequacy would be tested in the field. Jackson set out for the southern frontier on January 23, 1818.

The Negotiations

Simultaneous to the War Department's plans to stabilize the border, negotiations between Secretary of State John Quincy Adams and the Spanish minister to the United States Don Luis de Onís strained to produce a treaty ceding Florida to the United States. Logic suggested that outcome: the Spanish government was tired of maintaining the expensive Florida colonies and was inclined toward such a treaty, but with a qualification—and there was the rub. Spain would leave Florida to the United States *if* the Americans would promise not to provide aid to Latin America.

It was a risky game for Onís. Spain had no resources to stop the United States from taking Florida by force and could only hope that British misgivings about American expansion would cause them to intervene. Relying on the Royal Navy and British soldiers to stitch up the Spanish Empire was as precarious as it was galling for the Spaniards, but they had little choice. As it turned out, Britain would not help, and Onís probably suspected as much, just as he bitterly suspected that the U.S. government in Washington was laying plans to take Florida.

Onís was right about the British but wrong about Monroe, Adams, and Calhoun. All evidence indicates that the U.S. government believed the coming campaign was to eliminate the Seminole problem on the Florida border. Onís, however, was unwittingly on the mark about Andrew Jackson, a man he had never met. Jackson represented those southwestern Americans who wanted southern expansion, and they would have Florida sooner rather than later if he had anything to do with it.

The Invasion

Jackson arrived at Fort Scott on March 9, 1818, and began final preparations for the invasion of Florida. He and his little army could not linger because the garrison at Fort Scott was already near starvation before his arrival. Jackson knew that Gaines had arranged for supplies to come out of Mobile and up the Apalachicola, but the boats would have a difficult trip past hostile Seminoles. Driven by hunger more than tactics, within two days Jackson and his men set out for Florida to meet the boats. (See Map 3.1.)

Jackson's 1818 invasion of Florida was not a new war. Partly, it was a continuation of those Creek and Seminole clashes that stretched back to the War of 1812. Jackson found it easy to recruit Creeks from Georgia and Alabama because they wanted to plunder former enemies. The invasion also became a continuation of the unrealized dream of expansion left over from the War of 1812. Jackson found it easy to recruit Georgians and Tennesseans to march into a dense and danger-ous Spanish wilderness because they wanted Florida.

Jackson's little army soon met the supply boats coming up the Apalachicola. Fed and rested, the army then moved down to the remains of Negro Fort at Prospect Bluff where engineers constructed a new fortification. Named Fort Gadsden after Lieutenant James Gadsden, the chief engineer on the project, it became Jackson's principal supply depot as he headed east to nearby Seminole towns. Before marching toward those targets, however, Jackson ordered the naval forces that had brought the supplies back into the Gulf of Mexico. They were to stand off the Spanish fort at St. Marks, ostensibly to prevent the escape of Seminole leaders or Alexander Arbuthnot. Rumors correctly placed the old Scot at the fort, and his days of being ignored by Americans were almost over.

Jackson's disorganized, ill-trained force then proceeded to stumble through the wilderness. The army found a few empty Seminole towns, most Indians having fled before Jackson's arrival, and the best it could do was capture a few prisoners, burn the towns, and pillage or destroy food stores. Having swiped at some Indians, Jackson then set about the real business of the campaign. He turned his army toward St. Marks.

The small American flotilla, its ensigns tucked away to conceal its identity, had already arrived off St. Marks. The Spanish garrison watched the vessels with mounting curiosity until the fort's commander nervously sent a boat to investigate. The American commander, Captain Isaac McKeever, then raised a British flag and assured his nervous visitors that the Royal Navy had at last arrived to help defend Spanish Florida. As St. Marks breathed a sigh of relief, two Red Stick Creeks, the prophet Josiah Francis and the headman Homathlemico, rowed out to greet their "British friends."[4] Thus lured aboard a U.S. naval vessel flying false colors, the two Indians were imprisoned below decks.

The Seizure

Jackson arrived at St. Marks on April 6 and demanded that commander Don Francisco Caso y Luengo surrender the fort. Luengo refused, and Jackson promptly sent four companies of regular United States infantry through the fort's main gate—Luengo had left it unsecured—so surprising the garrison's seventy Spanish soldiers that they never even came close to their guns. In case any doubt remained about what had happened, Jackson personally lowered the Spanish flag and replaced it with the Stars and Stripes.

It was time to settle scores. Informed about McKeever's two Indian prisoners, Jackson had them brought ashore and hanged. Bearing out the rumors, Jackson also found Alexander Arbuthnot at St. Marks and ordered him arrested to be dealt with later.

Other scores were settled, too. Seminole towns to the east of St. Marks along the Suwannee River, for instance, had been for years sheltering countless fugitive slaves from Georgia and Alabama plantations. On April 9, Jackson moved east with the bulk of his army toward those towns, his soldiers eager to bag the numerous runaway slaves who had taken refuge among the Seminoles. Two days' march brought them to the village of Red Stick Creek leader Peter McQueen, who had led his followers into Florida after the 1813–14 Creek War. McQueen's warriors mounted a fierce rearguard action as their families scattered into the nearby swamps. At the end of it, some forty warriors lay dead on the field and about one hundred women and children fell prisoner. In a surprising development, the white woman captured during the attack on the Scott party in November 1817 turned up in McQueen's village, abandoned by her captors and, save for her considerable emotional ordeal, otherwise unharmed.

Jackson hurried his army eastward, concerned that the fleeing Red Sticks would warn the Seminoles on the Suwannee about his approach. The Indians easily outpaced him, however. When he reached the Suwannee, he found towns peopled only by a few warriors to hold off his advance while the last of their women and children crossed the Suwannee. As Jackson's men looted and burned the towns, they captured Robert Chrystie Ambrister, formerly an officer of the British Royal Marines and now a soldier of fortune. In fact, Ambrister was in Florida helping George Woodbine arm Indians and runaway slaves to aid Latin American revolutionaries. Ambrister was taken back to St. Marks as a prisoner, his sins in the eyes of Americans even greater than the letter-writing of Arbuthnot.

The Executions

Jackson' brief war against the Seminoles was over, but he still had important work in West Florida. First, he sent most of the Georgia militia and Creeks home, taking only his regulars and Tennessee volunteers back to St. Marks, where he appointed a military court to try Arbuthnot and Ambrister. They were charged with inciting enemies of the United States (meaning the Seminoles and Red Sticks). With his judges hand-chosen and his desires clearly evident, the verdict was a foregone conclusion. Both defendants were found guilty and sentenced to death. Perhaps because of his plea for mercy, the court recommended that Ambrister be flogged and imprisoned instead. Jackson, however, insisted that both men be executed. Arbuthnot was hanged from the yardarm of his own trading schooner. A firing squad shot Ambrister. By then, Andrew Jackson was already headed toward Fort Gadsden and from there west to Pensacola, the capital of West Florida.

The Capital

Jackson sent a report of his campaign to the War Department that described Florida as pacified and the Indians suppressed. Technically, the expedition was over. Yet, Jackson was determined—perhaps he had made the decision even before he left Tennessee—to take Pensacola and end Spanish rule in West Florida. He wrote to Calhoun that the war in Florida was over, but he also wrote to José Masot, the governor of West Florida, accusing him of aiding hostile Indians. Jackson also instructed Edmund Pendleton Gaines to clear the Apalachicola region of Indians. Gaines was "to view them as enemies and treat them accordingly" if they sought refuge with a Spanish garrison.[5] Such instructions were an additional violation of Calhoun's orders to limit the campaign, but after St. Marks, nothing the War Department had said mattered. On May 7, Jackson led most of his army out of Fort Gadsden toward Pensacola.

When Jackson marched into Pensacola on May 23, the Spanish garrison and Masot evacuated to Fort Barrancas. Jackson threatened dire consequences if Masot did not surrender the fort, but the governor was stubborn. On May 27, 1818, as the Americans trained their artillery on the fort, the Spaniards in Barrancas gamely fired on the U.S. batteries, but the devastating American bombardment persuaded Masot to surrender. Jackson's terms allowed the Spanish garrison to remove to Cuba and required U.S. forces to respect Spanish property in Pensacola.

Pensacola saw more than just a switching of flags. By the time Jackson departed for home just two days later, he had established a substantial garrison to retain Pensacola and had set up a United States Customs House to collect American duties on all imports into the city. While on the way home, Jackson paused to write his final, amended report to the War Department. In it, he proudly boasted that he had "planted the Star Spangled Banner on the ramparts of" Fort Barrancas.[6]

To say the least, the Monroe administration would be surprised.

Aftermath

Jackson had clearly disobeyed orders by attacking Florida's Spanish garrisons, but the possibility of serious objections to his conduct apparently did not occur to him. He assumed that most Americans were eager for new territory and that their representatives in Washington would applaud the accomplishment. Yet, the grave implications of what had happened—a general brazenly violating the government's orders, making war on a foreign power without congressional authorization, executing two British subjects on Spanish soil—greatly troubled official Washington. President Monroe and his cabinet were disturbed. Some in Congress were livid.

Congress

Jackson's actions prompted Congress to launch a formal investigation in early 1819, the first such proceeding in American history. Jackson partisans charged that Congress was simply engaging in cynical and politically motivated bluster, but the legislature was not merely posturing. Many representatives found Jackson's behavior troubling on several levels. One was the justifiable fear that the incident signaled an untoward expansion of executive authority when Jackson made war on a foreign power without congressional authorization. Other motives were not so dignified, particularly among those from the Northeast who opposed territorial expansion because new states would diminish their section's political influence. Other congressmen, Henry Clay prominent among them, appeared willing to exploit the incident to embarrass the Monroe administration. Speaker of the House Clay was certainly protective of congressional prerogative, but he also wasted few opportunities to discomfit James Monroe. Clay also probably numbered among those who resented the growing popularity of Andrew Jackson and feared the political career such acclaim was certain to launch.

In short, considerable congressional opposition decried what Jackson had done, albeit for a variety of reasons. Yet, after a flood of speeches, in the end Congress did nothing.

The inaction represented a bow to the evident and widespread popular approval of Jackson's conduct. Most Americans in 1819 already saw expansion as a natural expression of their control over the continent bordering their republic. In their view, Jackson in Florida had merely begun what should have begun long ago. They did not call it Manifest Destiny yet, but it was a big continent and plenty of time remained for someone to come up with the vocabulary. For the time being, even those congressmen with justifiable misgivings about Jackson's exploits refused to challenge the popular trend. Consequently, after all the ominous warnings about unchecked executive power and reckless expansionism, Congress did nothing. Jackson, who emerged from the incident even more popular than before, had won a great personal as well as political victory, rivaling even the one over the Spaniards in Florida.

Diplomacy

Domestic difficulties with Congress were significant, but the international repercussions over the invasion could have proved more harmful. Spain's anger halted the Adams-Onís negotiations, and the British public's reaction to the Arbuthnot and Ambrister executions was fierce.

Fortunately, the British government was more interested in stabilizing relations with the United States, especially by resolving issues persisting after the War of 1812. The 1817 Rush-Bagot agreement disarming the Great Lakes was one example of that spirit. Another accord in 1818 established mutual rights to the Pacific Northwest for ten years, temporarily resolving the awkward question of who owned the Oregon Country. British foreign secretary Lord Castlereagh wanted no crisis with the United States to disturb this new amity, especially one over two British subjects whose careless activities had apparently invited their unfortunate fate.

After an uneasy few weeks in the summer of 1819 during which the administration boldly asserted to foreign embassies that Jackson's behavior was justified, it gradually emerged that Spain would be the only foreign power intent upon causing trouble over the invasion. Secretary of State Adams assured the president that even the Spanish fury would wane in time and be of no consequence.

The Transcontinental Treaty

Adams was right. Spanish Minister Don Luis de Onís vociferously protested Jackson's violation of Spanish territory and threatened to break off negotiations, but Madrid eventually gauged the U.S. threat to Florida as irresistible. It was at last time to cut colonial losses. Onís received instructions to negotiate the sale of East and West Florida and, for good measure, to settle the boundary between the United States and Spanish holdings farther west. The result was the Adams-Onís Treaty of 1819, frequently called the Transcontinental Treaty because its terms extended the U.S. border with Spain's North American colonies to the Pacific.

The Spanish government would truculently delay ratification of the treaty for two years, but once ratified, it gave the United States not only Florida but also Spanish recognition of American rights to the Pacific Northwest above the forty-second parallel. It was not a clear title to the so-called Oregon Country, as the British would repeatedly point out, but it was an important step in broadening America's westward reach.

Conclusion

After 1815, American desire for access to the Gulf of Mexico coincided with a growing and uncontrollable American settlement in southern Georgia and Alabama. As settlers clashed with Indians and Spain's impotence was worsened by erupting Latin American revolutions, the Florida border became more violent and the frontier it straddled more volatile. The arrival of the U.S. Army to protect survey crews, control squatters, and discourage Indians, heightened tensions. The provocative policies of American officers such as Edmund Pendleton Gaines and Andrew Jackson toward both Indians and Spaniards finally sparked incidents serious enough to compel the U.S. government to authorize an invasion of Florida. The operation as described by Washington had limited objectives, but Jackson exceeded his instructions and seized Spanish posts and towns against orders. Although his Florida adventure caused heated domestic and international disapproval, his popularity shielded him from serious personal consequences. Meanwhile, Secretary of State John Quincy Adams mixed finesse, glib verbal defenses, and blunt expressions of the truth to maneuver Spanish envoy Don Luis de Onís into a treaty that legitimated Jackson's conquest.

Leaving aside the unique features of this expansionist episode, its general aspect reveals a pattern in American territorial growth. Settlements either tied directly to the United States or composed of those sympathetic to American ideals would spread to the frontier. As this American presence increased, abrasive incidents with the people of bordering provinces ultimately prompted U.S. intervention responding to a perceived need to secure national boundaries. The result could be a diplomatic solution, as in Oregon, or it could be a martial one, as with Florida or Mexico, but the result would be the same: the expansion of U.S. territory and the corresponding expansion of U.S. power and interests.

As Americans learned, also, acquiring territory was only the first part of the arduous process of settling, developing, and governing it. As the country entered the 1820s, a growing refrain among expansionists was the obstacle to orderly settlement and economic development posed by Indians. In only a few years, that sentiment produced one of the most significant policies in American history, the wholesale relocation of Indian tribes to a region west of the Mississippi.

Notes

1. Jackson to Mauricio de Zúñiga, 23 April 1816, in *American State Papers: Foreign Relations,* 6 vols. (Washington: Gales and Seaton, 1834), 4:499.

2. Gaines to John Williams, 12 July 1817, Letters Received Adjutant General's Office, National Archives, Washington, D.C.

3. Curiously, some authors such as Robert V. Remini in *Andrew Jackson and His Indian Wars* (New York: Penguin, 2001), 137–38, claim that, without evidence that Jackson did not receive authorization to take Florida, no one can say that he did not have such authorization.

4. Josiah Francis had recently returned from an extended visit to Great Britain where he had unsuccessfully courted British support for his people. See David S. Heidler and Jeanne T. Heidler, *Old Hickory's War: Andrew Jackson and the Quest for Empire* (1996; reprint, with a foreword by the authors, Baton Rouge: Louisiana State University Press, 2003), 54.

5. Jackson to Gaines, 5 May 1818, Letters Received Adjutant General's Office.

6. Jackson to Gaines, 2 June 1818, Andrew Jackson Papers, Library of Congress, Washington, D.C.

CHAPTER 4

DOMESTIC IMPEDIMENTS:
INDIAN REMOVAL

Problems between American Indians and whites over land began with the settlement at Jamestown in 1607. In the ensuing years, European colonization gradually shoved many Indians west of the Appalachian Mountains, but they could never move fast enough to outpace the spreading white tide. By the American Revolution, settlements were across the Appalachians, too.

The Revolution, in fact, foretold the Indians' fate. Many sided with the British to fight colonists' relentless expansion, but it was an unwise alliance that alarmed and enraged white Americans and left the Indians abandoned and friendless when the British lost the war. American revolutionaries banded together to quell the domestic Indian threat even more eagerly than they had fought redcoats. At war's end in 1783, they nursed memories of Indian depredations, frequently seeking revenge as they steadily encroached on Indian lands.

Purpose and Policy

Under the Articles of Confederation, the national government assumed jurisdiction over Indian affairs, a policy that continued after the Constitution was adopted and the new government established in 1789. George Washington's administration thus controlled all relations with Indian tribes, including the purchase of their lands through treaty negotiations. The government did not formally recognize Indian land ownership, but treaties were an easy way of placating natives while promoting white settlement. This worked for a while because demand for national expansion was steady but not frantic, as it would become in the ensuing decades. The government consequently had as its main task preventing conflict between Indians and whites or ending it when it occasionally broke out.

Separation, Force, and Acculturation

The Washington administration believed that keeping Indians and whites separated would best preserve the peace. Perhaps the most typical agreement to achieve this goal was the 1790 Treaty of New York with the Creek Indians. In addition to setting boundaries separating the Creek nation from white settlements, the treaty promised "perpetual peace and friendship between . . . the United States of America, and . . . the Creek nation of Indians."[1] To reduce the chance for tensions arising from the wrong kind of contact, Congress passed a series of statutes known as the Trade and Intercourse Acts that required government approval of all commercial relations with Indians.

Other measures, however, were not so peaceful. The government increased military spending on temporary regular forces and authorized Major General Anthony Wayne's successful campaign against a large Indian confederation in the Northwest Territory. The resulting Treaty of Greenville in 1795 ceded much of modern Ohio to the United States. Despite such occasional shows of force, the government's goal during this early period was permanent peace between Indians and whites. The aspiration prompted the Washington administration's policy known as the civilization program, an acculturation plan to encourage Indians to live and work like their white neighbors. Agents were assigned to each tribe to establish schools and foster significant cultural transformations that would make Indians acceptable as future U.S. citizens. Some of these efforts succeeded, especially among southern Indians, but much of the success derived from the fact that southern Indians had adopted a sedentary lifestyle that predated even the earliest European settlements in North America. That lifestyle employed a mix of agriculture and hunting and featured residence in permanent towns. Such customs of the southeastern Indians probably account for early European assessments of them as the most intelligent native people in North America.

European contact affected these people, of course, but more materially than culturally, and in the long term, such material intrusions would be more destructive of native societies than any civilizing program. White traders purchased deerskins with metal pots, guns, and ammunition. By the end of the eighteenth century, the deerskin trade became so brisk that Indians were gravely over-hunting deer and glutting the pelt market even as they were increasingly dependent on the goods white traders provided. In addition to this material dependence, blood ties developed as well. Indian women married traders and had children who could and did live in both white and Indian worlds, speaking both languages, and sometimes attending white schools. The matrilineal tradition of southern Indians made these mixed heritage children thoroughly Indian in the eyes of the tribe. Frequently they wielded extensive political and religious influence within Indian culture.[2]

Meanwhile, white settlement inexorably crept closer. As part of the civilization program, the government established stores to control trade with the Indians. But with the deerskin market in decline, Indians sank into hopeless debt buying goods on credit, and the government persuaded tribes to relinquish land to satisfy those obligations. Although not necessarily malicious by design, the gradual nature of the process disguised its ominous implications for everybody. The government assumed that as Indians relied more exclusively on farming, livestock husbandry would provide them meat and diminish the need for large hunting preserves. For their part, the Indians did not realize until too late the importance of land as a birthright. Before then, they carelessly continued to sell that birthright for nothing more than pots and pans.

The Origins of a Removal Policy

At the opening of the nineteenth century, state governments began demanding that the federal government extinguish Indian land claims in the East. Georgia was especially insistent about the matter, and shortly after assuming office, the administration of President Thomas Jefferson complied. In return for Georgia's relinquishing claims to the territory west of the Chattahoochee River, the U.S. government promised to negotiate the gradual termination of all Indian land ownership within the state. The arrangement, called the Compact of 1802, did not specify a schedule for the negotiations, but Georgians expected the pact to be fulfilled sooner rather than later.

Part of the reason was economic. Ten years after its invention, the cotton gin was making short-staple cotton a major cash crop, fueling calls for ever larger tracts of land to grow this white gold. As Georgia's demands to implement the 1802 agreement grew louder, the government continued to rely on its civilization program and an occasional Indian land cession to keep the peace. How long such gradual measures could ward off Georgian impatience was a difficult question.

Jefferson believed that a permanent solution was imperative, especially as rapidly expanding white settlement threatened a war that might wipe out the Indian nations and their cultures. To Jefferson's thinking, the plentiful lands of the Louisiana Purchase provided a happy solution. The government could relocate eastern Indians to lands west of the Mississippi, buying them time for acculturation while opening their vacated lands to white settlement. Jefferson never acted on this plan, but he always regarded the idea of using western lands as a permanent home for eastern Indians as a benign solution to an ugly problem. He believed that the eastern Indians would "in time either incorporate with us as citizens . . . or remove beyond the Mississippi."[3]

Eventually the plan would appeal to those with less than benevolent motives. In later years, advocates of Indian removal would cloak their desires with mock concerns about preserving Indian culture, but their real goal was the land.

The War of 1812 and Indian Lands

As with the American Revolution, the War of 1812 left American Indians weaker than before. The war itself was in part caused by the American belief that the British were inciting Indian violence against the United States, but Indians needed no such encouragement. The subsequent defeat of both northwestern and southwestern Indians spelled disaster for their extensive land claims. More white settlers poured into former Indian holdings even before the government could survey the regions and put parcels up for sale.

In the South, this flood of squatters proved especially provocative because many Indians had not yet left the vast region acquired by Andrew Jackson in the Treaty of Fort Jackson. The situation became so volatile that it led to the American invasion of Spanish Florida and the purchase of that territory from Spain.[4]

Removal

The pace of American settlement after the War of 1812 amplified whites' calls for a solution to "the Indian problem." Their problem was not complicated, and consequently their solution was simple. In fact, the hard part was dressing it up with palatable and high-sounding oratory, but that too would be accomplished. Removal, proclaimed Andrew Jackson, would allow Indians "to pursue happiness in their own way and under their own rude institutions."[5]

In simplest terms, Indians occupied lands that whites wanted, and no matter how isolated or remote the Indians believed themselves, federal agents would eventually visit almost every tribe east of the Mississippi. The circumstances for individual groups would differ in time and place—some would try forceful resistance and others would appeal to the white man's own laws—but the result was always the same. The Indians lost their land and were moved west of the Mississippi River.

Seminoles and Creeks

The United States' 1821 acquisition of Florida placed the Seminole Indians in an unhappy position. They were few and unable to resist several American invasions during the previous decade. Understandably, they regarded the United States as an enemy, and after 1821, they were justifiably alarmed at being under American dominion. Most disturbing of all, the first Florida territorial governor was Andrew Jackson.

During Jackson's brief tenure as governor, one of his primary goals was removing Seminoles from valuable agricultural lands in the northern part of the territory. Jackson failed to complete the task before stepping down as governor, but his efforts led to the Treaty of Moultrie Creek in September 1823. Under its terms, most Seminoles moved into south central Florida to scratch out an existence in swampy regions far different from the fertile lands in the northern part of the territory. Those would be set aside for whites.

Similar arrangements were made throughout the Southeast in the 1820s with the primary goal always being additional acreage for white settlement at the expense of Indian country. Georgians remained especially impatient for this process to be completed. In 1825, federal negotiators bribed Creek headman William McIntosh to persuade his followers to accept the Treaty of Indian Springs. Not only were the treaty's terms objectionable—they ceded to Georgia all remaining Creek lands within the state—the blatant fraud surrounding negotiations discredited both them and their principal organizer, McIntosh. Worse, the Creek National Council had not approved the cession, and McIntosh had violated Creek law by acting without the council's approval. It was not his first such offense, but it would be his last. The council sentenced him to death for his treachery.

Even as the executioners were carrying out their grim chore, the United States repudiated Second Indian Springs because McIntosh had not possessed the authority to cede tribal lands. The mess, however, did not daunt fuming Georgians. The state continued to pressure the federal government for another and equally extensive treaty with the Creeks. In 1826, just one year after the notorious agreement at Indian Springs, Creeks relinquished all their lands in Georgia. After that, only the Cherokee remained, their homes restricted to the northern part of Georgia on land that nobody wanted, at least for the time being.

President Jackson

When Andrew Jackson was elected president in 1828 small groups of southern Indians had already migrated to Arkansas and a region designated as the Indian Territory (present-day Oklahoma). In the upper Midwest, other Indian groups had also been pushed off their lands by treaties immediately following the War of 1812 and had migrated to lands west of the Mississippi. Those Indians who remained east of the river were mostly determined to remain on what land they had left.

By 1829, southern states, with Georgia in the lead, had begun passing laws that further encouraged Indians to migrate westward. For instance, the Cherokees were placed under the jurisdiction of Georgia laws although doing so violated U.S.-Cherokee treaties. Another Georgia statute prohibited Indians from testifying against whites, and an 1830 law required whites who entered the Cherokee nation to obtain a license from state authorities. Georgia clearly wanted to limit the activities of northern missionaries who helped the Cherokees with their legal battles and encouraged them to resist removal. When missionaries Samuel Worcester and Elizur Butler were arrested for refusing to comply, the case reached the United States Supreme Court where a majority ruled in favor of the missionaries and the Cherokee nation. Speaking for the majority, Chief Justice John Marshall in the case of *Worcester* v. *Georgia* declared the Georgia licensing statute as unconstitutional because "the treaties and laws of the United States contemplate the Indian territory as completely separate from that of the states."[6] In response, Andrew Jackson allegedly muttered, "Well: John Marshall has made his decision: *now let him enforce it.*"[7] Possibly Jackson never said those words, but he did make it clear from the moment he assumed office that he supported the states' desire to rid themselves of Indians.

While Jackson no doubt wanted the eastern Indians removed beyond the Mississippi, his motives have been variously interpreted. In his first annual message, Jackson outlined his proposal for Indian removal, claiming that such a policy would benefit the Indians as much as it would the whites. His declaration that Indians could develop the arts of civilization only if removed from corrupt white influences had an insincere ring, but whatever his reasoning and rationale, the results would be the same. The following year, at Jackson's urging and after considerable debate, Congress passed the Indian Removal Act, its terms appropriating $500,000 for the administration to negotiate removal treaties with the Indians. Jackson immediately sent emissaries to the various tribes to begin the process. (See Map 4.1.)

The Black Hawk War

The South contained the largest concentration of Indians east of the Mississippi River, so removal efforts focused on that region. Yet, in the 1820s and 1830s, Indians in the upper Midwest also came under increasing pressure to abandon their lands in Illinois, Wisconsin, and Minnesota. Unintended consequences of removal immediately appeared in these instances.

Indians lived where they did based on the logic of survivability. The presence of game and fertile soil and the absence of enemies dictated habitat and home. The dislocation of removal, however, completely disrupted such logic. When uprooted from their natural habitats, Indians were removed not just from their land but from the reasons they had made it their home. Sparse game and arid earth awaited them. Worse, they were no longer separated from hereditary enemies. The general nature of removal uprooted all Indians, placing traditional antagonists into unexpected proximity where cycles of violence and retaliation that had been quiet for generations flared anew.

The fate of the Sauk-Fox Indians perfectly illustrates this unfortunate circumstance. In 1831, government negotiators intimidated the Sauk-Fox into relinquishing all of their lands in Illinois. Their aged leader Black Hawk had resisted such a move for years, but in the face of the government's menacing insistence, he led his people westward. The

experience became a nightmare when they found only impending starvation and hostile enemies on the other side of the Mississippi. In only
a year, Black Hawk led about five hundred men, women, and children
back across the river into Illinois.

The reappearance of this small band of Sauk-Fox sent the people
of Illinois into a panic. Frantic pleas for government action against the
perceived Indian menace brought militias and regular army units to
fight what became known as the Black Hawk War. Like most removal
incidents, it was a sad and shameful affair. Black Hawk, as astonished
by the reaction to his return as whites were frightened, tried to surrender to protect his women and children, but edgy militiamen apparently
misinterpreted the gesture despite the standard white flag. The militia
opened fire, and Black Hawks' warriors did so as well. The militia ran.

So did the Sauk-Fox because growing military forces were soon
pursuing them all the way to Wisconsin. As Black Hawk directed rearguard actions, his people reached the Mississippi River in early August
and were attempting to cross it when U.S. Army and Illinois militia
forces fell upon them. The Battle of Bad Axe on August 2, 1832, left
about 70 percent of the Sauk-Fox men, women, and children dead,
mostly killed by unruly militiamen. Black Hawk escaped, but Win-
nebago Indians soon turned him over to the government. Kept prisoner
in the East for several years, Black Hawk finally returned to his people
shortly before his death in 1838. By then, they were eking out a meager
existence in Iowa.

Choctaw Removal

The Choctaw Indians in Mississippi were the first southern Indians
to enter into a removal agreement under the 1830 law. In that year, a few
Choctaw leaders signed the Treaty of Dancing Rabbit Creek, believing
they had little choice because U.S. negotiators said Mississippi would
insist on enforcing state laws within Choctaw territory. The agreement
did not reflect the will of most Choctaws, however, and even the treaty's
pliant signers required liberal federal bribes before agreeing to it. Under
Dancing Rabbit Creek, Choctaws could remain in Mississippi and
receive a land allotment for each head of household. Some would not be
allowed to leave, however, if they were indebted to white Mississippians
until all such obligations were met. Those who could leave and chose to
would be provided with land in the West and an annuity.

Map 4.1
Results of the Indian Removal Act of 1830

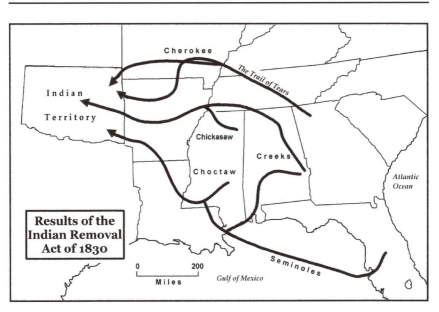

Neither those who stayed nor those who departed fared well. Even before the U.S. Senate ratified Dancing Rabbit Creek, white squatters were rushing onto Choctaw land, worsening an already confused situation. Choctaws who remained in Mississippi often became aware of unknown debts that allowed whites to defraud them of their allotted lands. Meanwhile, the first Choctaw migration commenced during the winter of 1830–31, described as "one of the severest winters ever experienced in the south or west."[8] There were few roads and sometimes not even paths to ease the journey, and provisions were both inadequate and inferior.

Perhaps recalling the fate of the Creek treaty of 1825, most Choctaws remained in Mississippi until the following year to see if the U.S. Senate would ratify Dancing Rabbit Creek. When it did, dashing all Choctaw optimism, plans went forward to remove at least one-third of the remaining Choctaws, beginning in the fall of 1831. More elaborate preparations envisioned better supplies and transportation for this second migratory trek, even to the point of delaying it until the Choctaws had harvested their crops. Nevertheless, the Indians again endured appalling hardships. The government also decided that relocated Chick-asaws should occupy part of the land promised to the Choctaws, so even before they reached their new home along the Red River, it was shrinking.

Large emigrations like that of the winter of 1831–32 were repeated over the next few years until most Choctaws were gone forever from Mississippi. Bad food, little shelter, poor transportation, inadequate clothing, and disease made these people refugees rather than migrants. Even small improvements suggested by experience were offset when whites took to accosting Choctaws and looting their possessions at ren-dezvous points. Herded like cattle through areas afflicted with cholera, they died in droves en route to their new homes.

By the middle of 1833, about seven thousand Choctaws had under-gone this ordeal and about seven thousand remained in Mississippi enduring harassment and victimization that left them landless and hope-less. The government in the 1840s sought to remove these destitute peo-ple to lands occupied by the other Choctaws in Arkansas. Only the more acculturated Choctaws, most of mixed heritage, remained in the state as citizens, legatees of the original civilization program begun so many years before. It was hardly what George Washington had had in mind.

Creek Removal

While Choctaw removal proceeded, federal agents visited other southeastern tribes seeking similar removal treaties. Pressure from the states speeded the process. By 1831, Alabama had emulated Georgia's practice by extending its authority over the Creek Nation. White squat-ters continued to move onto Creek land, assaulting and stealing at will, impervious to any efforts to control them. In fact, when Creeks appealed to the federal government for protection from these interlop-ing marauders, federal agents merely shrugged and advised that the Indians would be better off moving west. The Creeks also appealed to their sympathetic agent John Crowell, but he lacked any authority to punish or remove offending whites.

Desperate for some measure of security, the Creeks sent a delega-tion to Washington at the end of 1831 to seek help from President Jack-son. The envoys should have saved themselves the trip. Not only would Jackson not see them, their meeting with the secretary of war was most gloomy. The only topic for discussion was Creek removal, and in the face of Creek persistence—additional delegations were sent to Washington the following year—the administration proved equally dogged. Finally in March 1832, the Creeks agreed to the land allotment scheme that had mollified the Choctaws. Within the boundaries of the Creek Nation, heads of households would receive parcels of acreage, and all remaining land would be ceded to the United States. Allotments could be sold, in which case, the government would provide land west of the Mississippi, transportation, supplies for the journey, and subsistence to help transplants become established in the West. The process was to span five years.

The government quickly put into operation a plan to survey Creek land, count Creek heads (about 23,000 in 1832), and transport Creeks west, beginning in 1833. White squatters and traders spent this time among these dispossessed and friendless people fleecing them out of their lands and money. When swindles failed, force worked even faster. Creeks appealed to the federal government for protection, but the only response was to suggest immediate removal rather than the five-year schedule of the original agreement.

Encouraged by apparent government indifference, white outlaws went on a rampage that shocked even government agents. Fearful that Creeks might be driven to defend themselves and thus delay the removal plan, army officers and civilian officials tried to intervene, but white Alabamians threatened them for their trouble. Efforts to control the chaos were redoubled. Some Creeks who had already migrated west were brought to Alabama to persuade their eastern cousins to quit their lands immediately. By the end of 1833, small groups of Creeks began moving west.

That number increased during the winter of 1834–35. Although the government had prepared a route and sought to provide sufficient supplies, the journey was horrific. Winter weather, poor provisions, and the inevitable diseases killed about one-third of the Creeks who made the trip.

Rapacious white settlers and unscrupulous businessmen continued to victimize those Creeks who remained in Alabama. They purchased land allotments for a fraction of their value, sometimes with nothing more than whiskey. Finally, the threat of Indian violence and the complaints of honest whites who deplored such fraud prompted the government to suspend sales of Indian lands in the spring of 1835 and conduct an investigation, but it was too little action coming too late for angry Creeks. Occasional retaliation against white speculators set off vengeance raids against remote Indian homesteads. Forced off or cheated out of their farms and livestock, by 1836 many Creeks were near starvation. Their restlessness frightened white settlers who called for immediate removal of all Creeks. It was either that, they said, or war.

The Creek War of 1836

The crisis divided Creek leaders. Some believed that immediate removal was their only option, but others insisted that the government should uphold the terms of the original treaty of 1832. Government agents, on the other hand, were of one mind. They told the Creeks that the only choice was removal and began distributing money for supplies to sustain the Indians during the journey. As swindlers again descended on the Creeks to pick them clean of this latest government bounty, the Indians had hard evidence that the government was as unlikely to protect them during the journey as before it. Many Creeks tried not to think about the fate awaiting them at the end of their trek.

Instead, quite a few began to run away. By early 1836, about 2,500 Creeks had already moved among the Cherokees in north Georgia. Georgia militia attempts to drive them back into Alabama started the Creek War of 1836, but it was hardly a war. Georgia militia was responsible for most of the violence, while most Creeks ran to refuges in any isolated place they could find, pathetically trying to avoid the horrors of a forced march. They preferred to starve in the forests and pine barrens of Alabama if that was the only way for them to remain on the land of their ancestors.

Several hundred Creeks made the journey west in 1836. Those who remained were forced into petty theft to feed their families, acts that the white population exaggerated as warlike. Finally, in east central Alabama, small groups of Creeks accommodated the label by mounting attacks that put settlers in rural areas to flight. Most Creeks, however, were adamantly opposed to this belligerent behavior, certain that it would provoke even more wrath from whites. To demonstrate their commitment to peace, Creek leaders sent warriors against those responsible for the attacks. By this time, even many white settlers had come to realize that the real authors of the unrest were the unscrupulous men who had preyed on the Creeks in their time of distress. If those people were punished, they said, the violence would stop.

Nevertheless, the governor of Alabama prepared to call out the militia while others, including many in Washington, thought the attacks merited deploying troops to force remaining Creeks to leave the state. Federal troops under the command of Brigadier General Winfield Scott were dispatched, ostensibly to capture the perpetrators of the attacks but actually to facilitate rapid Creek removal at gunpoint. By the summer of 1836, more that two thousand Creek men, women, and children had been rounded up and sent west. Not only did this end the Creek War of 1836, it made it easier for the army to begin removing the remaining Creeks in Alabama, even though many had helped the government capture their own brethren. Rather than winning American gratitude, however, the Creeks had given American authorities an idea. With astonishing audacity, government agents requested that during the forced Creek removal, Creek warriors should help the army capture Seminoles in Florida where removal had ignited a real Indian war.

By the end of 1836, most of the Creek Nation had been driven west from Alabama. The only Creeks who remained fell into four categories, two of them troublesome to Alabamians. Those who had not yet disposed of their property and those of mixed heritage who had gained title to their lands posed no problems, but those who hid in swamps and forests to avoid their removal as well as families of the warriors who had gone to fight the Seminoles were most unwelcome.

Roving mobs could do little about Indians who hid in remote areas, but the others were kept in camps maintained by the government. Armed rabble descended on these camps and forced Creek women and children to clear out. Conditions during this impromptu 1837 removal were simply abysmal. Without their husbands and fathers to shield them, women, children, and the elderly were mercilessly abused as they were driven to embarkation points in Mobile. When Creek warriors returned from Florida, they were stunned by this latest outrage, but the government, without apology, simply transported them to south Alabama where they were placed on the steamboats with their families and shipped west. By the end of 1837, Creek removal was essentially complete.

Chickasaw Removal

The Chickasaw Indians, who lived in eastern Mississippi and western Alabama, were accorded a special privilege in 1830 when some of their headmen personally met President Andrew Jackson in Tennessee. The occasion was far from festive. Jackson solemnly told them that he could not prevent Mississippi and Alabama from assuming jurisdiction over them. It was a sobering interview, and on the weight of it, the headmen agreed to removal. They did stipulate that they would tour their prospective home in the West before entering a final agreement. When it became clear that the government intended to place them within the Choctaw domain, the Chickasaws refused to move to that location, but such objections were pointless. White settlers were already moving onto Chickasaw lands, and the Mississippi and Alabama governments had assumed authority over them.

Helpless before this physical and legal onslaught, Chickasaws agreed in October 1832 to the Treaty of Pontotoc Creek. One of the more straightforward of the removal agreements, the treaty relinquished all Chickasaw land to the United States with the understanding that the proceeds from its sale would belong to the Chickasaws once they settled in the West. In an apparent concession, the Chickasaws would also be allowed to choose where they would settle in the Indian Territory.

The treaty caused a tremendous division within the Chickasaw nation that pitted Indians of mixed heritage against their more traditional brethren. The latter felt that they had not been adequately represented at the negotiations and resented the extra monetary considerations given to those Chickasaws who signed the treaty. These Chickasaw nativists wielded considerable influence among their people, so when the government rebuffed their objections, most Chickasaws suddenly balked at removal. The delay was of little consequence to government agents who placidly watched white settlers pour onto Chickasaw lands while government surveyors plotted sections of it for sale. The Chickasaws watched, too, but not at all placidly. Most of them, in fact, concluded that they had no choice but to leave. During the summer of 1837, the process began in earnest.

As in other removals, poor supplies, disease, and inadequate shelter beset Chickasaw migrations. By early 1839, most of them had relocated to their new homes. Over the next few years, most of the rest would find their way west as well, leaving their prosperous lands under the cabins and plows of white settlers.

Cherokee Removal

Although the process of removal was a horrid ordeal for all tribes, Cherokee removal from Georgia has always been regarded as especially infamous. It has certainly received more attention than that of any other Indian group. The Cherokees were numerous, numbering at least sixteen thousand at the time of removal, prosperous, and more inclined to adopt white cultural ways than any other southeastern tribe. They welcomed white Protestant missionaries into their communities, encouraged the construction of schools within their territory, and acquired land as individuals rather than as a tribe or clans. Wealthier Cherokees, emulating wealthy white neighbors, owned slaves. During the first quarter of the nineteenth century, the Cherokees also began adopting a system of written law and developed a central government in 1827 with a constitution closely modeled on that of the United States. It was a unique accomplishment among Indians, for the Cherokees were exceptional in having developed a written form of their language, even founding a national newspaper, the *Cherokee Phoenix*.

Here was a matchless example of success for the civilization program, but Georgians were neither impressed nor pleased. Instead, they expected the federal government to honor the Compact of 1802 and extinguish Cherokee land claims within the state. The Cherokee obviously had other ideas, as when they adopted a law that made the alienation of any Cherokee land a capital crime.

For a time, the marginality of the rough hill country the Cherokees occupied protected them, but then gold was discovered in north Georgia, and everything abruptly changed. The state's leaders increased demands that the federal government remove the Cherokees immediately, and Andrew Jackson's election in 1828 meant that those demands would have a friendly ear in the presidency. Meanwhile, the Georgia legislature began a systematic legal program to harass the Indians. They were prohibited from mining gold, even on land recognized as Cherokee territory by the United States. Georgia also organized a state lottery to distribute Cherokee lands to Georgia citizens. Another law required all whites to swear allegiance to the state of Georgia as a condition for obtaining a license to enter the Cherokee nation. The Georgia government believed that limiting white access to the Cherokees would stem the irritating interference of northern missionaries who were stirring up trouble by encouraging the Indians to mount legal challenges against the state.

The Legal Battle

Georgia's claim of legal jurisdiction over Cherokees, the lottery to distribute their lands, and the passage by the U.S. Congress of the Indian Removal Act in 1830 caused the Cherokee nation to turn to the courts. In their first effort, the Cherokees asked the Supreme Court to enforce their treaty rights by prohibiting the enforcement of Georgia law within their territory. In *Cherokee Nation* v. *Georgia,* the Supreme Court declined jurisdiction because the Cherokees only resided within the borders of the United States but were not citizens. Despite that disappointing result, Chief Justice John Marshall expressed his belief that the Cherokees were in the right. Georgia, he said, could not violate U.S. treaties by asserting jurisdiction over the Indians. Marshall's sentiment, however, was only that—a sentiment. The Supreme Court's ruling that Indians could not sue in federal courts simply emboldened Georgia to intensify its program of harassment. The state began arresting missionaries who were encouraging the Indians in their legal fight. State courts subsequently convicted Samuel Worcester of violating the state licensing law, and thus the case was appealed to the Supreme Court as the famous *Worcester* v. *Georgia.* Unlike the purported restraints dictating judicial inaction in the Cherokee Nation case, *Worcester* fell within the court's jurisdiction because the missionary was an American citizen.

This time the court handed the Cherokees a victory by declaring that Georgia laws did not apply to the Cherokee nation. Speaking for the court, Chief Justice Marshall stated that the Georgia law was "repugnant to the Constitution, treaties, and laws of the United States."[9] The plain language of Marshall's ruling, however, masked the ambiguous nature of the Cherokees' legal triumph. There was no question that the highest American court in the land supported their right to be left alone, but in practical terms, the ruling meant little. Some scholars have argued that the Worcester decision did not really order the state of Georgia to do anything positive in the way of restitution. The court merely told Georgia it was wrong.[10] Even if this actually was the intentional legal limit of the decision, Andrew Jackson, no matter what he did or did not say regarding Marshall's ruling, did not think Georgia was wrong at all. Neither the Cherokees nor Samuel Worcester needed a remark from the president to clarify matters. Jackson acceded to Georgia's wishes to punish the troublesome Worcester by removing him from his postmastership. Georgia would not likely be forced to leave the Cherokees alone.

Disappointed over the lack of tangible relief from the courts, many Cherokees lost hope that they could avoid removal. Soon the Cherokee nation became deeply divided over the issue as a Treaty Party began urging negotiations with the United States for the most favorable terms in their unavoidably bad situation. Hundreds of Cherokees were already leaving the nation for the Indian Territory by the end of 1832, and the following year Georgia sought to prove the wisdom of the Treaty Party by confiscating Cherokee property and distributing it to whites in the state lottery.

Such a blatant violation of property rights was more than some Cherokees could bear, and envoys of the Treaty Party traveled to Washington in the spring of 1834 to negotiate a removal agreement. The Treaty Party's ascendancy, however, was short-lived because this accord was never ratified and only left the Cherokee nation more divided over the removal question. The following year another Treaty Party delegation went to Washington, but this time a rival group of anti-removal Cherokees led by John Ross, the principal chief of the nation, shadowed it. The Treaty Party again negotiated a removal treaty, but Ross's party blocked its ratification in the Cherokee Council. Georgia promptly confiscated Ross's property and placed it in the state land lottery.

The Jackson administration finally lost patience. Government agents arranged a meeting at the former Cherokee capital of New Echota in December 1835. Although only about 3 percent of the Cherokee nation came to New Echota, and none was authorized to negotiate for the entire nation, federal negotiator John F. Schermerhorn was undaunted in concluding a removal agreement that the U.S. government would regard as final and binding. After a stormy debate, the U.S. Senate ratified the Treaty of New Echota.

Using this dubious document over the strenuous objections of virtually the entire Cherokee nation, the government deployed the army to force the Cherokees west. General John Wool had the disagreeable and unpopular task of disarming and rounding up these Indians while sympathetic Americans bombarded the administration and Congress with petitions of protest. The few hundred Indians who had agreed to New Echota had already started west, but fifteen thousand Cherokees who opposed removal were resolved to stay put. To his credit, Wool gave the Cherokees as much time to file their appeals as he could and tried to protect their property while they awaited word from Washington.

These last requests for relief went unheeded as all had before, and soon all appeals were exhausted. By then, Martin Van Buren had succeeded Andrew Jackson in the presidency and found himself under immediate and significant pressure both to speed removal and appoint someone other than the exasperatingly compassionate Wool to run it. Van Buren complied on both counts, setting removal to begin in May 1838 and replacing Wool with General Winfield Scott, fresh from his humiliation at the hands of warring Seminoles in Florida.

That spring and on a rapid schedule, regular and militia troops forcibly rounded up the Cherokees and herded them into camps. Just weeks later, parties ranging from several hundred to several thousand began the westward journey, first by boat and then overland in wagons and on foot. The rigors of the trip were the same as elsewhere and perhaps worse as food scarcity and the elements cut a wide swath through the refugees' ranks. About one-fourth of the Cherokees died along what became known as "the Trail of Tears." Most of the casualties were the very young and the very old, so the journey had the cruel irony of wiping out both large portions of the tribe's future and its past. The survivors straggled into the Indian Territory in the spring of 1839 as white settlers streamed onto neat, fertile Cherokee farms. Thus, after all the arguments, legal battles, and sad hopes for justice, the great civilization program of the Early Republic came to this sorry end, its most successful exemplars bleak victims, its most avid and idealistic proponents dead and forgotten.

The Seminoles of Florida

One group of Indians would not prove so docile when confronted by the U.S. removal policy. Before the War of 1812 and afterward, the United States had viewed the Seminoles of Florida as enemies. After the United States acquired Florida from Spain in 1821, the government exerted steady pressure on the Seminoles to relinquish their lands. After being limited to small patches of land in the panhandle and the south central part of the peninsula, the Seminoles enjoyed only a brief lull before the government renewed its insistence that they diminish their holdings. Large numbers of slaves and free blacks among the Seminoles also attracted greedy speculators planning to take advantage of rising slave prices in the southern United States. That was the situation when Congress passed the Indian Removal Act in 1830. The Seminoles, like all other southeastern Indians, met with abrupt demands that they cede all of their Florida lands and move west.

At first, the Seminoles were malleable, because a severe drought was threatening them with starvation. The government thus found it relatively easy to negotiate a treaty with the Seminoles in May 1832 at Payne's Landing. Reminiscent of the terms set for the Chickasaws, the agreement did not require immediate cession and departure but only called for a delegation of Seminoles to travel west to determine if lands reserved for them in the Creek preserve were acceptable. The Seminoles were assured that under this provision, the entire Seminole leadership would decide whether to emigrate after hearing the report from this delegation.

It was all a lie. When the Seminole delegation arrived in the West, they were compelled to sign the Treaty of Fort Gibson authorizing the removal of all Seminoles from Florida. There would be neither a report on prospective home sites nor a vote of the entire nation.

As far as the Seminoles in Florida were concerned, there would be no removal, either. Hearing about the duplicity at Fort Gibson, they refused to recognize the treaty as valid. They scoffed at the paltry compensation offered for their lands, and caviled at the thought of being forced to live among the Creeks, many of whom were former enemies, where they would likely be treated as a subject people. Finally, they worried about what would happen to their slaves and black allies during the upheaval of relocation. Undistracted by such objections, the government advanced its plan to put the Seminoles on boats at Tampa Bay and move them out of Florida. Forced evacuation was to begin in early 1836, or so American planners thought.

The Second Seminole War

With the exception of a few hundred Seminoles who prepared to move, most continued to tend their fields, hunt the swamps of central Florida, and generally live as they had before Payne's Landing. Yet passive resistance obviously could not last, and Seminole men more attentively listened to warriors who plainly stated that unless the tribe opposed removal, the U.S. government would eventually insist on having its way. Led by a charismatic figure named Osceola, these warriors not only prepared for the day when active resistance would be necessary, they mounted a campaign of vengeance against traitors in their midst and American interlopers.

In November 1835, the killing of a Seminole leader who had agreed to removal sent other removal proponents scurrying into white forts for protection. Now purged of all pro-removal elements, Osceola declared war on the white presence in Florida by killing U.S. Seminole agent Wiley Thompson. It was in part a personal vendetta, for Thompson had humiliated Osceola the previous summer by chaining him until he agreed to removal. Warriors also attacked a party of soldiers commanded by Major Francis Dade en route from Tampa Bay to Fort King near present-day Ocala, killing all but 3 of 110. Thus on December 28, 1835, the Dade Massacre sent whites flying in terror to forts throughout the peninsula, marking the start of the Second Seminole War.

The government called up militia from surrounding states and dispatched more regular forces to Florida, but the war went badly for the United States from the start. In February 1836, Indians besieged more than a thousand regulars and volunteers under Brigadier General Edmund Pendleton Gaines on the Withlacoochee River. To rescue his force, Gaines had to agree that the Seminoles could live south of the Withlacoochee, a promise quickly broken by the army. Meanwhile, to prevent the army from rounding up noncombatants, Seminole warriors hid their families in the impenetrable swamps of south central Florida.

The war in Florida quickly became a mess. General Winfield Scott could not subdue the Seminoles, and command fell on General Thomas S. Jesup, who watched with dismay as Seminoles confused the army with hit-and-run attacks on isolated detachments. Jesup tried to destroy the Indians' food supplies and diminish Indian forces by capturing stragglers, but the army could tally no better than a few hundred Seminoles, not a single leader among them.

Most Seminoles evaded capture, but they were hungry, homeless, and increasingly dispirited. Finally, in March 1837, some leaders entered into an agreement with Jesup to quit Florida if they could take their slaves and black allies with them to the Indian Territory. Rapacious whites spoiled the bargain, though. As Seminoles gathered at embarkation points on Tampa Bay that spring and summer, slave hunters descended on the camps to claim the black people there. The Indians rightly feared that they would be forced to emigrate without their slaves, and most of them fled back into the interior.

Seeing his designs frustrated, Jesup was desperate to show some positive gains for his year in Florida. He began using questionable methods to apprehend Seminole leaders, summoning them in small groups to putative parleys and then clapping them in irons. Some were shipped west. Others saw their families held hostage to persuade them to bring in other leaders. The unsavory ruse of pretending to hold peace talks allowed Jesup to capture Osceola in October 1837. Expansionists hailed Osceola's arrest as a great victory, but many others condemned it as a cowardly and dishonorable act.

The great war chief would spend a year behind bars at Fort Moultrie near Charleston, South Carolina, before dying, but by then he had already become both a symbol and an inspiration for continued resistance, steeling the resolve of those Seminoles still at large. In the face of such defiance, Jesup blended his hoax of peace talks with renewed and concentrated military actions, a strategy systematically applied by him and his second-in-command, Colonel Zachary Taylor. The army suffered badly from both fighting and disease, but it captured scores of Seminoles, although they were mostly hungry women and children.

American officers found serving in Florida increasingly repugnant. Coping with unhealthy conditions was one thing, but reconciling themselves to the government's policy toward the Seminoles was quite another. To them, it seemed less and less in the national interest to harass these poor people merely to extend national control over the trackless wilderness of central and southern Florida. When they were bold enough to say this, they were disciplined. When Jesup sided with them, he was removed from command.

Florida was, in fact, becoming the graveyard of military careers. The next commander in Florida was General of the Army Alexander Macomb, who briefly and unsuccessfully tried to renew talks with Seminole leaders for a negotiated settlement. Zachary Taylor then succeeded Macomb and commenced establishing forts throughout central and south Florida so that soldiers could more thoroughly scour the countryside, but he also grew tired of the disagreeable chore and asked to be relieved. By 1841, Florida had become a dreary chronicle of futile negotiations, indecisive military actions, and plummeting morale. The government ordered the army to "find the enemy, capture or extermi- nate them."[11] Colonel William Jenkins Worth accordingly conducted a scorched-earth campaign to destroy Seminole food before it could be harvested. That winter hundreds of starving Seminoles finally faced the inevitable and gave up. Worth declared the war over the following year.

Nonetheless, several hundred Seminoles remained in Florida after the official termination of hostilities, and they would remain there, in perpetual defiance of Indian removal. Most of their brethren had already died or were long gone to the Indian Territory, and most Semi- nole land was already opened to white settlement, but unlike the home- steading frenzy that occurred in other areas of removal, the remote and steamy Florida wilderness attracted little interest. The Second Seminole War, the longest Indian war in United States history, had cost the lives of more than a thousand soldiers, countless Seminoles, and millions of dollars, all to open a wilderness that nobody wanted.[12] Removal policy in Florida in the end was not so much about expansion as it was about a test of wills. In that respect, the handful of Seminole holdouts who remained in south Florida won the point, if not the war.

Conclusion

Many white Americans in the 1830s and 1840s saw Indian removal as necessary to eliminate a major obstruction to the country's destiny. Proponents of Indian removal, such as Andrew Jackson, justi- fied their actions by arguing that Indians' communal agriculture and hunting traditions did not use the land efficiently. They solemnly declared God intended white Americans to assume stewardship over that land and by doing so, they were not only exercising their rights, they were fulfilling a higher duty. Simultaneously, they intoned how the Indians needed to be isolated from the pressures of white settlement if they were ever to learn the arts of civilization.

Perhaps such rationalizations actually did ease the consciences of some, but the simple reality was that land hunger had gripped the country, and the Indians were in the way. Many whites were troubled by the inherent unfairness and the physical sufferings caused by Indian removal. During the debate on Indian removal, Massachusetts con- gressman Edward Everett had passionately condemned the proposed policy. "The evil, sir, is enormous," he said, "the violence is extreme; the breach of public faith deplorable; the inevitable suffering incalculable." Everett pleaded with his fellow representatives to "not stain the fair fame of the country."[13] Such moral protests were lost, however, in the noise of restless settlers and the politicians who did their will.

Notes

1. Treaty of New York, 7 August 1790, in Charles J. Kappler, ed. and comp., *Indian Affairs: Laws and Treaties,* 7 vols. (Washington: GPO, 1904), 2:26–29.

2. Mixed-heritage children's influence within Indian society resulted for several reasons. First, marriages between Indian women and white traders were probably arranged alliances, so these women likely came from prominent clans whose status the children would inherit. Second, the children's paternal ties would make them valuable assets in establishing trade relationships with the white world. Finally, the children's fluency in both English and their mother's language made them indispensable as translators for both groups.

3. Quoted in Anthony F. C. Wallace, *Jefferson and the Indians: The Tragic Fate of the First Americans* (Cambridge, MA: Harvard University Press, 1999), 273.

4. American actions in Florida are discussed in Chapter 3.

5. James D. Richardson, comp., *A Compilation of the Messages and Papers of the Presidents, 1789–1908* (Washington: Bureau of National Literature and Art, 1908), 2:520

6. Quoted in Richard P. Longaker, "Andrew Jackson and the Judiciary," *Political Science Quarterly* 17 (September 1956), 334.

7. Jackson was quoted, some say erroneously, in Horace Greeley, *American Conflict: A History of the Great Rebellion in the United States of America, 1860–65,* 2 vols. (Hartford, CT: Case, 1864), 1:106.

8. Quoted in Grant Foreman, *Indian Removal: The Emigration of the Five Civilized Tribes of Indians* (Norman: University of Oklahoma Press, 1956), 41.

9. Theda Perdue and Michael D. Green, *The Cherokee Removal: A Brief History with Documents* (Boston: Bedford-St. Martin, 1995), 75.

10. Charles Warren, *The Supreme Court in United States History,* 3 vols. (Boston: Little, Brown, 1922), 2:224.

11. Quoted in James W. Covington, *The Seminoles of Florida* (Gainesville: University Presses of Florida, 1993), 101.

12. Much of the Florida peninsula would remain a sleepy backwater until the late nineteenth century when railroads made resorts viable and tourism attractive to investors and entrepreneurs. Even then, many years and several cycles of boom-and-bust and the invention of air conditioning would at last make the state the success story it is today.

13. *Register of Debates,* 21st Cong., 1st sess., 1079.

CHAPTER 5

SANTA ANNA MEETS MANIFEST DESTINY: TEXAS

Expansionism after the War of 1812 caused white Americans to turn their attention not only to the absorption of eastern Indian lands but also to regions beyond the Mississippi River. The 1803 Louisiana Purchase secured the western bank of the Mississippi, but restless settlers looked even farther west to a place Americans would come to call Texas. Some Americans believed that Texas had been part of the Louisiana Purchase and therefore belonged to the United States anyway. Such was the opinion of Andrew Jackson, who insisted to his dying day that when John Quincy Adams was concluding the Transcontinental Treaty, the Sabine River was the actual U.S.-Spanish border, a situation that Jackson accused Adams of deliberately ignoring. Jackson also claimed that Adams was lying when he said that Jackson had been consulted about the matter in 1819.

Americans in Texas

Although the U.S. government abandoned any claims to Texas in the Transcontinental Treaty, adventurous Americans regularly took advantage of Spain's indistinct administrative presence in the region to defy U.S. laws with extensive smuggling operations. Spain's lax enforcement of customs regulations along the Texas coast allowed smugglers to operate with impunity out of Galveston and other ports. Goods came into Galveston duty free and then were transported overland into Louisiana. The most lucrative smuggling operation involved the foreign slave trade, long outlawed by the United States. Louisianan Jim Bowie, most famous to later generations for his invention of a broad-bladed knife and for his presence at the doomed Alamo, was a typical slaver and smuggler of the period. He would purchase smuggled slaves in Galveston, perhaps from the Lafitte brothers of Battle of New Orleans fame, and move them overland for sale in Louisiana. Clever operators like Bowie worked the game both ways, avoiding capture by vigilant U.S. patrols by turning their contraband over to government agents when the caper became too hot. They would then collect the reward for apprehending smuggled slaves. Both Spain and the United States realized that such antics made Texas a problem, but Spain lacked the energy and the United States lacked the will to do much about it.

American Settlements

Shortly after gaining independence from Spain in 1821, the Republic of Mexico sought to solve the Texas problem it had inherited from languid Spanish administrators. Mexico would encourage Americans to settle in Texas, hoping to attract pioneers far different from Bowie and his ilk. Because Texas was so sparsely populated, smuggling and other illegal activity thrived in the vacuum. Bolstering the population by allowing honest and hardworking Americans into the province seemed a sensible arrangement at the time. Desirable immigrants would move to Texas permanently, bringing their families and putting down roots to stabilize the meagerly peopled, remote land. Larger and more enduring settlements could also provide a buffer against hostile Indians while strengthening Mexico City's brittle administrative hold on the region. For their part, restless Americans proved eager to seek their fortunes in Texas. "Texas fever" gripped the U.S. frontier, particularly in the southwest where the countryside was soon dotted by empty cabins with GTT (for "Gone to Texas") scrawled on their walls.

The Mexican government even devised a system to promote large American migrations of the right kind of people, contracting with American entrepreneurs Moses Austin and his son Stephen to arrange the details. The elder Austin received a grant of twenty thousand acres in return for the promise that he would bring three hundred families to Texas, all of them willing to become Mexican citizens and convert to Catholicism. The Austins led the way, but other so-called *empresarios* were soon obtaining similar grants.

The scheme worked wonders to swell the population. Within a decade, former U.S. citizens in Texas numbered nearly twenty thousand, and more were on the way. At first, the growing population pleased the Mexican government, but soon it became apparent that other parts of the plan were not working. Migrants remained American in custom, language, and often refused to convert to Catholicism. When they began openly to disobey Mexican laws, particularly those restricting slavery, the Mexican government tried to regain control of the situation by stopping additional emigration from the United States, but by then it was too late.

Changes in Policy

In 1830, the Mexican government clamped down on Texas. It sought to stop violations of the law, tried to establish control over the U.S.-Texas border, and revived previously waived Mexican tariffs on imports into the region. Texans brooded over this drastic change in Mexican policy that effectively ended the freewheeling economic autonomy they had enjoyed for almost a decade. As resentment grew, the situation in Texas became volatile.

In May 1832, Mexican officials learned just how explosive Texas had become when they tried to crack down on smuggling by arresting several Texans, including William Barret Travis, a fortune-hunting immigrant who had abandoned a wife and family in Alabama. Although Travis and his fellow prisoners were hardly the stuff of martyrdom, armed mobs nonetheless demanded their release with such vigor that war nearly broke out. It was averted when a new government assumed power in Mexico and at least seemed more flexible about policies net-tling Texans. In the hope of preventing additional incidents, Stephen Austin traveled to Mexico City to meet with the new president, Antonio López de Santa Anna.

Americans in Texas might have become raucous and uncoopera-tive, and they certainly included shady elements, but Santa Anna was a scoundrel without peer. After keeping Austin waiting for several months, Santa Anna finally granted an interview in which he pretended to sympathize with Texan grievances. The Mexican president, however, was indulging his habit for duplicity. As Austin cheerfully headed home, Santa Anna ordered his arrest and renewed strict measures to stop smuggling and collect tariffs.

On the face of it, Santa Anna's insistence on the strict enforcement of Mexican law was just and reasonable, even if it was politically unpopular in Texas. But Santa Anna lied, even when telling the truth would have served him better, and he adopted a dictatorial method bound to offend the democratic sensibilities of former U.S. citizens in Texas. Worse, he sustained his authoritarianism with a swaggering brutality that occasionally disgusted even his supporters. For a while, both Austin's arrest and the insidious way Santa Anna's central administration exerted its will in other parts of Mexico cowed enough Texans to restrain proponents of revolt. Soon, however, Santa Anna's combination of despotism and cruelty pushed even moderate Texans to consider a war of independence.

Revolution

It was out of character for Americans to tolerate a government based on fear and repression, and when Santa Anna eventually pushed too hard, Texans abruptly pushed back. In the summer of 1835, Santa Anna sent more troops to Texas to curb any unrest, but this last resort to force convinced even the most cautious Texans that immediate revolution was the only answer. For a fraction of a moment, Santa Anna stopped blustering and took stock of the worsening situation. He released Stephen Austin, perhaps as a show of conciliation, but Austin's months in a Mexican prison had both wrecked his health and made him righteously angry. As soon as he was back in Texas, he sided with the revolutionaries.

The explosion came in October 1835 with an incident strangely reminiscent of the confrontation at Lexington and Concord that set off the American Revolution forty years earlier. The commander of Mexican troops in San Antonio de Bexar sent a party of soldiers under Lieutenant Francisco Castañeda to Gonzales, Texas, to confiscate a cannon there. In response, the Texan Americans in Gonzales organized themselves into a militia of sorts and trained the cannon on approaching Mexican soldiers, repulsing them with a series of sputtering discharges. It was October 2, 1835, and the Texas Revolution had begun.

With remarkable speed and unity, Texans rallied behind Stephen Austin and other leaders to expel Mexican military forces from the territory. A week after the fracas at Gonzales, Texans took control of Goliad and its store of munitions. That November, a diverse jumble of Texans that included Anglo and *tejano* (a Texan of Mexican origin) vol-

Map 5.1
The Texas War of Independence, 1836

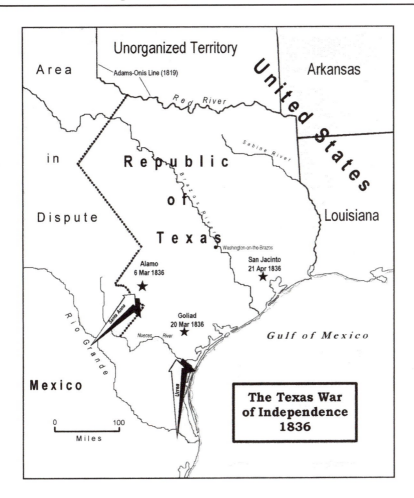

unteers besieged the Mexican garrison at San Antonio de Bexar. Gentle-men farmers in their carefully tailored waistcoats stood with frontiers-men in buckskin, electing the ailing Austin as their commander.

Despite their brashness, none of them, including Austin, had the slightest idea of what to do. They were few in number, and they were not soldiers. Moreover, they found San Antonio well fortified, armed with artillery, and supported by cavalry. The Texans had none of these, but their biggest problem was lack of leadership. Stephen Austin pro-vided a measure of coherence to the disparate group gathered around

San Antonio, but little else. His inability to end the stalemate lost his men's confidence, and they finally refused to follow his orders. Austin dejectedly turned command over to Edward Burleson, an uninspiring old fellow who talked a lot and did little. Austin then applied himself to something he knew about. He left for the United States to raise much needed men and money for the coming fight.

Finally, impatience got the better of the little army outside San Antonio. When an old Texan named Ben Milam offered to lead an attack, the gesture resulted in an impromptu assault on December 4, 1835. About three hundred men attacked the town and drove the Mexicans before them in heavy hand-to-hand fighting. On December 9, the Mexican force surrendered, and San Antonio was in Texan hands. Nobody could have known it, but this opening and seemingly small victory had set the stage for the most profound event in Texas history.

Enter Santa Anna

Texan defiance outraged the Mexican government. By late January 1836, Santa Anna had raised an army of four thousand soldiers to enter Texas from Saltillo. Other Mexican forces were also assembling. Abysmal weather and poor provisions greatly discouraged many of these men, however, and as Santa Anna's army moved toward San Antonio in February, they dwindled to about twenty-five hundred. It was still more than enough. Of those men who had impulsively taken San Antonio, most had come to Texas in search of easy fortune. Risking their lives fighting a Mexican army promised to be neither painless nor profitable. Consequently, many of them ran away, stealing what they could carry as they did so. Those who remained were mostly mercenaries, and they planned to pillage the Mexican city of Matamoros several hundred miles away, an enterprise that pulled much needed men and supplies away from already vulnerable points, including San Antonio.

To make matters worse, squabbles were developing over command of Texan troops. A hastily assembled citizens' council tried to organize a territorial defense by naming Tennessean Sam Houston as overall commander, but it then distributed authority among several others as well. The result was chaos. When Governor Henry Smith tried to bring order to the situation, the council tried to remove him from office. Against this backdrop of confusion and petty bickering, the revolutionaries faced grave peril with the impending arrival of Santa Anna's armies. (See Map 5.1.)

The Alamo

In early 1836, Texas military forces consisted of three small, ill-supplied, disorganized bodies of troops. One was the 100-man garrison at San Antonio under the command of Col. James C. Neill with head-quarters at a former Catholic mission called the Alamo. Another was a small group at Goliad under the command of James Fannin, and the third was composed of the mercenaries heading for Matamoros. In the middle of January, Houston sent a small detachment under Jim Bowie to the Alamo, apparently with orders that if Bowie deemed the fort inde-fensible, he was to destroy it and pull everybody northward. Exercising judgment that can only be described as profoundly significant, Bowie not only decided the post was sound, he resolved to help defend it. He immediately sent out calls for reinforcements. Davy Crockett was one of the adventurers whose arrival with a small band of companions boosted the small garrison's morale. Crockett had traveled all the way from the United States to participate in the Texas Revolution, while oth-ers came from closer locales. While he held no command at the Alamo, "Crockett was seen at all points, animating the men to their duty."[1] William Barret Travis, the same man arrested four years earlier for smuggling, was now a lieutenant colonel in the Texas regular army, and he brought thirty additional men to the Alamo. Plucky as these men were as they gathered in the path of thousands of Mexican soldiers, they were fewer than a hundred and fifty.

Short of men, the Alamo began to boast an awkward abundance of commanders. When a family emergency called away Neill in mid-February, Bowie the volunteer and Travis the regular, both with more than a measure of pride and vanity, were on the verge of butting heads when they arranged a compromise. The plan was for them to share command, but this cumbersome arrangement was never tested. Bowie became so ill with typhoid that Travis exercised sole command during the ensuing events.

Santa Anna and his army arrived at the end of February to occupy San Antonio and lay siege to the Alamo. While he still could, Travis continued to call for reinforcements, but it was obvious that the garri-son was courting calamity. Santa Anna hoisted a red flag on the town's church to announce that no quarter would be given to the defenders. For two weeks, the Alamo's defenders shored up the defenses of their makeshift fort while Santa Anna's cavalry tightened the siege. The Texans sustained their courage with the belief that reinforcements were on the way, especially the two hundred men from the garrison at Goliad who they supposed must have heard of the Alamo's predicament. At Goliad, however, James Fannin had decided to hold his position, a decision that Santa Anna's patrolling cavalry soon made binding. Thirty-two men trudged into the Alamo from Gonzalez, but they would be the last to enter Travis's doomed command, still tiny in contrast to the Mexican multitude it would fight.

Almost constant bombardment from Santa Anna's artillery tore at the Alamo's walls and rattled its occupants' nerves. It was only a matter of time before the Mexicans mounted an irresistible assault, and when it came at last on March 6, the garrison never had a chance. Before dawn, Mexican soldiers crept close to the fort and attacked at several different points before the Texans could sound an alarm. They put up a stout defense, desperately fighting in small pockets that were quickly isolated from each other by the overwhelming number of attackers. Travis fell dead early, leaving the men no central coordination, but it hardly mattered. Their fate had been sealed weeks before, when Santa Anna had first appeared from the South. At the end, fighting was especially vicious as the Mexicans swamped the Texans in hand-to-hand combat. Finally subdued, the few surviving Texans were taken prisoner, Davy Crockett reportedly among them. Some Mexican officers urged Santa Anna to spare these brave fighters, but he refused. The prisoners were hacked to death with swords. That brought the toll to 182 Texans. Santa Anna had lost 600 soldiers.

The Texans' corpses were piled up and burned. Santa Anna spared the one woman in the fort (Suzanna Dickenson, wife of one of the defenders) and Travis's slave Joe, less from compassion than to have them bear witness to revolutionaries elsewhere of what they had seen. This fate awaited the Texan rabble, Santa Anna decreed, if it continued its folly. Thus did word of the Alamo spread. Flushed with this "victory," Santa Anna was sure that his ferocity would terrify Texas into submission. He had no idea of the reckoning that it instead would summon.

Goliad

Rather than staying in the fort constructed at Goliad for their defense, Fannin and his men tried to reach safety after learning of the fall of the Alamo. With the army of Mexican general José Urrea racing out of Matamoros toward him, Fannin began evacuating Fort Defiance on March 19. The next day, Urrea caught up to him on the open prairie and immediately sent in the Mexican cavalry. Fannin, who failed to move his men to a nearby creek and the cover of trees, was soon surrounded and commenced a stout but hopeless defense. The following morning, the little army decided its only option was surrender, even though Urrea insisted that it be unconditional and that the Texans would be considered pirates. Under such terms, they could be executed with no more ceremony than Urrea's order, but Fannin and his men put their faith in the Mexican general's compassion.

Taken back to Goliad, they were imprisoned in a burned-out church while their wounded were tended in a makeshift hospital. Other Texans were also rounded up during the next few days, including part of the aborted expedition to Matamoros. Almost everybody—even the Mexican officers—believed that the prisoners would be conveyed to the United States, but on the night of March 26, orders arrived from Santa Anna with shocking instructions. All prisoners were to be executed. That night, strains of "Home Sweet Home" could be heard coming from the prisoners' enclosure.[2]

Unaware of their imminent fate, all prisoners able to walk were marched out of Goliad in three separate columns the next morning. They were apparently told their destination was the Gulf coast, so they were bewildered when the Mexican escort first separated and then halted the columns. Infantry took up positions in front of the puzzled men, and on orders barked by their officers, opened fire. Those who survived this initial volley were bayoneted to death. The bodies were burned. Later that day, the wounded in Goliad were also killed, and Fannin fell before a firing squad. More than four hundred revolutionaries died in this appalling display of brutality. With the blood of almost six hundred Texans on his hands, Santa Anna headed north.

Independence and Retreat

Santa Anna thought he was destroying Texans' will as well as their ability to continue the revolt, but important events occurring elsewhere in Texas were solidifying revolt into revolution. Even as the Alamo lay under siege, a constitutional convention met at Washington on the Brazos and on March 2 boldly declared Texas independent. Delegate Sam

Houston was appointed commander of all Texas forces, this time with full authority. He immediately took all available troops toward Gonzalez on the Guadalupe River northeast of San Antonio. His efforts to raise more volunteers to relieve the Alamo were meeting with some success when he learned from Mrs. Dickenson that he was too late.

Houston suspected that his little band of fighters would be Santa Anna's next target, so he retreated from Gonzalez, hoping his numbers would grow on the march. Unnerved by Houston's withdrawal, settlers fled from the path of Santa Anna's army, some all the way to the United States. The provisional Texas government and new president David Burnet took flight as well. Santa Anna, however, tarried, allowing Houston to pause for several weeks and put his raw recruits through rudimentary training. On April 12, word arrived that Santa Anna was on the move again, and Houston renewed his retreat, a move that drew criticism from members of the provisional government as it took up temporary quarters at Harrisburg. Soon the critics were silenced when Santa Anna learned of their location and sent a detachment to apprehend them as well. After that, the provisional government was too busy fleeing to complain about anything. In any case, Houston was not really running so much as searching. His eight hundred or so men were no match for Santa Anna's numbers unless he could fight on ground where the numbers would not matter. Then, he pledged, would come the reckoning.

San Jacinto

By mid-April, Houston had found his ground on the San Jacinto River. Part of the Mexican army, with Santa Anna himself in command, was coming right at him. On the morning of April 20, Houston placed his men along Buffalo Bayou, anchoring his right on the swamp and his left on the San Jacinto. A forest covered his rear; a prairie and a marshy lake stretched across his front, uninviting terrain that Santa Anna would have to traverse. The Mexicans appeared during the afternoon, but the battle did not commence until the following day. After all, Santa Anna at last had Houston's army where he wanted it. He saw no reason to hurry.

Houston waited most of April 21 before attacking at about 4 P.M. while the Mexicans were resting. The surprised Mexican soldiers simply ran from screaming Texans, whose guttural cries of "Remember the

Alamo!" and "Remember Goliad!" were as terrifying as their crackling rifles. Mexican officers lost control of their scattering men, and within twenty minutes, the battle was over. Enraged Texans continued killing Mexican soldiers and officers into the evening, committing barbarities that rivaled those at the Alamo and Goliad. At a cost of nine Texans, more than six hundred Mexicans were slain.

Santa Anna fled this disaster but was captured the following day in civilian clothes. His captors remained unaware of his identity until other Mexican prisoners began calling out, "El Presidente!"[3] When presented to Houston, Santa Anna explained, "That man may consider himself born to no common destiny who has conquered the Napoleon of the West."[4]

Texans wanted to execute Santa Anna to avenge the Alamo and Goliad, but Houston calculated the Mexican commander as more valuable alive than dead. During his captivity, he certainly seemed so. He agreed to order all Mexican armies out of Texas, and he signed two treaties that formally ended hostilities, that promised to recommend Mexican recognition of Texas independence, and that established the Rio Grande as the Mexican border.

Yet, these documents were only as valuable as Santa Anna's word and only as relevant as his influence. His word was always worthless, and after San Jacinto, his influence was waning. The Mexican government simply refused to recognize either agreement as legitimate. Moreover, Mexico believed that the entire revolution had been a plot by the United States to acquire Texas. Those suspicions were reinforced when U.S. troops under Brigadier General Edmund Pendleton Gaines entered northeastern Texas from Louisiana during the summer of 1836. Gaines was only briefly on Texas soil, but Mexico took it as hard evidence that American plans for Mexican territory included not only Texas, but probably the lands beyond as well.

Lone Star Republic

Mexico smoldered about Texas, but it had neither the will nor the wherewithal to do much else. Texas established a permanent republican government and conducted its first elections under its new constitution in September 1836. Sam Houston won 79 percent of the popular vote to defeat Henry Smith and Stephen Austin for the presidency. Texans also held a referendum to gauge sentiment on possible annexation by the United States. With more than 90 percent in favor, the vote further confirmed for Mexican officials that U.S.-Texas collusion had been in play all along.

When Houston was inaugurated a month later, he immediately began trying to secure U.S. annexation by corresponding directly with his old friend and mentor, President Andrew Jackson. Jackson waited several months, however, daring not even to recognize Texan independence until, as he said, "events shall have proved . . . the ability of the people of that country to maintain their separate sovereignty."[5] The best Jackson could do before leaving office in March 1837 was persuade a suspicious Congress to recognize Texas independence. Mexicans were not alone in smelling a rat in this business of Texas.

Annexation Deferred

For the United States, serious sectional issues complicated not only Texas annexation but a growing list of other national questions as well. Rapid westward expansion after the War of 1812 had also extended the reach of slavery, and a growing congressional minority became increasingly resolved to keep slavery out of new American territory. Antislavery advocates argued that a large reason for the recent Texas Revolution was to maintain slavery, and they were accordingly determined to keep Texas out of the Union. Andrew Jackson, old and weary from his two presidential terms, lacked the energy to mount the necessary political fight to secure congressional approval for annexation. His successor Martin Van Buren lacked the stomach for it, especially with former president and now Massachusetts representative John Quincy Adams in the opposition. Adams, described even by enemies as "Old Man Eloquent," was a formidable obstacle all by himself.[6]

Texans basked under U.S. recognition of their infant republic, but they wanted annexation. Van Buren could do little, though, for to move one way would alienate powerful political groups and to move in another direction would estrange others. He doubtless wished he had never heard of Texas. Much of the South and West strongly urged annexation, but many northeasterners protested that adding Texas to the Union was merely a brazen scheme to dilute their power with a flood of western territory full of southern slaves. Van Buren, a New Yorker, could only satisfy these northeastern interests by losing the already frail support of southerners. All arguments were beside the point anyway, because none of them could attract the votes in Congress necessary for annexation. That this political problem threatened to become a domestic storm seemed especially absurd to a man of Van Buren's practicality. Even discussing the matter under such circumstances was merely asking for trouble. Consequently, the matter was rarely if ever discussed.

An Unstable Republic

The fluttering Lone Star banner, the constitution, the legislature, and all the other trappings of a brave start for the new country would not long disguise the fact that Texas was in trouble. In fact, President Houston was having difficulty maintaining order. A lack of supplies had the army on the verge of mutiny even as its adventurous officers were trying to mobilize it to seize more land from Mexico. Houston furloughed most of the army in an effort to forestall such mischief, but the situation remained far from calm.

Skullduggery of all sorts flourished. Conflicting land claims generated bitter arguments, and swindlers preyed on unsuspecting settlers. The Lone Star Republic proved no more capable at enforcing its customs and trade laws than Spain or Mexico had been, and smuggling and privateering thrived along the Texas coast. President Houston was among those who thought U.S. annexation unlikely if Texas could not conduct its affairs any better than this. Ridding itself of lawless elements and building an economy on honest enterprise would be a start.

Garnering diplomatic recognition abroad would be even better. In 1837, Houston's government made a concerted effort to achieve that recognition, beginning with the appointment of a minister to Great Britain. Lone Star slavery, however, repelled enough people in London to thwart the diplomatic project until 1840, but British commercial interests were not so particular about opening a trade relationship with the new republic, a welcome relief to the failing Texas economy.

Of all its problems, the Texas Republic's finances were the bleakest. The government could not raise enough money to stop the spiraling debt, even as the population quickly grew because of cheap or free land. Continued immigration did little to ease Texas' economic plight. Through it all, many still clung to the prospective salvation of U.S. annexation, but as the Van Buren administration stumbled under its own economic problems with the Panic of 1837, Americans were even less likely to quarrel over Texas. Instead, new settlers from the United States created new problems. New arrivals regarded Indians and ethnic Mexicans as objectionable, and when they tried to run them off, nasty little fights broke out that the Texas government seemed powerless to prevent. In fact, the government seemed impotent on all levels.

One episode was typical. Before leaving office in December 1838, Houston's administration negotiated a treaty with Cherokees living in the northern part of the republic. The Cherokees, victims of removal, had spilled over from Indian Territory into northern Texas, and the treaty was meant to protect their lands from white encroachment. Houston had lived among the Cherokee for a time, and he was sympathetic to their plight, but in this matter, the Hero of San Jacinto found the limits even of his influence. He could not muster the political clout to persuade the Texas Congress to ratify the treaty.

The Lamar Administration

Houston's successor was Mirabeau Buonaparte Lamar, a transplanted Georgian with a big vision for Texas matched only by his lack of ability. He nursed a variety of reflexive prejudices, especially against Indians, and after inflaming white settlers for the chore, he began implementing an Indian removal policy for Texas. When the Cherokees resisted, Texans defeated them at the Battle of Neches on July 16, 1839. The Cherokees were then expelled from Texas.

To speed the removal of Texas's remaining Indians, Lamar and his faction encouraged white settlement ever farther westward by moving the capital from Houston to the newly named town of Austin, a costly and exceedingly irresponsible act for insolvent Texas. Even with the capital relocated, western settlements proved impossible to promote where Comanches habitually raided isolated homesteads. The Comanche custom of taking white captives to ransom back to the government dated from the days of Mexican rule, and it continued with a chilling persistence that the Lamar administration could not end and could only occasionally remedy.

While Comanches kept much of Texas empty, Lamar embraced the seemingly pointless goal of expanding the republic to the Pacific. Ignoring the fact that he could scarcely govern what he already had, Lamar believed such a vast area could become self-sufficient, thereby making U.S. annexation unnecessary. This delusion actually led to plans for a military expedition to seize Santa Fe, a campaign undertaken without consulting the Texas Congress, though that was the least of its problems. Sent on this fool's errand in early 1841, the expedition was promptly captured by Mexican forces in New Mexico and taken to Mexico City.

Houston Returns

Lamar's blustering administration accelerated the republic's economic disintegration, encouraged rather than controlled lawlessness and Indian depredations, and finally launched a disastrous military campaign against Santa Fe. With Lamar and his faction discredited, Sam Houston's return to power was inevitable. Houston's first priority was to revive the failed economy. Among its many other sins, the Lamar administration had printed so much paper currency as to make it worthless. The only reliable source of revenue for the republic was land, but no one was buying any of it. Houston knew that U.S. annexation could solve Texas's problems, but Lamar's misguided policies to make Texas self-reliant had not only eschewed annexation, they had made it less likely. Texas was a mess, and even if it had not held the potential to reanimate sectional animosity over slavery, it still would have been an unattractive prospect to add to the American Union. Fiscal irresponsibility, invasions of Mexican territory, and claims to even more Mexican territory caused many U.S. senators to ponder the wisdom of welcoming such irrational and irascible people into the national community. Furthermore, Texas seemed bent on provoking a war with Mexico, a war that the United States would inherit if it annexed the territory. It did not matter, then, that despite such worries, the new presidential administration of John Tyler seemed receptive to the idea of annexing Texas.[7] Nothing would happen without Senate approval.

That eventuality seemed remote. U.S. opposition to annexation had grown beyond the abolitionist minority. Even people who did not oppose the expansion of slavery feared the sectional rift that would come with a renewal of the Texas debate. Political parties might split along sectional lines, and the nation could hopelessly divide over the issue of slavery.

In 1842, the Mexican army began probing the Texas border, raising serious alarm throughout the republic. The resilient Santa Anna had returned to power and was seemingly intent on reclaiming Mexico's lost province. In quiet desperation, Texas turned to Great Britain whose foreign office offered to mediate the dispute. Santa Anna, however, would have none of it. Instead, he increased military activity on the Rio Grande, a move generally interpreted as foreshadowing a major invasion. Texas countered by threatening an invasion of its own, and went so far as to move what passed for an army across the Rio Grande to attack the town of Mier. It was a quixotic gesture in the first place, but it was especially rash because Mier was well defended. Outnumbered and outgunned, the 300 Texan attackers were soon undone, captured, and placed on a march to Mexico City. En route, they escaped, but 176 again fell to capture and were forced to endure a bizarre ordeal of deadly chance. Santa Anna first ordered them all executed, but he relented at least to the point of marking every tenth man for death. A bean for each prisoner was placed in a container, 159 of them white and the rest black. Those who drew black beans "were shot that evening within hearing of their companions."[8]

A full-scale war between Texas and Mexico seemed imminent, a conflict Texas was financially and physically incapable of fighting. Texans were urging Sam Houston either to make peace through the British or seek unconditional U.S. annexation. Because the United States seemed an unlikely option, Houston turned to Great Britain. British chargé d'affaires Charles Elliot seemed most willing to help.

The British Problem

Indeed, Elliot was eager to help. His superiors in London saw an opportunity to weaken the United States by establishing what would have amounted to a British protectorate on the Americans' southern border. The British were already edgy about American expansionism because of their dispute over the Oregon Country, so establishing a British foothold in the Southwest might provide a useful counterbalance.[9] Not only could Great Britain inhibit U.S.-Texas trade, it could advance an antislavery program, a pet project in British intellectual and political circles. British reformers could possibly persuade Texas to abolish slavery, creating a haven for runaway American slaves while setting an example of successful abolition right on the American doorstep.

Already at odds with London over Oregon, the U.S. government shuddered over the possibility of British influence taking root in the

Southwest. The potential for abolitionism following in the wake of that influence so distressed the Tyler administration that the president and Secretary of State Abel Upshur, both slaveholding Virginians, resolved to negotiate an annexation treaty with the Lone Star Republic and push it through the United States Senate, whatever the political cost.

Lone Star State

On February 28, 1844, the crème of Washington political society boarded the USS *Princeton* for a trial of the new ship. President John Tyler was playing host to his cabinet, various congressmen and senators, most of whom had brought family for the outing. It was an unusually pleasant day for that time of year, and the party was festive. Tyler and Secretary of State Upshur had been hard at work on the Texas annexation treaty, especially laboring to line up the necessary Senate votes for ratification. A boat ride on the Potomac afforded them a bit of relaxation as well as the opportunity to court influential members of Congress.

Upshur remained above decks to observe a gunnery demonstration and chat with congressmen while the president socialized below. Suddenly a deafening explosion violently rocked the ship. During a firing demonstration, one of the *Princeton's* guns had exploded. Several men lay dead, including Abel Upshur, now the former secretary of state of the United States.

The Treaty and the Resolution

The human tragedy of the *Princeton* accident was numbing, but Tyler was determined not to lose all the work on his Texas initiative. He quickly appointed South Carolinian John C. Calhoun as secretary of state, thus choosing a close adviser and reliable promoter of annexation. Although Calhoun completed negotiations with Texas on April 12, 1844, the administration found it impossible to secure enough votes in the Senate for ratification. Part of the problem was certainly caused by Calhoun's indiscreet declaration that Texas should be annexed to protect American slavery from British abolition.

In addition, recent studies have argued that at this time sectionalism was not yet the decisive factor it would later become. In short, senators voted for or against annexation not only because of slavery but also because of other, subtler reasons.[10] Both northern and southern

Whigs, for instance, were fairly united in their belief that the Union should consolidate and settle its current holdings before adding new territory. They were especially fearful that depopulating eastern states would harm the national economy. Many Whigs also worried that Texas annexation could cause a war with Mexico. Most northern and southern Democrats supported expansion into Texas and Oregon, but enough northern Democrats joined the Whigs to defeat ratification.

Tyler correctly saw this vote as a major setback, but treaty opponents both in and out of Congress had underestimated the country's enthusiasm for expansion, and senators were soon hearing complaints from the public. In the eyes of annexation advocates, the 1844 presidential election became a referendum on territorial expansion. Tyler had so alienated his Whig Party on this and other matters that he had no chance to win its nomination, but he became absorbed with resolving the Texas issue by asking for a joint House-Senate resolution calling for annexation. The presidential campaign between Whig nominee Henry Clay, who had initially opposed annexation, and expansionist Democrat James Knox Polk seemed to reveal the mood of the nation. Embracing the theory espoused by fellow Tennessean Andrew Jackson that Texas had been included in the Louisiana Purchase, Polk called for "the *re*annexation of Texas [emphasis added]."[11] When Polk narrowly won the election, Tyler interpreted it as a mandate on Texas. This interpretation of the election results caused considerable controversy, but John Tyler had grown accustomed to the role of political controversialist. He would have a new Congress to work with, if only briefly, before handing his office over to Polk, but he was confident that Texas would be his and the country's before his time ran out.

Annexation

Tyler was right. Just hours before he left office, he annexed Texas. The new Congress passed and the lame duck president signed a joint resolution that accomplished the deed, but in truth it accomplished little else. It would be up to Polk to secure agreement from Texas regarding specific annexation terms. The new president would also have to deal with Mexico's fury over what appeared to be the culmination of a long and carefully contrived American plan.

Nor was this all. The British tried to prevent Texas from accepting American annexation with promises to negotiate formal Mexican recognition of Texan independence. Polk's emissaries worked frantically to thwart the British initiative, but most instructive to Texans was the transparent British goal to establish an informal protectorate in the Southwest, entirely for London's commercial and diplomatic benefit. In that light, most Texans thought it more in their interests to accept the U.S. offer. On July 4, 1845, a popularly elected convention approved annexation.

Conclusion

The moment the first American immigrants set foot in Texas, it was only a matter of time before the region would come under the gaze of U.S. expansionists. The Mexican government in the 1820s certainly did not foresee this result of its policy to encourage American settlement in Texas. By the time Mexico tried to restrict such settlement and control the growing Texas population, however, it was too late. Steadfastly American in both sentiment and heritage, the Texans were sure to chafe under Mexican attempts to transform that sentiment and subsume that heritage. The Texan revolt that erupted in 1836 became a revolution without the help of the United States, but it was guided by the American example. U.S. sympathies naturally were with the Lone Star patriots, and their success was a cause for celebration that prompted a relatively quick recognition of their independence.

Sectional disputes, fueled by disagreements over slavery and less obvious arguments, prevented annexation for almost a decade, but the wishes of most Texans and the resolve of expansionist Americans finally overcame all obstacles. Just as opponents had predicted, Texas came with problems: Mexico was furious, American abolitionists were incensed, and Britain was irritated. President James Polk would have to deal with these and other difficulties to complete the continental mission that had been in some minds all along and was now being called the American destiny.

Notes

1. William Travis to Sam Houston, 25 February 1836, in John H. Jenkins, ed., *The Papers of the Texas Revolution, 1835–1836*, 10 vols. (Austin, TX: Presidial, 1973), 4:433.

2. Marshall De Bruhl, *Sword of San Jacinto: A Life of Sam Houston* (New York: Random, 1993), 212.

3. Ibid.

4. Marquis James, *The Raven: A Biography of Sam Houston* (Indianapolis: Bobbs-Merrill Company, 1929), 255.

5. Quoted in Eugene C. Barker, "President Jackson and the Texas Revolution," *American Historical Review* 12 (July 1907): 808.

6. Adams is the only president to have held elective office after leaving the presidency. He regarded his service in the House of Representatives as the greatest achievement of his career.

7. William Henry Harrison had been elected president in the fall of 1840 with John Tyler as his vice president. Harrison died a month after taking office, bringing Tyler to the presidency, the first vice president to take office on the death of a president.

8. Joseph D. McCutchan, *Mier Expedition Diary: A Texan Prisoner's Account,* Joseph Milton Nance, ed. (Austin, TX: University of Texas Press, 1978), 88.

9. The American-British dispute over Oregon will be discussed in Chapter 6.

10. Michael A. Morrison, *Slavery and the American West: The Eclipse of Manifest Destiny and the Coming of the Civil War* (Chapel Hill: University of North Carolina Press, 1997), 22.

11. K. Jack Bauer, *The Mexican War, 1846–1848* (New York: Macmillan, 1974), 7.

Andrew Jackson. Reproduced from the
Collections of the Library of Congress.

John L. O'Sullivan (ca. 1875). From the
collection of The New-York Historical
Society, etching from *Harper's Weekly*,
negative number 43507.

Seminole Warrior Osceola. Reproduced from the Collections of the Library of Congress.

A Parody of the Dispute over Texas Annexation. Reproduced from the Collections of the Library of Congress.

James K. Polk. Reproduced from the Collections of the Library of Congress.

COL. FREMONT
PLANTING THE AMERICAN STANDARD ON THE ROCKY MOUNTAINS.

John C. Frémont Lionized as Pathmarker of the West. Reproduced from the Collections of the Library of Congress.

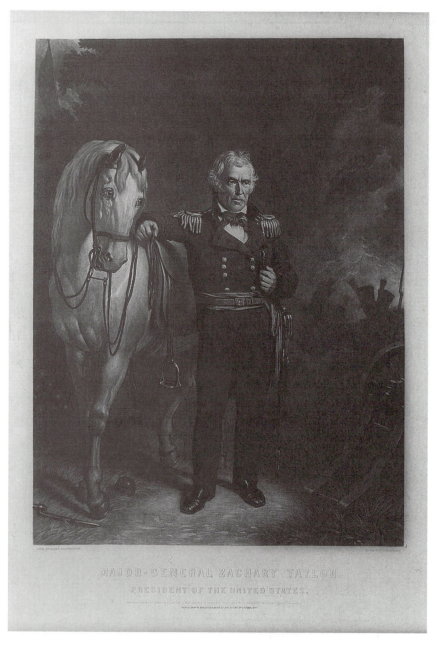

MAJOR-GENERAL ZACHARY TAYLOR.
PRESIDENT OF THE UNITED STATES.

Zachary Taylor. Reproduced from the Collections of the Library of Congress.

POLK'S DREAM.

A lampoon of the Oregon Question. Reproduced from the Collections of the Library of Congress.

MAJOR GENERAL WINFIELD SCOTT.
AT VERA CRUS MARCH 25 1847.

Winfield Scott. Reproduced from the Collections of the Library of Congress.

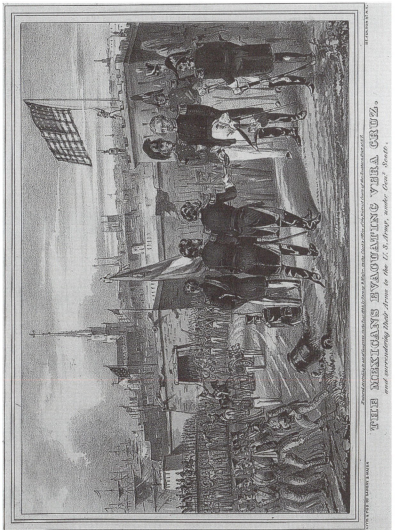

CHAPTER 6

OREGON

The great surge of migration toward the Mississippi paused on the edge of the enormous and inhospitable prairies that lay west of the river. Here trees were so scarce that fables took root and sprang up in the minds of a whole generation of American pioneers. They called it the Great American Desert in the erroneous belief that its arid, hard soil was sterile. It would be left to post–Civil War homesteaders to stake this land and dispel its myths with the help of sturdy plows and steel railroads.

For most people during this time, the Great Plains and Rocky Mountains remained obstacles to go around or struggle across, things in the way of people going someplace else. Consequently, during the first thirty years of the nineteenth century, American explorers west of the Mississippi mostly were legendary figures known simply as mountain men. Mountain men trapped beaver, taking advantage of a fashion boom that for a time enthralled high society in the eastern United States and Europe with elegant hats made shiny with stretched beaver skins. Their improbable connection to the well-dressed dandies thus prodded trapper-survivalists to explore otherwise inaccessible regions of the Rocky Mountain West. They traipsed independently through terrifying terrain in all weathers, loaded with paraphernalia and wearing the skins and furs of animals they trapped or hunted. Changes in fashion and the economic crash of 1837 soon brought down the curtain on one of the most colorful interludes in American history, but not before trappers had helped to show the way through the barriers that supposedly blocked American settlement west of the Rockies.

Just as economic troubles after 1837 helped end the era of the trapper, they also sent growing numbers of farmers toward the inviting fruitfulness of Oregon's Willamette River Valley. In turn, this influx of settlers prompted a serious diplomatic confrontation with Great Britain. The question, dormant for almost thirty years, finally had to be answered: Who owned what in the Oregon Country? Before it was resolved, the question animated American proponents and opponents of Manifest Destiny, stirred up anti-American sentiment in the British Parliament and public, and engrossed the highest councils in Washington and London.

The Land and Its Claimants

The Oregon Country was huge. It stretched west from the Rocky Mountains to the Pacific and from the Mexican border at 42° north to 54°40'. It covered about a half million square miles, a region larger than the combined area of Great Britain, Ireland, and much of northern Europe. Eventually it would constitute about half of British Columbia, the whole of Washington and Oregon on the coast and Idaho in the interior as well as parts of Montana and Wyoming.

Before the arrival of Europeans, no fewer than 125 Indian tribes composed a native population of about 180,000. Considerable differences in culture and custom distinguished these inhabitants of a region strikingly varied in its terrain and climate. The Nootka, for instance, who lived along the western coast of Vancouver Island, built permanent villages, fished from canoes fashioned from cedar trees, and stored smoked salmon, their principal dietary staple. On the other extreme, at the eastern edge of the Oregon Country near the Rocky Mountains, tribes such as the Nez Percé and Cayuse were hunters more like the Plains Indians in custom, skilled in the use of the horse to hunt buffalo.

As in other instances of contact between Europeans and Indians, the native peoples of the Pacific Northwest and the whites who began to appear in larger numbers during the nineteenth century clashed culturally and sometimes violently. The most tragic example is that of the Cayuse and the American missionaries who came to the region after the Nez Percé, according to some accounts, had asked for Christian instruction.[1] In 1836, the American Board of Commissioners for Foreign Missions dispatched a party led by Dr. Marcus Whitman and his wife Narcissa to these tribes. For eleven years they taught Christian doctrine, and then in 1847 a smallpox epidemic ravaged the Cayuse.

Surviving members of that tribe, believing white interlopers were the cause of the epidemic, fell upon the Whitman mission, killing fourteen whites including Marcus and Narcissa. In that far-flung land a continent away and two centuries removed from the Pilgrim settlements of Massachusetts Bay, the same sad chronicle of attack and reprisal was still being acted out.

Spain

Four nations at one time claimed the Oregon Country, and of them, the United States was literally the last on the scene. Spain's entitlement outranked all others. It dated from 1494 with the venerable Treaty of Tordesillas, a claim bolstered by subsequent voyages of discovery over a 250-year period. Yet, Spain's imperial reach grew less certain in the late eighteenth century, and it began a steady retreat from this part of the world where it had never firmly established a physical presence.

A sharp disagreement with Britain in 1789 over fur-trading rights in the Pacific Northwest led to the 1790 Nootka Sound Convention (named after an inlet on the western shore of Vancouver Island), in which Spain grudgingly consented to British settlement and commerce north of Spanish possessions on the Pacific Coast. Although Spanish settlements never spread farther north than the Sacramento Valley, the precise extent of Spain's North American possessions remained undefined until 1819. In that year, in addition to the agreement in the Adams-Onís Treaty to sell Florida, Spain formally ceded all claims above the forty-second parallel to the United States.

Russia

Russia's claim dated from the 1741 voyage of Vitus Bering, a Danish explorer under commission to the tsar, who named the strait between North America and Asia. At first, the Russians limited their activities to a profitable fur-trading business by hunting sea otters in the Aleutians and northward. The creation of the Russian-American Company in 1799 and gradual expansion of Russian commercial activity southward alarmed both Britain and the United States. Finally in 1821, Tsar Alexander I overstepped himself by claiming a Russian monopoly to the fifty-first parallel just north of Vancouver Island. The strong protest from Secretary of State John Quincy Adams—his note contained the principles later embodied in the Monroe Doctrine—and the potential displeasure of the British Royal Navy brought the Russians to the negotiating table. An 1824 treaty with the United States pushed back their holdings to north of 54°40'. The following year, an Anglo-Russian Treaty finished Russia as a possible claimant to any of the Oregon Country.

Great Britain

Second only to Spain's was the British claim, which dated from Sir Francis Drake's epic 1577–80 circumnavigation of the globe. In 1579, Drake put in just north of San Francisco in the shelter of Reyes Point at a spot still named Drake's Bay. Although he claimed the land for Queen Elizabeth, he was more interested in looting Spaniards' treasure ships rather than purloining their real estate. Not only had the Spanish preceded him, his brief halt in the land he called New Albion marked the shore with only a fleeting British footprint. It was certainly not a foothold.

Two hundred years later, though, the British came back. Captain James Cook landed farther north on what would become Vancouver Island and made the motions of again staking a claim for the British sovereign, by then George III. Cook also sailed away, soon to die at the hands of natives in Hawaii, but his 1778 visit theoretically justified a British commercial presence in the region. When John Meares established a trading post at Nootka Sound, Spain tried to run him off, and the confrontation resulted in the Nootka Sound Convention of 1790.

The desire to implement the Nootka accord and investigate more thoroughly the country led to Captain George Vancouver's voyage, the first substantial British attempt to lay claim to the Pacific Northwest. Vancouver, in addition, was on a quest to find the geographical Grail of the Western Hemisphere. He hoped to discover the western opening of the fabled Northwest Passage, a navigable watercourse leading to the inland lakes of North America and providing an avenue between the Atlantic and Pacific oceans.

Arriving off the Pacific Coast in the spring of 1792, Vancouver sailed north. He passed by indications of an opening in the coast because a tentative inspection by Meares several years earlier had concluded that it did not mark a navigable river's mouth. Reflecting his frustration, Meares had given the surrounding features discouraging names such as Cape Disappointment and Deception Bay. In any case, breakers disclosed the presence of a sandbar that ran parallel to the coast, an impressive obstacle for any deep-draft vessel.

On April 29, Vancouver met an American merchant vessel commanded by Boston mariner Robert Gray. It was a fateful meeting, because Gray was reputedly knowledgeable about the waters farther north that held promise as gateways to the interior. Convinced he was on the right track, Vancouver headed north while Gray went south along the seemingly impenetrable coast. Near the island that would bear his name, Vancouver sailed through the Strait of Juan de Fuca to discover Puget Sound, named after Peter Puget, an officer of his crew. Vancouver concluded, however, that it was not the Northwest Passage, a prelude to the Lewis and Clark expedition's definitive verdict twelve years later that such a waterway simply did not exist.

Two weeks after his meeting with Vancouver, Robert Gray gazed at the forbidding surf crashing against the sandbar off Cape Disappointment. He ordered his ship's helm put over to direct her bow through the foam. His crew thought he had lost his mind, but actually, he was on the verge of finding the entrance to the second greatest river in North America. Gray named it after his ship, the *Columbia.*

Although Gray's exploit was a setback for the British, they were not idle. Vancouver followed Gray's discovery by exploring a hundred miles up the Columbia River. In 1793, the indomitable Alexander Mackenzie, agent for the Montreal-based North West Company of fur traders, made history by leading a party to the Pacific, the first white men in North America to complete the continental passage. Upper Canada's lieutenant governor assessed Mackenzie as being "as intelligent as he is adventurous," an observation that could have described other intrepid Northwest agents who blazed trails through the region in years to follow.[2] Simon Fraser trekked the northern reaches of the Oregon Country and beyond to the Arctic, while in the south David Thompson stumbled onto the headwaters of the Columbia. By 1810, British trading posts dotted the landscape from the Kootenai River west of the Continental Divide to the Spokane River as the North West Company's agents continued to bestow their names on landmarks both prominent and trifling. Thus, on the eve of the War of 1812, by means of a diplomatic accord, exploratory voyages, physical presence, and cartographic place names, the British claim to the Oregon Country was well established.

The United States

Robert Gray and his crew were not the first Americans to visit the Pacific Northwest. Two others traveled with James Cook in 1778. One, New Englander John Ledyard, reported a profitable China trade in sea otter pelts that roused the interest of Boston merchants. True to the astute sense for commercial opportunity that personified the go-getting Yankee trader, two Boston merchantmen appeared off the coast of the Oregon Country within ten years. One of the ships was the *Columbia*. Under Gray on the trip home, she became the first American vessel to circumnavigate the earth. On May 11, 1792, during Gray's return voyage to the Pacific Northwest, she rolled through the surf into the great "River of the West."

Gray did not formally claim the Columbia River for the United States—the United States in 1792 would likely have had little interest in it—but he did establish that an American was the first to put a vessel on its waters. For years afterward, however, little other than Gray's exploit upheld a U.S. claim to Oregon. The Lewis and Clark expedition did not arrive in the region until the winter of 1805, and even then, none of its members ventured north of the Columbia.

The first sustained American presence came in 1811 with a venture promoted by the New York fur-trade tycoon John Jacob Astor, who intended to establish a settlement on the south bank of the Columbia near the coast. Named Astoria, it was meant to test the heretofore-unchallenged British and Russian control of the region's fur trade.

Astoria, however, was founded at the worst possible time. After the outbreak of the War of 1812, its nervous founders tried to cut their losses by selling the post to the North West Company. The arrival of HMS *Raccoon* shortly thereafter made the sale of Astoria seem prudent, but the Royal Navy's behavior in this instance actually complicated matters for the British. The *Raccoon's* captain formally seized Astoria, despite the North West Company's purchase of it, an act that adversely affected British fortunes south of the Columbia. The Treaty of Ghent, which restored all territory captured during hostilities, destined Astoria (or Fort George, as the British renamed it) to be returned to the United States. Thus, although the British postponed the transfer until 1818, the U.S. flag again flew at the mouth of the Columbia. Astoria's return did not alter the fact that the North West Company had bought the trading post. Astor argued that the expected threat from the Royal Navy had tainted the transaction, but the British continued to operate the post even after 1818.

More changes bolstering the British presence were in store for the region. As the fur trade's focus shifted from the oceangoing sea otter to the inland beaver, the venerable and influential Hudson's Bay Company absorbed the North West Company in 1821, including Astoria among its assets. Lavished by the Crown with broad licenses that increased its already sizable power in Canadian provinces, the company would be the sole economic engine as well the only law and order in the Oregon Country for the next twenty years. In 1824, the company, under the direction of George Simpson, moved its headquarters from Astoria to build Fort Vancouver upriver at Belle Vue Point just across from the mouth of the Willamette River. From there, Hudson's Bay chief factor John McLoughlin ruled the region as a sort of benevolent dictator. As Fort Vancouver became a bustling emporium, the company expanded its influence in all directions. Dr. McLoughlin—he had trained as a physician in his youth—sent out agents to explore, trap beaver, set up company farms, herd company livestock, net company salmon, even plant company apple orchards.

Over the years, the few Americans who came into the region, such as the occasional grizzled mountain man or missionaries like those led by Marcus and Narcissa Whitman, usually found McLoughlin friendly and generous.[3] He was under orders from London to discourage Americans from setting up rival establishments along the Columbia, but he and his subalterns were usually pleasant as they did so. McLoughlin saw no reason not to be. At Fort Vancouver, his empire—and by extension, Britain's—seemed well entrenched and impressively secure.

Diplomacy and Delay

McLoughlin's affability was more than a product of his temperament; it was the Hudson's Bay Company policy as set by its board of directors in London. When he and his subordinates tried to extend the company's reach into American territory, those directors rebuked the chief factor with instructions to cease such activities or risk incurring their "serious displeasure."[4] Fearful of losing its broad charter in North

America, the Hudson's Bay Company eagerly conformed to the British government's conciliatory American policy that took shape after the War of 1812.

That policy was fashioned within the framework of a burdensome empire and the potentially unstable situation in post-Napoleonic Europe. The result was a series of important and largely amicable agreements with the United States. In 1817, Acting Secretary of State Richard Rush and British minister Charles Bagot halted a naval arms race on the Canadian border by demilitarizing the Great Lakes. In addition, during the following year the two countries began their first serious talks about ownership of the Oregon Country.

The Treaty of 1818

After the War of 1812, British foreign secretary Lord Castlereagh wanted to avoid Astoria's return to the United States looking like a surrender of British claims south of the Columbia. Yet, when British representatives failed to deliver Castlereagh's stipulation to American authorities, the United States felt free to presume that the restoration of Astoria signaled a formal British retreat to the region north of the Columbia.

There the situation stood when Richard Rush and Albert Gallatin began talks with British counterparts in Britain about, in part, the Oregon Boundary. The American envoys proposed that the forty-ninth parallel serve as the border from the Lake of the Woods to the Pacific Coast. Although the suggestion was somewhat audacious in assigning American rights to the region north as well as south of the Columbia River, it was not a new claim. In 1807, envoys James Monroe and William Pinkney had suggested the same boundary during negotiations over an assortment of differences with Britain. The forty-ninth parallel was erroneously believed to be the traditional boundary between French and British provinces as established by the 1713 Treaty of Utrecht.

Gallatin and Rush had not pulled forty-nine degrees from thin air, but they had proposed an impossibility as far as the British were concerned. The British balked at abandoning their substantial claim north of the Columbia. They would only agree to the boundary set at forty-nine degrees from the Lake of the Woods to the Rockies. West of the mountains, both countries would have equal access to Oregon for ten years, after which the issue could be revisited.[5] Thus, the 1818 treaty

Map 6.1
The Oregon, Santa Fe, and California Trails

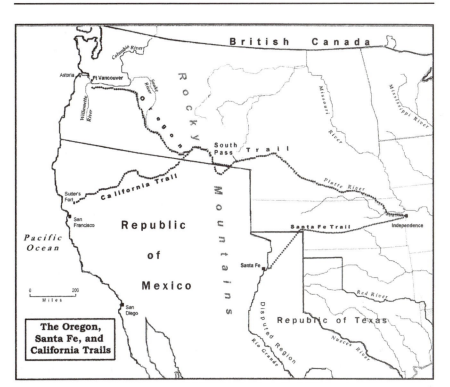

settled part of the western Canadian border and avoided by postponement a dispute over the remainder.

By the time the ten-year period neared its end, at least some
aspects of the Oregon question had been simplified. Spanish and Russian claims were eliminated in 1819 and 1824–25, respectively, and the
United States asserted in the Monroe Doctrine the principle of no additional European colonization in the Americas. But as the number of
claimants narrowed in the Oregon Country, British attitudes, under the
influence of the Hudson's Bay Company, hardened. Embracing the idea
that the Columbia would be for western North America what the St.
Lawrence River was for eastern Canada, they proposed that the border
be the forty-ninth parallel to its intersection with a tributary of the
Columbia and then follow the river to the Pacific. The United States
would not accept such a settlement.

When the 1818 treaty was due to expire, Gallatin again represented the United States in a series of unproductive talks aimed at resolving the border. In 1827, after a flurry of unacceptable proposals and counterproposals, the diplomats simply renewed the 1818 agreement indefinitely. Either party could terminate it after one year's advance notice. Under those imprecise provisions, the fate of the enormous region remained uncertain for almost two decades.

Boosters and Missionaries

While U.S. diplomatic representatives wrestled over the dry data of longitude and latitude, the American public displayed only casual interest in the distant Oregon Country. It was, as the Lewis and Clark expedition had shown, remote, isolated, and almost impossible to reach. The expedition's official journals, published in 1814, described a trek so long and a land so exotic that for ordinary Americans, the Corps of Discovery might as well have visited the moon.

Some legislators began trying to change that impression in the years after the War of 1812. In Congress in 1821, Virginia representative John Floyd began making speeches, forming committees, and sponsoring resolutions avowing American rights in the Columbia Basin. In 1825, in the upper house, Missouri senator Thomas Hart Benton proclaimed the belief that no European power should be in Oregon. Floyd's interest perhaps stemmed from his friendship with people connected to John Jacob Astor, but both he and Benton acted sincerely from the same convictions expressed in the Monroe Doctrine. It was not necessarily an expansionist message. Benton, with many others, believed that the Rocky Mountains posed such a barrier to westward migration that they marked the natural limit of U.S. growth. "Along the back of this ridge [of the Rocky Mountains]," he proclaimed in 1825, "the Western limit of this republic should be drawn, and the statue of the fabled god, Terminus, should be raised upon its highest peak, never to be thrown down."[6]

They wanted an independent republic in the American image to take root in Oregon and thus serve as another outpost of liberty by blocking the spread of monarchical imperialism. Yet, many other Americans disagreed. Some held positions of authority, such as John Quincy Adams (secretary of state, president, and finally Massachusetts congressman) who objected to the notion of American interests hemmed in by any barriers, including the mountainous kind. In addition, voices in the public gradually formed a growing chorus that rejected any suggestion of American limits, both in reaching Oregon and in spreading out once there. In 1830, Bostonian Hall J. Kelly commenced churning out widely read books and pamphlets to promote the Oregon Colonization Society, and the appearance of Washington Irving's two-volume *Astoria* in 1836 further heightened popular interest in the region. Boston merchant William Sturgis, who had been trading in the Pacific Northwest for more than twenty years, publicly insisted that owning Puget Sound was paramount if the United States wanted success in the trans-Pacific trade. U.S. Navy lieutenant William Slacum seconded that opinion in 1837, and an investigative voyage commanded by Charles Wilkes in 1841 confirmed it. Wilkes assessed the Columbia River as having limited value and went so far as to say that the United States should expand its claim all the way north to 54°40'—possibly the first call for "All Oregon" that later produced the political battle cry "Fifty-four Forty or Fight!"

Meanwhile, a noticeable American presence in Oregon was gradually gathering south of the Columbia River. In 1834, Jason and Daniel Lee led a party of Methodist missionaries to settle in the Willamette Valley. Two years later, the ill-fated Whitman party of missionaries also traveled to the Oregon Country to establish a mission among the Nez Percé, Cayuse, and Walla Walla. Seemingly slight at first, this missionary work in Oregon would have an important impact on both the character and pace of American settlement.

That reality eventually dawned on the watchful Hudson's Bay Company. It became apparent, for example, that the people who came to preach the Gospel were different from itinerant trappers or commercial-minded entrepreneurs. Lack of pelts or profits usually persuaded those types to move on. Missionaries, however, established permanent settlements and planted crops. Moreover, they stirred curiosity in the East about the distant land. In addition to saving the souls of Oregon's native inhabitants, both the Lees and the Whitmans eventually wanted to sponsor American immigration to the region. Methodist authorities in the East so disapproved of the idea, however, that they ended up recalling Lee from his Willamette Valley ministry. Marcus Whitman returned to Boston in 1842 to argue against a similar fate for his Walla Walla mission. Successful in his plea, he returned to Oregon in 1843 at the head of a sizable party of settlers.

Only a few years earlier most Americans had thought of Oregon, when thinking of it at all, as impossibly remote. As the East slid into economic depression after the Panic of 1837, Oregon was suddenly being thought of almost all the time by countless dispossessed farmers down on their luck and searching for a second chance. The question for them was how to get there. Mountain men had early found the passes through the Rockies to this paradise, but their persistent isolation and usual illiteracy had limited that knowledge to a small circle of people. Missionary journeys in the 1830s signaled a rapid change in that, too.

The Oregon Trail

The path across the plains and through the mountains, eventually named the Oregon Trail, was pieced together by a century of stumbling explorations dictated by the logic of topography and terrain. In the 1740s, French Canadians trudged part of the trail in Montana, and in 1805 Lewis and Clark journeyed over another part through the Snake River country. When John Jacob Astor sent agents to set up Astoria in 1811, the expedition found the key component of the route by discovering a practical way through the Rocky Mountains. Called the South Pass, it rose about 7,500 feet above sea level and thus made possible travel through the treacherous landscape. (See Map 6.1.)

Mountain men came to know the route well, but information about it was not common until the 1830s. Trappers and traders then began serving as guides for the occasional intrepid settler. Literate migrants also began to write guidebooks describing the trail, sometimes in remarkable detail. The colorful narrative about Lieutenant John C. Frémont's 1842 expedition into the Wind River Mountains further fueled interest and disseminated information.[7]

Once the route of the Oregon Trail became well known, scattered American settlements south of the Columbia began to increase at a remarkable rate. In the early 1840s, "Oregon Fever" spurred hundreds to take up the 2,000-mile journey to this new Promised Land. Starting across the plains from Independence, Missouri, rolling through the mountains at South Pass, and braving the obstacle of the formidable Blue Mountains, wagon trains brought about five thousand Americans into the region south of the Columbia by 1846. The cost was high. At best, these pioneers covered about 10 miles a day, leaving along the trail countless animal carcasses and rudely marked shallow graves, makeshift monuments to the human toll of this epic trek.

Those who made it mostly settled in the Willamette Valley. Finally, the Hudson's Bay Company north of the Columbia had to concede that it could not compete with the swelling American population. The region was nearly trapped out anyway, and in the face of growing settlement to the south, the maintenance of Fort Vancouver became a burden not worth the cost or bother. When American settlers formed a provisional government, it became apparent that McLoughlin's paternalism would no longer work to restrain needy American migrants. He laid plans to move the company's headquarters to Vancouver Island, a move accomplished in 1845. By then, American settlers were beginning to eye the region around Puget Sound.[8]

In the face of these developments, the British government had good reason to settle the Oregon question on lines favorable to the border Americans had suggested at forty-nine degrees. Yet, they still were unable to do so. A series of unfortunate incidents along the eastern Canadian border seriously disturbed Anglo-American relations during the late 1830s, including an argument over the northeastern U.S. boundary with New Brunswick. American settlers in Oregon were ready for a settlement, and the Hudson's Bay Company at last was willing for a resolution. Unfortunately, the politicians on both sides of the Atlantic were not.

Crises and Compromise

By 1844, the Pacific Northwest controversy actually concerned a relatively small section of the vast Oregon Country. Specifically, it involved an area bordered by the Columbia River, the line of forty-nine degrees latitude, and the Pacific Ocean. (See Map 6.2.) Even after the withdrawal of the Hudson's Bay Company headquarters, Britain insisted that the Columbia form the border. Some in the United States began to push for a settlement beyond forty-nine degrees all the way to the Russian line of 54°40′. These mutually inflexible stands partly resulted from a worsening relationship between the two countries during the late 1830s.

The Webster-Ashburton Treaty

During the 1830s, Canadian uprisings against the Crown sought help from Americans all too willing to disobey U.S. neutrality laws. All manner of trouble resulted. In 1837, the British sank the American vessel *Caroline* on the Niagara River because it was purportedly running

Map 6.2
The Oregon Question

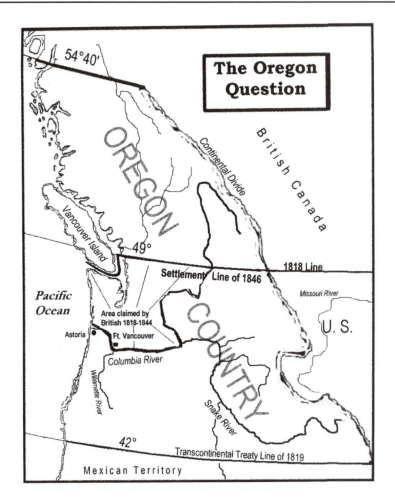

guns to Canadian rebels. A year later, New York authorities arrested and
put on trial British subject Alexander McLeod because he had boasted
of murdering a crew member aboard the *Caroline*. McLeod, who had
made the claim in a barroom, was probably guilty of nothing more than
whiskey-soaked braggadocio, but by the time a New York jury acquitted
him, Anglo-American relations were at low ebb. Then in 1839, a long-
standing border dispute between Maine and New Brunswick threatened
to turn violent when Maine authorities tried to bar Canadian lumber-
jacks from the state's Aroostook Valley.

Secretary of State Daniel Webster met with special British envoy Lord Ashburton in 1841 to resolve the many disagreements before matters deteriorated further. The talks resulted in the Webster-Ashburton Treaty that more or less split the difference in Maine, a compromise much criticized in both Britain and America. Webster was unfairly accused of giving away a sizable section of the United States, his harshest critics claiming he was bribed by Ashburton to do so. Anti-American sentiment in the British Parliament found loud voice in the caustic Lord Palmerston, who condemned what he regarded as a gross betrayal of British-Canadian interests. Aware that they were already tackling a ticklish issue in the Northeast, Webster and Ashburton thought it wise to let Oregon wait. At most, Webster proposed an odd scheme that would link the resolution of Oregon to a British assurance that it would help the United States acquire San Francisco from Mexico. This unlikely suggestion came to nothing. "The Oregon Territory and the Columbia River question," John Quincy Adams noted in his diary, "remain open."[9]

In spite of their denigration by partisans in Washington and London, Webster and Ashburton had at least laid aside confrontation and launched a spirit of conciliation based on compromise. For the settlers in Oregon and the coiling spring of Manifest Destiny, it was not much, but it was a start. As it happened, it was a fortunate one. The two governments would need all possible conciliation and compromise during the next few years.

"Fifty-Four Forty or Fight!"

Another postponement meant that the Oregon question became embroiled in the presidential election of 1844 and by virtue of that, it became interwoven with Texas annexation.[10] The Whig Party's nominee, celebrated Kentuckian Henry Clay, wavered on Texas in an attempt to appease both the proslavery South and antislavery North. Ultimately, his vacillation cost him too many voters, and New York State narrowly went for the Democratic Party's nominee. Clay lost the election.

The Democrat nominee, James Knox Polk of Tennessee, emerged from a deadlocked convention as the country's first "dark horse" presidential contender.[11] Polk was certainly not as renowned as Clay, despite a long career in state and national politics that included a stint as Speaker of the U.S. House of Representatives. Campaign biographers portrayed Polk, a follower of Andrew Jackson, as "Young Hickory," but even most Democrats believed the label an exaggeration.

Almost everyone, however, misjudged Polk as he moved into the presidency. True, he was no Andrew Jackson. He lacked that man's forthright if frequently blunt method of dealing with both friends and foes. In the first place, Polk had no friends, and second, he saw everyone as a possible enemy. The outlook made him a master manipulator and careful schemer with both foreign as well as domestic opponents. Suspicious by nature and under no illusions about his natural talents, Polk worked especially hard at every task he tackled. Because he was an unqualified expansionist, he applied himself with unwavering determination to an expansionist agenda, confident that he was doing not only the American people's will, but God's also. Although the narrowly won 1844 election questionably revealed the will of the people, and the pulpit was mixed on God's opinion, Polk's presidency fulfilled what newspaper writer John L. O'Sullivan described as the United States' "Manifest Destiny" to expand to the Pacific Ocean.[12]

Polk closely resembled Andrew Jackson in another way. He was impetuous and quick to anger. Solving the Oregon question would involve surmounting considerable domestic as well as foreign obstacles, and throughout negotiations, Polk stubbornly held to inflexible positions because he regarded British behavior as a personal affront.

The 1844 Democratic Party platform included a boldly expansionist plank that announced an American "title to the whole of the Territory of Oregon." It also declared "that the re-occupation of Oregon and the re-annexation of Texas . . . are great American measures."[13] On the face of it, the statement was rife with audacious abandon, for with no historical justification the Democratic Party placed a claim to Oregon all the way to 54°40' and imprudently tied settlement in the Pacific Northwest to the acquisition of Texas. But beneath such apparent irresponsibility lay a fairly cynical compromise required by sectional concerns over slavery. In simplest terms, southerners wanted Texas, which already had slavery. Northerners wanted Oregon, which never would have slavery, as a counterweight. Texas was huge, so the bigger Oregon was, the better.

Aside from the mischief of promoting an "All Oregon" agenda that risked war with Britain, the platform fed the emotions of a sharply heightened and aggressive American nationalism. Young America was the label for this sentiment that felt it could whip all creation. Itching for a fight over anything, but especially over slights to national honor, hotheads (and even cooler ones who should have known better) were brashly proclaiming the intention to acquire "All Oregon" with the motto "Fifty-four Forty or Fight!"[14]

Unclear about how much of this was bluster and how much was consequential, the British government of Sir Robert Peel watched with increasing discomfort. When the British proposed the Oregon question be submitted to arbitration by a third party, John Tyler's lame-duck administration declined. After the House of Representatives passed a bill in February 1845 to establish a territorial government over "All Oregon," Peel was startled that the United States might violate the 1827 agreement without formally ending mutual access to the territory. Such a breach might require a response in force. He wrote to his foreign secretary Lord Aberdeen, "Might not a stout frigate be immediately sent [to Oregon] . . . ?"[15] Aberdeen, normally conciliatory even in the face of American rhetorical excess, agreed. Fortunately, the House's bill died when the Senate adjourned before acting on it.

On March 4, 1845, however, Polk made matters worse by pledging in his inaugural address "to assert and maintain by all constitutional means the right of the United States to that portion of our territory which lies beyond the Rocky Mountains." Polk went on to state that the U.S. title to Oregon was "clear and unquestionable" and advocated extending American laws to citizens who immigrated to the region. America's sloganeering public and the boisterous Congress alarmed the British, but Polk's formal inaugural statement openly dismayed them. Robert Peel somberly informed Parliament that he and his advisers were "resolved—and we are prepared—to maintain" Britain's rights in the region.[16]

Such careless strides and reflexive gestures can have awful and disproportionate consequences, putting prideful nations at war over trivial matters while larger disagreements fade. In 1845, it appeared that such might be the fate of the United States and Britain. As the British and American press traded snarls, it became obvious that most Britons cared little about Oregon, but they greatly resented impertinent treatment by insolent Yanks. On the American side, many in the Whig Party and its newspapers began to counsel caution. The question was whether President Polk could resolve the matter and placate his own Democratic Party.

The distraction of potential hostilities with Mexico over Texas was a potent incentive to solve the Oregon problem with Britain. Polk was especially troubled by rumors that the British had plans for Mexico's province of California. Searching for a way to duck his party's pugnacious platform, he fell back on the argument that no fewer than three previous proposals made by prior administrations required him to negotiate an Oregon border at forty-nine degrees. On July 12, 1845, Secretary of States James Buchanan offered that boundary to British minister Richard Pakenham and was surprised when Pakenham instantly rejected it without consulting London.

Perhaps Pakenham, frustrated by more than a year of unproductive dealings with the Tyler administration, was irritated by the tone of Buchanan's proposal—the secretary had begun with a long lecture about the validity of the U.S. claim to 54°40'. Whatever its cause, Pakenham's outright rejection infuriated President Polk, who apparently expected at least a counteroffer. London was unhappy, too. Aberdeen intimated to American minister Louis McLane that Pakenham's action deeply troubled him. Finally taking the measure of the prickly Polk, Pakenham was reduced to renewing suggestions that the Oregon question be arbitrated while begging Aberdeen to bring him home. Aberdeen kindly sent calm reassurances to his minister, but Pakenham's hasty act had done great damage.

Polk not only rebuffed arbitration, he withdrew the offer of the forty-ninth parallel and thereafter obstinately embraced 54°40'. "The only way to treat John Bull," he told South Carolina congressman James A. Black, "was to look him straight in the eye."[17] In his annual message to Congress that December, Polk recommended giving Britain the year's notice required by the Convention of 1827 to end mutual access to the Oregon Country. He asserted that "both national honor and interest" required the United States to possess all of Oregon, and by affirming the principles of the Monroe Doctrine, he indirectly indicated that its preservation compelled a steadfast resistance to Britain in the Northwest and in California.[18]

Although both president and country seemed to have their blood up, the congressional debate over terminating the 1827 agreement droned on for sixteen weeks. Polk, who had promised to serve only one term, believed that politicians posturing for the 1848 presidential contest mostly caused the delay. In the interim, sectional differences gradually seeped into the discussion. After the United States annexed Texas, southerners became increasingly indifferent about gaining free territory in Oregon. Not until April 27, 1846, did Polk have a congressional resolution that allowed him to put the British on notice that in one year, the United States would consider their presence in the Oregon Country to be trespassing.

Britain Seeks Peace

Despite a good deal of chest thumping in the British press, Peel's government was glum as it contemplated the possibility of war. Resolving the matter while preserving British honor, however, presented a difficult dilemma, especially when critics such as Palmerston remained poised to rail at the government for allegedly giving away large chunks of the empire.

Britain was powerful, but it was not without problems. British textile manufacturers relied on southern cotton and faced grave economic injury in the event of a rupture with the United States. Other domestic concerns also absorbed the government. A nasty political argument over Britain's policy of employing high tariffs to shield grain growers from foreign competition had seriously divided the country. By 1846, these measures, called Corn Laws, would intensify a horrible famine in potato-blighted Ireland and gravely damage Britain's progressive reputation both at home and abroad. The impossible political challenge the Corn Laws presented prompted Peel to resign in December 1845, necessitating the formation of a new government by the opposition Whig Party. The Whigs, however, could not accomplish the task because Palmerston's belligerent attitude alarmed even his own party members. After weeks of trying to overcome this handicap, the Whig leadership agreed not only to Peel's return but also promised to discipline Palmerston for his tirades. By the end of 1845, the Peel ministry had a new if limited lease on its political life.[19]

In addition, Peel's preoccupation with securing the repeal of the Corn Laws allowed Lord Aberdeen even greater leeway to attempt a compromise with Americans, no matter how feisty and difficult they appeared. To prepare public opinion for such an effort, Aberdeen had been directing a skillful campaign in the British press to describe the area south of forty-nine degrees as unessential to British interests. He also cultivated and encouraged those members of Parliament called

"Little Englanders," a faction anxious over the growing burdens of empire, especially after the costly Canadian uprisings of the late 1830s. Finally, Aberdeen could point to the Hudson's Bay Company's relocation to Vancouver Island, a signal that even the region's British inhabitants regarded it as unworthy of continued occupancy.

With its domestic house prepared for compromise, Britain could then look to the United States for the next move. The April 1846 congressional resolution to terminate the 1827 agreement for mutual access provided the opening, especially because Congress had softened the gesture by including a call for negotiation. On June 6, 1846, Richard Pakenham appeared at the State Department to propose talks aimed at replacing the Convention of 1827. He presented to James Buchanan a plan that would finally and permanently divide British and U.S. territory in the Oregon Country. Deserting their stand of almost thirty years, the British offered to draw the boundary at the forty-ninth parallel from the Rocky Mountains to the Pacific.

The Oregon Treaty

Polk heard about this potential breakthrough days before Pakenham formally offered it, but the president disliked some of the terms. While forty-nine degrees would give the United States the region north of the Columbia and Puget Sound, the British proposal carefully preserved exclusive right to Vancouver Island by dipping the line around Vancouver's southern tip. Polk was especially resistant to the British proposal that the Hudson's Bay Company receive navigation rights on the Columbia. His first impulse was to stand firm and reject Britain's offer, but when most of his cabinet disagreed, he reconsidered. Great perils awaited a hasty decision that might prove disastrously wrong, and Polk, though obstinate, was canny at avoiding political pitfalls. Consequently, he consented to a unique plan to shift responsibility elsewhere for accepting or rejecting the British proposal.

The Constitution instructs the president to seek the "advice and consent" of the Senate in the making of treaties. While the "consent" stipulation had been scrupulously maintained (treaty ratification requires a two-thirds Senate majority), only once had a president sought the advice of the Senate before signing a treaty. George Washington brought a prospective Indian treaty before the Senate early in his administration, but he became so incensed by both the Senate's semi-chaotic hubbub and members' reluctance to debate in front of him that he never sought the Senate's advice again. In fact, no subsequent president had done so, until James K. Polk used the provision for the Oregon Treaty.

The Senate debate lasted two days at the end of which the die-hard proponents of "Fifty-four Forty" lost the fight. Midwestern senators attacked Polk for sacrificing American interests to political expediency, but the administration had a powerful argument for ratification in that Congress had declared war on Mexico just a month before. As the American military prosecuted that conflict, it seemed sensible to remove the potential for one with Britain. On June 18, 1846, the Senate ratified the treaty without alteration as Pakenham had proposed it twelve days earlier, and just that quickly, the decades-old Oregon question was settled. The treaty established the border at forty-nine degrees and granted both countries free navigation of all rivers, including the Columbia, that crossed the boundary. In spite of barbed protests from abolitionists and ardent expansionists, most of the public received the Oregon settlement favorably. By the time of its ratification, the country's concentration was increasingly focused on Mexico.

Conclusion

Oregon was the first major territorial settlement under the newly minted designation of Manifest Destiny. During the Anglo-American newspaper war that accompanied the mounting crisis over Oregon, journalist John L. O'Sullivan had written a column for the *New York Morning News* in which he had proclaimed, "In the growth of our nation . . . we seem to have reached a period . . . stamped with distinct features of expansion, change, development."[20]

A growing number of Americans heard more than a ring of truth in these words. Part of their validity rested in the continental logic of American expansion. The British claim to the region north of the Columbia had always been more substantial than that of the Americans, but increasing American settlement in the Willamette Valley made the claim of contiguity the one that trumped all others. John McLoughlin realized the fact when he moved the Hudson's Bay Company headquarters to Vancouver Island, and Lord Aberdeen comprehended it as he weighed American sentiment from distant London. In the great balance of empire, Oregon had become more trouble than it was worth, especially when the balance of empire was more or less given symmetry by Daniel Webster's concessions over the Maine boundary in 1842.

In his handling of the Oregon question, President Polk's vacillations between forty-nine degrees and 54°40' appeared to charitable assessments as marking both his inexperience and uncertainty about the valid extent of Manifest Destiny. Others were less kind. Thomas Hart Benton accused the president of weakness and jeered that Polk's nickname would forever afterward be "fifty-four forty."[21]

Yet, Polk's defenders have since described his conduct in the affair as a masterful blend of aggressive rhetoric and flexible negotiation. After taking office, he broke from the impossible platform of the Democratic Party and made a responsible offer that accorded with previous presidential diplomacy. The British rejection allowed him to preserve his standing in his party, however, by taking up its call for a boundary at 54°40'. When the British regarded this extravagant position with growing apprehension, their ultimate offer embraced a boundary at forty-nine degrees, which happened to be the long-standing American desire. Polk then arranged to have the settlement initially approved by the Senate to absolve him of abandoning the claim to 54°40'. The outcome was a peaceful settlement that avoided domestic political disaster and foreign territorial war. Instead, the United States emerged from this delicate situation with its honor intact, its territory reasonably enlarged, and its improving relations with Britain further bolstered by a peaceful border stretching from the Atlantic to the Pacific oceans.

Whether President Polk accomplished all this by accident or by deliberate and shrewd design can be debated. Those critical of Young Hickory maintained that he had been more lucky than capable, and events in another setting seemed to be proving their point. Even as the Oregon question reached resolution, muttering guns in Mexico suggested that Polk's luck could only run so far before running out.

Notes

1. The Nez Percé wore ornaments dangling from their noses, hence the French trappers' name, which means "pierced nose." A generation after the ordeal of the Cherokee in the Southeast and the Sauk-Fox in the Midwest, the

Nez Percé would mirror those experiences in the Northwest. In 1855, they ceded most of their land to the United States for a reservation in Oregon's Wallowa Valley region. Yet, the presence of gold there prompted the government to force the Nez Percé from those lands as well.

In 1877, Nez Percé Chief Joseph mounted a briefly successful resistance before leading his followers and their families on a thousand-mile trek toward the safety of Canada. The pursuing U.S. Army captured them less than fifty miles from the Canadian boundary, and they were transported to Indian Territory, a relocation during which many perished.

2. Lt. Gov. J. Graves Simcoe is quoted in Oscar Osburn Winther, *The Old Oregon Country: A History of Frontier Trade, Transportation, and Travel* (Lincoln, NE: University of Nebraska Press, 1950; reprint, Bison, 1969), 26.

3. An attitude of compassionate paternalism toward American settlers persisted even after the formal settlement that established forty-nine degrees as the U.S.-Canada border. In 1847, the famous Hudson's Bay agent and explorer Peter Skene Ogden rescued the survivors of the Whitman Massacre.

4. Quoted in Frederick Merk, *The Oregon Question: Essays in Anglo-American Diplomacy and Politics* (Cambridge, MA: Belknap-Harvard University Press, 1967), 83.

5. Frequently referred to by historians as establishing "joint occupation," the 1818 treaty did not in fact use this language nor did it likely intend to institute a concept of "occupation," which has military connotations. Anders Stephanson better, though not perfectly, describes the arrangement as an "open-door policy." See Stephanson, *Manifest Destiny*, 35.

6. *Register of Debates in Congress* (18th Cong., 2nd sess., 1825), 712.

7. Frémont's 1842 journey, as well as his subsequent explorations, are described in *Narrative of the Exploring Expedition to the Rocky Mountains in the Year 1842, and to Oregon and North California in the Years 1843–1844* (London: Wiley and Putman, 1846). Most historians agree that Frémont's wife, Thomas Hart Benton's daughter Jesse, was responsible for the flamboyance, and hence popularity, of the writings.

8. Historians have long debated the effect of American migration to Oregon in spurring a settlement favorable to the United States. Fredrick Merk, for instance, pointed out that even as McLoughlin moved to Vancouver Island, only eight Americans had settled north of the Columbia River. Nonetheless, the rapidly expanding American presence in the Willamette Valley and its potential to spill north toward Puget Sound prompted a change in Hudson's Bay Company strategy during these crucial years, and that change helped to shape British government policy.

9. Entry of 24 July 1842, in Allan Nevins, ed., *the Diary of John Quincy Adams, 1794–1845: American Diplomacy, and Political, Social, and Intellectual Life from Washington to Polk* (New York: Scribner, 1951), 542.

10. Texas annexation is discussed in Chapter 5.

11. Like much else in the vocabulary of politics during that period, the term "dark horse" derived from horse racing. A dark horse, not favored to win, nonetheless came from far behind to prevail.

12. *New York Morning News,* 27 December 1845.

13. Kirk H. Porter and Donald Bruce Johnson, comps., *National Party Platforms, 1840–1956* (Urbana, IL: University of Illinois Press, 1956), 4.

14. Expansionist William Allen, Ohio senator and member of the Senate Foreign Relations Committee, coined the phrase.

15. Peel to Aberdeen, 23 February 1845, quoted in Frederick Merk, *The Monroe Doctrine and American Expansionism, 1843–49* (New York: Knopf, 1966), 74, fn. 11.

16. The quotation from Polk's inaugural is in Richardson, *Messages and Papers,* 4:381; Peel is quoted in Howard Jones and Donald A. Rakestraw, *Prologue to Manifest Destiny: Anglo-American Relations in the 1840s* (Wilmington, DE: Scholarly Resources, 1997), 206.

17. James K. Polk, *Polk: The Diary of a President; Covering the Mexican War, the Acquisition of Oregon, and the Conquest of California and the Southwest,* Allan Nevins, ed. (New York: Longmans, Green and Co., 1952), 42.

18. Richardson, *Messages and Papers,* 4:397, 398–99.

19. It was generally agreed that after cooperating with Whigs to repeal the Corn Laws, the Peel government would step aside for the Whigs. This indeed occurred in the summer of 1846, just after ratification of the Oregon Treaty.

20. *New York Morning News,* 5 January 1846.

21. *Cong. Globe* (29 Cong., 1st sess., 1845), 853.

CHAPTER 7

MR. POLK'S WAR:
MANIFEST DESTINY AND THE ACQUISITION OF THE SOUTHWEST

As the Polk administration wrestled with the final stages of the Oregon controversy, problems caused by Texas annexation simmered. Mexico had responded to Congress's vote in early 1845 by recalling its minister to the United States, Juan Amonte, a move that exceedingly complicated Polk's plans to complete the Texas annexation and solidify the Rio Grande as the established border. In addition, and just as important for the new president, he had become engrossed with the prospect of acquiring Pacific Coast ports to promote American trade with the Orient. Any hope of purchasing California, however, had suddenly become most unlikely. Military action was always an option, but Polk knew world opinion would condemn a war of conquest. He was certain that Congress would, making the required congressional declaration of war impossible—unless Mexico could be goaded into striking first.

Even before Texas agreed to annexation, Polk took steps to secure the Mexican border. Ships under Commodore David Conner patrolled the Gulf of Mexico, and Brigadier General Zachary Taylor marched the so-called Army of Observation to Fort Jesup on the Louisiana-Texas border. After annexation was formally approved in Austin, the War Department ordered Taylor overland and by ship via New Orleans to Corpus Christi, Texas. Clearly, the military option remained open.

Diplomacy

With Texas secure, Polk tried to open a diplomatic initiative to purchase California and perhaps New Mexico. In his view, such a transaction was a practical solution to the huge debt Mexico owed American creditors. Mexico's payments on these obligations were in arrears, so the president presumed that Mexico would see the wisdom of ceding its western territories to the United States in exchange for the assumption of Mexico's American debts. That Polk embraced such a simplistic formula revealed his greatest weaknesses—inexperience in foreign affairs and the tendency to adopt an artless approach to complex problems. Polk never understood how deeply the loss of Texas had wounded Mexican pride, and he completely misapprehended Mexico's political dilemma stemming from that humiliation. No Mexican government could either cede or sell additional territory to its powerful northern neighbor and expect to remain in power. The entire contents of the United States Treasury could not change this basic reality; no blandishments in the diplomatic lexicon could alter this fact.

The Slidell Mission

Nonetheless, Polk was determined to try. More or less ignoring the fact that Mexico had broken diplomatic relations, Polk dispatched John Slidell to Mexico City with instructions to purchase New Mexico and Upper California and to obtain recognition of the Rio Grande as the U.S. border. Slidell arrived in Mexico at the end of November 1845. The Mexican government under President José Joaquín de Herrera was not entirely averse to talking about unresolved disputes, but Herrera could not even think about selling New Mexico and California to the United States. Doing so would have brought down a political death sentence and, given the mood of Mexico at the time, would have likely meant a real death sentence for Herrera. In addition, Slidell was designated by the United States as a "minister," a technical point of terminology over which the Mexicans took issue. Receiving a minister would signify the reestablishment of diplomatic relations, but Mexicans wanted redress of their grievances as a condition for renewing those relations. Slidell, they said, should have been an envoy empowered to resolve issues that had caused the breach in the first place, and they would not receive him under his official designation. It was an exacting point, perhaps, but Mexico was in an exacting mood.

In fact, Herrera's enemies were up in arms that he had allowed a U.S. diplomat in the city at all. They seized upon Slidell's arrival as a way to topple the government. Although Herrera refused to receive the American minister, Major General Mariano Paredes y Arrillaga marched his army on Mexico City at the end of December and deposed the president. Paredes's military coup laid claim to power by accusing Herrera of toadying to the Americans, a pronouncement that made clear the general had no intention of negotiating with Slidell or any other agent the American government sent his way.

Soldiers on the Rio Grande

Slidell's failure left Polk dejected but no less determined. In early 1846, Polk ordered Taylor down from Corpus Christi to the Rio Grande, a move so apparently confrontational that arguments over Polk's motives have divided students of the period ever since. Was he trying to bait the Mexicans into attacking Taylor and starting a war? Alternatively, was he merely trying to demonstrate American intentions to uphold Texas's claims to the Rio Grande? Given Polk's limited understanding of the political situation in Mexico, perhaps he saw Taylor's maneuver as more a gesture of resolve than a provocation. More likely, however, he rather expected something to happen that would open a way to intimidate the Mexicans into giving him what he wanted.

Whether Polk intended to start a war or simply blundered into one, the result was the same: one month after Taylor arrived on the Rio Grande opposite the Mexican town of Matamoros, a Mexican cavalry patrol attacked sixty-three of his dragoons. Eleven of them were killed and most of the remainder, including their commander Captain Seth Thorton, were captured.[1]

The Mexican-American War

If such was what Polk had intended to happen, he must have despaired that it took an unexpectedly long time to occur. The Mexicans took a full month to rise to Taylor's provocation, and before Polk received the news of the attack, he grew so impatient that he decided to ask for a declaration of war anyway. Slidell had returned with his tale of diplomatic rejection, which was not much, but at the time it was all Polk had. He carefully prepared his message to Congress by outlining U.S. grievances against Mexico, stressing the large debts owed American citizens and Mexico's snub of Slidell. Even Polk must have realized that these were thin grounds for hostilities. He was essentially asking Congress to make war on Mexico because it was a rude spendthrift.

Nevertheless, the timely arrival of Taylor's report describing the Mexican attack saved him the embarrassment. Polk drafted another message declaring that a state of war already existed because the Mexican army had "shed American blood upon the American soil."[2]

The president wanted only enough volunteers and money to prosecute what he described as a conflict not of his choosing but already underway. Put that way, his request for men to reinforce Taylor and ten million dollars to supply them placed his congressional opponents squarely on the defensive. To vote against a war resolution required a vote against providing American boys what they needed to defend themselves on the Rio Grande. Few congressmen wanted to appear insensible to the needs of American soldiers in harm's way, and vote tallies consequently gave the impression that Congress stoutly supported Polk's war. The House of Representatives voted 174–14 and the Senate 40–2 in favor of the resolution, but those figures represented a reflexive resolve temporarily buoyed by patriotic posturing.

In relatively short order, more than a few congressmen wavered and their posturing gave way to contemplation and finally to protests. In their minds, the lopsided vote for war signified nothing more than the manipulations of that moment when the administration told them that American soldiers were under attack. Soon they would ask what kind of attack and why it had occurred. They would ask where it had happened, intimating that it was the American military, not the Mexicans, who had invaded foreign soil. They would come to wonder, once the dust settled and the facts gradually emerged, who were the patriots and who were the scoundrels in that fateful spring of 1846.

Palo Alto and Resaca de la Palma

Taylor tried to strengthen his position by erecting a bastion of sorts that he dubbed Fort Texas, but the large Mexican force at Matamoros continued to threaten his supply line to the coast. Leaving five hundred men under Major Jacob Brown to hold Fort Texas, Taylor took the rest of the army—about three thousand men—to Point Isabel to obtain supplies and secure his communications with the gulf. For Major General Mariano Arista, the Mexican commander at Matamoros, Taylor's move was an opportunity to catch the Americans in the open and destroy them. However, because Arista could not cross the river in time to catch Taylor, the American army reached Point Isabel without incident. Returning to Fort Texas, though, was another problem altogether.

As Taylor started back, Arista moved to block his advance, positioning his army on a grassy plain near Palo Alto and setting the stage for the first battle of the Mexican-American War on May 8, 1846. It began about 3 P.M., primarily as an artillery duel in which highly mobile American batteries demonstrated clear superiority. Arista unsuccessfully tried to flank the American right with his cavalry, so the guns continued their pounding until nightfall halted the battle. The next morning Arista withdrew to more defensible ground, placing his men along dry riverbeds called *resacas,* thus giving the battle of May 9 the name Resaca de la Palma. When American infantry captured several Mexican batteries and turned them on Arista's troops, it sent them in full retreat.

Taylor then moved his army back to Fort Texas where he found a weary and beleaguered garrison. Steady Mexican bombardment had inflicted relatively little damage, but it had claimed a few casualties, including the fort's commander, whose death prompted the renaming of the post Fort Brown.[3] Although the garrison was relieved to see Taylor return, it need not have worried. Arista had removed his beaten army from Matamoros into the interior of Mexico.

Taylor soon crossed the river and occupied Matamoros in preparation for moving upriver to Camargo. As soon as he could, he planned to begin a campaign against the city of Monterrey. (See Map 7.1.)

Political Considerations

When word of Taylor's victories reached Washington, the news set off wild celebrations throughout the country. Predictions of a quick capitulation on the part of the Mexican government, however, failed to take into account the fierce pride of the Mexican people. Few Americans understood that it would be politically impossible for the Mexican government to make peace with the United States after Mexican blood had been shed on what Mexicans viewed as their soil. If Polk at last realized differently, he at least now knew that he would have little trouble raising the necessary volunteers to fight in northern Mexico.

Polk's concerns were actually closer to home. The growing popularity of Zachary Taylor and whispers of a Taylor presidential candidacy in 1848 vexed the president, and he considered replacing Taylor with his senior, Major General Winfield Scott. Plans to do so were advanced to the point of issuing Scott orders to travel to Texas, but then Polk began pondering the wisdom of the change. The president had plenty of time to think over the matter because Scott so indulged his penchant for planning and precise organization that he lingered, seemingly inert, in the capital. Polk thus had time to become suspicious of Scott's political ambitions, and when hints of the president's displeasure reached Scott, the general sent an impolitic letter to Secretary of War William Marcy accusing the president of bad faith. Polk exploded at the impertinence and promptly cancelled Scott's orders. Not only deprived of his impending command, but also now clearly in disfavor, Scott wrote a plaintive defense that detailed the extraordinary efforts he had made to plan the coming campaign. So diligent had he been at his labors, he said, that he had practically resided at the War Department, only leaving "to take a hasty plate of soup."[4] Scott would wish he could take those words back, for they caught on in the newspapers, and soon "a hasty plate of soup" became a popular catchphrase, its author depicted as a pompous whiner aptly nicknamed "Old Fuss and Feathers." In many minds, the episode was enough to prove that Taylor—"Old Rough and Ready" to his men—was the better soldier.

An Unprofessional Army

While this drama played out in Washington, Taylor took up positions in Camargo's, where volunteers began arriving in droves. In fact, Taylor soon had more men than he could feed, and as his army awaited supplies, Camargo's summertime heat devastated it. Disease killed a considerable number, and many of the rest proved unmanageable. Most of the volunteers had no military experience and made plain their contempt for soldierly discipline. Many were robustly independent frontiersmen temperamentally unsuited to taking orders from anyone. A criminal element, both in fact and aspiration, committed abuses on the Mexican population ranging from petty cruelty to rape and murder. Taylor tried to banish the worst offenders from the army, but such incidents continued throughout the war.

Such inexcusable American outrages against the Mexican people are difficult to explain unless one takes into account the nineteenth century's prevailing opinions on race. Scholars have ably demonstrated that American attitudes toward Mexicans stemmed from a deeply ingrained racism that in its extreme form viewed people of non-Germanic heritage as less than human. Some scientific studies even went so far as to delineate the different races as different species. The same justification for the forced removal of thousands of Indians framed the thinking of American soldiers in Mexico during the war, and some of them behaved abysmally. That behavior was, in fact, the most glaring indication of something sinister occurring in conjunction with American expansionism. Early supporters of what became known as Manifest Destiny had seen the American mission as spreading the virtues of liberty, democracy, and free market capitalism to less fortunate people. By the Mexican War, however, that noble calling had been replaced in the minds of many with the brazen belief that American racial superiority simply entitled them to the lands of "inferiors."[5]

Monterrey

Most of Taylor's volunteers were either too ill-trained to be of any use or too sick to travel. When Taylor moved toward Monterrey in September 1846, he left many of them behind. By the time the American army was approaching the city on September 19, Mexican commander Pedro de Ampudia had made Monterrey a fortress. Because a direct assault would have been lethal, Taylor sent Brigadier General William Jenkins Worth southwest of the city to attack Ampudia's works in an area called Federation Hill. As Worth began his assault on September 21, Brigadier General David Twiggs's regulars and Brigadier General John A. Quitman's volunteers mounted a diversion from the northeast and ran into a formidable obstacle called Fort Tenería. The diversion, in fact, became a major effort that cost Taylor hundreds of casualties. Nonetheless, American success at the outlying forts caused Ampudia to fall back into the town, and by September 23, the two armies were fighting from house to house in Monterrey. The next day, Ampudia requested terms for surrender.

His losses mounting and eager to end the costly fight, Taylor made generous terms. He allowed Ampudia to march his men out of the city and declared an eight-week armistice so both generals could determine their governments' wishes. When Polk learned of Taylor's terms, he exploded. He wanted California, and possessing Monterrey in northern Mexico would not move him an inch closer to having it. He considered the Mexican government's wishes immaterial once the shooting had started. Instead, the Mexican government must be forced, through the destruction of its armies, to see that it had no choice but to accept James K. Polk's terms, not Zachary Taylor's.

New Mexico and California

Polk had already taken steps to secure physical control of the territory he wanted to buy. Even while at peace, instructions went overland to Commodore John Sloat of the United States Pacific Squadron that if war came, he should blockade Mexico's western ports, including those in California. In June 1846, Polk ordered Colonel Stephen Watts Kearny at Fort Leavenworth to take possession of New Mexico and, if possible, Upper California.

U.S. interest in New Mexico stretched back to the early days of the century when the Santa Fe Trail became the main thoroughfare for trade in the Southwest. After Mexico won its independence from Spain, commerce blossomed between Missouri traders and Santa Fe merchants. Mexican anger over American intentions toward Texas prompted official attempts to stop the trade in 1844, but western American merchants such as those at the fortified frontier trading post called Bent's Fort continued a clandestine exchange of goods in New Mexico. Meanwhile, a liberal reading of the Rio Grande boundary led the Texas Republic to claim that Santa Fe fell within its boundaries and resulted in an ill-fated effort to seize the town.

Already in a shooting war with Mexico, Polk and the U.S. Army had a better chance to make good on the old Texas claim. Kearny left Fort Leavenworth at the end of June 1846 with about seventeen hundred regulars and volunteers, an aggregate force styled the "Army of the West," to take Santa Fe. A month-long arduous journey through desert and grassy prairies put the army at Bent's Fort. After less than a week's rest, Kearny again started his men toward Santa Fe, bracing for the Mexican resistance he expected to find in the rugged canyons and rocky terrain outside the city. As it happened, though, the journey was the hardest part of the campaign because the Mexicans lacked sufficient men to hold the passes. Their withdrawal allowed Kearny to march into Santa Fe unmolested. He promptly declared the area American territory and placed the people there under the authority of the U.S. government.

From Santa Fe, Kearny sent most of his volunteers under Colonel Alexander Doniphan south to Chihuahua where they were to cooperate with regulars under Brigadier General John Wool. Doniphan's amazing trek through more than 3,500 miles of Mexico was all the more remarkable because it was accomplished by about 800 volunteers rather than professional soldiers. For his part, Kearny took about 300 handpicked dragoons to seize Upper California, leaving the balance of his now fragmented Army of the West to hold Santa Fe. The trip to California rivaled Doniphan's to Chihuahua in its difficulty. Luckily for Kearny, his small army came upon legendary mountain man Kit Carson en route. With Carson as guide, the Americans reached San Diego, where Kearny discovered that events had overtaken him.

Captain John C. Frémont of the United States Army Topographical Engineers, under instructions to explore the Oregon Country, had instead entered northern California with a small party of engineers and scouts. Frémont then took it upon himself to lead a group of American and foreign immigrants in a rebellion against Mexican authorities. The bizarre initiative was so unexpected that it succeeded, at least to the extent of allowing the insurrectionists to dub their new little country the Bear Flag Republic after a crude banner they had fashioned depicting a grizzly. By then, Commodore Sloat was in the midst of establishing his blockade of California ports. Surmising that Frémont's surprising actions had changed matters, he promptly seized Monterey, California. Frémont apparently realized his government would question the rectitude of a U.S. Army captain who declared himself a part of a revolutionary republic, so he traveled to Monterey and put himself under Sloat's command.

Sloat was an elderly, careful man, and this entire business made him most uneasy. He regarded it as a stroke of good fortune that he was soon relieved of command by Commodore Robert Stockton. Fortunately for Frémont, Stockton turned out to be an energetic officer every bit as ambitious as the army captain. They soon became fast friends and quickly formed an alliance to expel Mexican administration from all of Upper California. It looked to be an easy task, because Mexican authorities could barely sustain themselves at Los Angeles, let alone mount an effort to retake the rest of Upper California. Indeed, they could not even defend Los Angeles. Stockton and Frémont took the city and proceeded to govern California in the name of the United States.

The young American officers were more than feeling their oats. They were also becoming careless about the measure of their enemy as they indulged in a fit of self-congratulation. Mexican forces reorganized and in September 1846 descended on the American occupiers with a vengeance, retaking Los Angeles and much of southern California.

That was the situation when Kearny arrived with his exhausted force in December 1846. After consulting with Stockton, Kearny organized a campaign to retake Los Angeles in January, but no sooner had the military again gained control of Upper California than its officers commenced to quarrel about who was really in charge of the occupation. Kearny had been promoted to brigadier general during the operation. Even better for his case, he had orders explicitly instructing him to form a California government. Stockton was unimpressed by Kearny's rank and unmoved by his orders. Ostensibly refusing to relinquish what he styled his command, the commodore found an ally in Frémont, probably because Stockton had named him military governor.

Such command confusion could not last, of course, and its resolution was not long in coming. When Commodore W. Branford Shubrick replaced Stockton, he properly deferred to the legitimate authority of Kearny's written orders. As for Frémont, the ambitious junior officer who had impulsively made the California revolution and then had fallen prey to his own arrogance, the game was up. He was arrested and returned to Washington where a court martial convicted him of disobeying orders and of mutiny.[6] Frémont's exploits had cost him his army career, but they had helped the United States gain California a full year before it would obtain legal title through a treaty with Mexico.

Sectional Politics and International Intrigue

While California was being secured, President Polk and Secretary of War William Marcy were reassessing American strategy in Mexico. Finally, they decided to launch a new campaign that would originate on Mexico's east coast at Vera Cruz and march inland on the capital at Mexico City. Once they settled on this new initiative, it remained for them to choose a commander, a task that turned out to be fraught with difficulty. The administration also had to cope with growing opposition to the war in Congress. Almost nonexistent when the war vote had been taken in May 1846, a chorus of dissent had since grown, especially when events in California suggested that territorial gain, not protection of American soil, had always been Polk's primary goal.

Map 7.1
The Mexican-American War

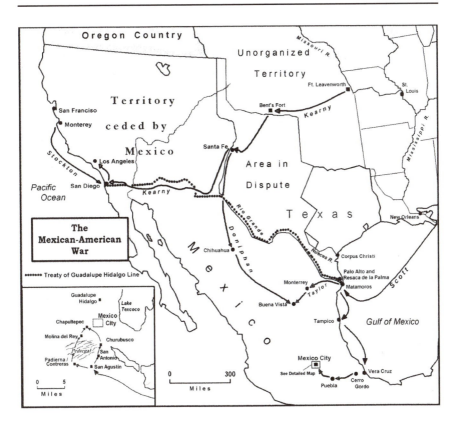

It was not just the Whigs making noise, either. Elements in Polk's own party were growing restive. Northern Democrats felt constituents' pressure to prove untrue Whig descriptions of the war as a way to extend slavery. Fearful that their entire expansionist agenda might be at risk, several northern Democrats decided to sponsor an amendment to an appropriation bill for two million dollars that Polk requested in August 1846. Polk wanted the money to entice Mexico away from the battlefield and up to the negotiating table, but that objective was immediately lost when Pennsylvania congressman David Wilmot offered the amendment that would become known as the Wilmot Proviso. The Wilmot Proviso called for a prohibition on slavery in any territory acquired from Mexico because of the war. It set off a firestorm of debate in Congress that irreversibly linked slavery and expansion in the public mind. The House managed to approve the proviso, but southern strength in the Senate killed it. That is to say, the Senate killed it as a political measure, but as a popular cause that called for no more slave territory in the United States, the Wilmot Proviso refused to die.

President Polk at first regarded the proviso as an annoying distraction. He especially fretted over the possibility of political disarray costing him a grand opportunity to end the war while achieving his original purpose. Antonio López de Santa Anna, so fallen from Mexican favor that he had become an exile in Cuba, sent an emissary to the administration with a tempting proposal. For a price and with the assurance that the U.S. Navy would not hinder his return to Mexico, Santa Anna promised to seize power and immediately make a treaty ending the war and ceding to the United States all the territory Polk desired.

It was, of course, too good to be true, and considering the pledge came from Santa Anna, almost none of it was. The only part of the plan that came to fruition was Santa Anna's return to Mexico—the U.S. Navy allowed him to land at Vera Cruz in August 1846—and his relatively easy return to influence. Within a month, Santa Anna took advantage of the Paredes government's unpopular conduct of the war and was invited by a new government under José Mariano Salas to take command of the Mexican army. Returned to Mexico and on the path to power, Santa Anna soon made it clear that he did not intend to surrender an inch of territory to the United States.

Fuss and Feathers over Rough and Ready

Although Polk had foresworn a second term, he bristled at the thought of a Whig succeeding him in the presidency. Whig talk of nominating Zachary Taylor as their presidential candidate for 1848 convinced Polk that it would be folly to give Taylor more opportunities for military glory. In any case, even Polk's supporters in Congress and most of the public had expected a short war, and this one was dragging on. Even if Taylor had been politically acceptable to the president, "Old Rough and Ready" was poorly situated in Mexico to bring a speedy conclusion to the fighting. Polk's decision to launch the Mexico City campaign was a tactical one dictated by a desire to end the war quickly, but his choice of its commander was a political judgment guided by the principle of "anybody but Taylor."

For a while, that guiding rule hobbled the administration with indecision. At one point, Polk even contemplated making Democratic senator Thomas Hart Benton a lieutenant general and giving him the command, but the president finally and more prudently decided upon the senior general in the army, Winfield Scott. Ironically, Scott's embarrassing letter that had so angered Polk ultimately made him politically acceptable to the president. The newspapers' ridicule had removed any chance for Scott to win the Whig nomination.

Scott, thrilled by his military resurrection, set out in November to meet with Taylor and arrange the transfer of most of his regulars for the Vera Cruz landing. The conference was supposed to take place on the Rio Grande, but Taylor did not show up. Scott had no choice but to issue written instructions to Taylor ordering the release of his regulars. They were to march to Tampico on Mexico's east coast.

Taylor had not been delayed; he was livid. Convinced that Scott's expedition was a Polk scheme to diminish Taylor's chances for a presidential bid, Old Rough and Ready denounced "Scott's sugared letter."[7] Moreover, Taylor was unwilling to be written out of the war. While Scott organized his growing forces at Tampico and prepared landing craft for an amphibious assault on Vera Cruz, Zachary Taylor prepared his dwindling roster of men for a fight.

Buena Vista

Few rogues could claim the resilience of Santa Anna. In short order, he parlayed his command of the Mexican army into a revived political career, again winning election as president of Mexico. Resolved to double-cross Polk, Santa Anna temporarily relinquished the presidency to his vice president, Valentín Gómez Farías, and set out to destroy the American invaders in detail. Taylor would be first. Then Santa Anna would race to repel Scott's invasion at Vera Cruz.

Taylor was situated near a ranch called Buena Vista just south of Saltillo at Angostura. Although Santa Anna's approximately fifteen thousand men outnumbered Taylor's army more than three to one, Taylor's position helped to even the odds. Santa Anna would have to attack either through a narrow pass or by executing a series of wide flanking maneuvers. The first option was perilous, and the second was complicated and difficult to coordinate.

Preliminary skirmishes preceded the battle, but it finally commenced in earnest on the afternoon of February 22, 1847. Santa Anna's main thrust tried to gain high ground on the American left flank, but he ran out of daylight before completing the maneuver and had to wait until the next morning to finish the job. With his left in danger of collapsing, Taylor rushed reinforcements to shore up his flank. Thanks partly to the efforts of Colonel Jefferson Davis of the Mississippi Rifles the Mexican attack was halted. That afternoon, Santa Anna tried his luck against the American center, and Taylor again rushed up artillery, cavalry, and infantry to the new salient. The Americans not only prevented Santa Anna from breaching their line, they threw back the Mexican charge. On what would have been the third day of the Battle of Buena Vista, Santa Anna decided he had seen enough of Zachary Taylor. The Mexican army withdrew.

It was a costly fight for both sides. Taylor lost almost 15 percent of a force already considerably reduced by detachments to Scott. Santa Anna's casualties were high as well, but the most serious one for him was the blow Buena Vista dealt his reputation. As for Taylor, his political future was sealed at the little cattle ranch near Angostura. Victory in the face of such tremendous odds made him the premier Whig candidate for the presidency, and he would win that party's nomination for the 1848 election.[8]

Vera Cruz

The loss at Buena Vista was bad enough, but as Santa Anna pulled back toward Mexico City, Scott's threat to the Mexican coast was developing much more rapidly than the Mexicans had expected. Scott moved his army to Lobos Island. Swelled with additional volunteers, the army was ferried to a position off Vera Cruz. Once in place, it prepared to assault the beaches in specially designed landing craft.

Scott and his staff conducted a reconnaissance to find the best spot for the landing, steaming close in along the shore aboard the small *Petrita*. The Mexican fort San Juan de Ulúa splashed some shells near enough to spray the vessel's decks and provide historians with one of American history's biggest what-ifs. Aboard with Scott were such junior officers as Lieutenants P. G. T. Beauregard and George Gordon Meade and Captains Joseph E. Johnston and Robert E. Lee, whose greatest fame lay years later in the American Civil War. Had Mexican marksmanship been better, not only might Scott's loss have altered the course of the Mexican-American War, the course of the Civil War too, in the absence of Robert E. Lee for one, would have been much different.

The trip ended, however, with everyone dampened but otherwise unscathed. In addition, Scott had found his spot—a beach south of Vera Cruz. On March 9, 1847, his landings began and to his surprise were unopposed. Because Mexican soldiers in the walled city of Vera Cruz did not come out to make a stand on the beaches, the United States Army's first amphibious landing in its history succeeded without a single American casualty. In relatively short order, Scott had ten thousand men ashore to take Vera Cruz and then march on Mexico City.

Scott took several days to move his army in an arc around Vera Cruz while positioning his artillery as well as guns on loan from the navy to bombard the town into submission. Vera Cruz was defiant at first, but when the American bombardment began exacting heavy casualties, the city surrendered on March 29, 1847. For Scott, it was not a moment too soon. Warmer weather was sure to bring yellow fever, the ravages of which were graphically described by the Mexican name "vómito." Yellow fever had the potential to destroy Scott's army more effectively than any Mexican foe could. Scott needed to move rapidly toward Mexico City in the interior where higher altitudes would make an outbreak of the disease less likely.[9] On April 8, Brigadier General David Twiggs led his division of regulars out of Vera Cruz toward the highland town of Jalapa.

Cerro Gordo

Mexico's National Highway provided Scott's men with a firm marching surface into the highlands where they would briefly rest at the charming town of Jalapa before pushing on first to Puebla and then to Mexico City. Reaching Jalapa, however, required travel through a pass flanked by several hills on its right and a ridge on its left. Santa Anna intended to use this terrain's ideal defensive features to stop Scott dead in his tracks. The hill closest to the road was named Cerro Gordo, and there would unfold Scott's first real test of the campaign.

Twiggs's division was in the vanguard, and his scouts soon discovered that the ground overlooking the pass was teeming with Santa

Anna's army. American engineers ranged through the surrounding countryside to find a way around Cerro Gordo to nullify Santa Anna's defensive advantage, and Captain Robert E. Lee further explored Lieutenant P. G. T. Beauregard's promising discovery of such a route. On April 17, Lee was guiding Twiggs's division on this path when Mexican soldiers atop Atalya, a hill to the northeast of Cerro Gordo, spotted them. With perilous impetuosity, the American ranks began to advance toward Atalya, even though it was well short of their objective. Bending to his men's irresistible will, Twiggs shouted, "Charge them to hell!" and that is almost what they did.[10] At the least, the Americans took the hill. The following day, while the rest of the army staged a diversionary attack farther down the road, Twiggs, reinforced with volunteers, took Cerro Gordo and cut the road to trap much of Santa Anna's force. More than half of Santa Anna's men were captured, and the remainder fled in disarray, Santa Anna among them.

Mr. Trist and General Worth

Although victory at Cerro Gordo had opened the way to Jalapa, Scott rightly worried about his vulnerable supply line to the coast. Mexican guerrillas and bandits would find that lengthening route easy to plunder, especially because Scott could not spare men to patrol it. Many of his volunteers' enlistments would soon expire, and he faced the prospect that in about a month almost a third of his army would be going home. Jalapa was pretty and pleasant, but Scott took little comfort in his surroundings as he contemplated this ugly development. He brooded that the War Department was not adequately supporting him while the administration had apparently begun to question his conduct of the war. Scott's suspicions regarding this latter point seemed confirmed when an emissary from the State Department arrived to accompany the army. His name was Nicholas Trist, and his purported reason for showing up was to negotiate with the Mexican government should it seek to end the war. Scott thought Trist was actually Polk's spy, and the two men accordingly got off to a bad start. The relationship was not improved by Trist's imperious bearing. General Scott, perhaps the most imperious man ever to wear the United States Army uniform, matched Trist's arrogance gesture for gesture. Scott continued to prosecute the war as he saw fit and simply ignored Trist, a signal that the State Department's envoy was too insignificant to merit notice.

In fact, a troubling internal squabble in Scott's official family probably made Trist seem the lesser of two evils. From Jalapa, Scott sent William Jenkins Worth's division ahead to Puebla where Worth arranged the town's peaceful surrender and secured the cooperation of its citizenry by granting extremely generous concessions. For instance, Mexicans accused of crimes against American soldiers, even the charge of murder, would be tried in Mexican courts. American soldiers naturally presumed that such an arrangement gravely imperiled them. Soon rumors told of Puebla citizens poisoning food and water supplies. Worth's official warning about possible poisonings made matters worse by giving credence to the rumors while appearing helpless before their threat.

Scott had to come to Puebla to straighten out the mess, and Worth construed the intervention as a personal insult. Worth requested a court of inquiry, which only extended the quarrel while worsening its rancor. When the court recommended that Worth be reprimanded, he accused both Scott and the court's panel of conspiring to humiliate him. The high command of the American army would be at each other's throats for the remainder of the war.

Padierna and Churubusco

Scott could at least take comfort that not all of his personal relationships need be stormy. While the army rested and awaited reinforcements at Puebla through July, circumstance and proximity revealed to Scott and Trist their unexpected compatibility, and they became good friends. Now in a spirit of cheerful amity they shared the hope that as the army approached the capital, Santa Anna's government would sue for peace. Trist would then use his diplomatic skills to secure the cession of California and New Mexico.

They were encouraged in that hope in July when a messenger relayed Santa Anna's willingness to negotiate if the Americans provided money to bribe the Mexican legislature and other government leaders. Scott discussed the proposition with his generals, but none of them apparently yet had the measure of the crafty Mexican president. Scott consequently sent Santa Anna a down payment, which he openly used to strengthen his defenses of Mexico City.

Poorer but wiser, Scott planned to force a military decision. Just after dawn on August 7, 1847, Twiggs took the lead division of Scott's army out of Puebla, urging the men to give the town "a Cerro Gordo shout" as they began the last leg of their journey to the valley of Mexico City.[11] The remainder of the army followed over the next few days while Scott pondered where and how to attack the fearsome defenses around the Mexican capital, especially those to its west. Scott tentatively elected to make his attack from the south.

After establishing headquarters at San Agustín, Scott deployed scouting parties to determine Mexican strength and find a way over or around one of the most eerie stretches of terrain in the Western Hemisphere. It was an ancient lava bed called the Pedregal, described by observers as resembling a stormy sea frozen motionless. After riding repeatedly though this disturbing landscape, Captain Lee at last found a path across its far western edge that would allow the Americans to threaten the Mexicans at Padierna.[12] It was an important tactical advantage because the army could not move on Mexico City from the south without securing Padierna. Otherwise, Scott risked an attack on his rear. On August 20, American forces used Lee's route to gain the Mexican rear, attack Padierna, and rout its defenders.

The fall of Padierna gave Scott the opportunity to smash Mexican positions at San Antonio just north of San Agustín, a feat that would open the way to the capital. Most of all, Scott wanted to prevent their retreat to Mexico City where they could regroup. Santa Anna countered this potential collapse by moving San Antonio's defenders across the Churubusco River toward the capital while part of his army at the Convent of San Mateo guarded the retreat. Those defenders furiously resisted repeated American assaults. Even after running out of ammunition, many died swinging their musket butts. The survivors of Churubusco were taken prisoner. Soon it became clear why many of them had preferred death to capture. Many were American deserters from the San Patricio Battalion, mostly Irish Catholics who had forsaken the American cause partly from sympathy for fellow Catholics, partly because of Mexican promises of free land. Whatever their motives, their fate as captured traitors was foreordained. They too would die as the U.S. Army raised the flag over Chapultepec.

From Molino del Rey to Chapultepec

Scott had paid a high price to hand Santa Anna these defeats outside of Mexico City, but they caused the Mexican leader to ask for a cease-fire, ostensibly to negotiate a peace treaty. When Scott realized that Santa Anna again was using this latest truce to strengthen Mexico City's defenses, he cancelled it on September 7. The following day he hurled Worth's regulars with some volunteers against Mexican lines at Molino del Rey west of the capital. Scott had not yet firmly resolved to attack Mexico City directly from the south, but he considered Molino del Rey an important salient. In addition, rumors reported that the foundry there was converting church bells into cannon. The tale turned out to be false, as Worth discovered after a particularly ferocious fight gave the Americans the position.

Three days later Scott could no longer postpone his decision about the assault route on the Mexican capital. On September 11, he summoned his division commanders and staff to discuss the matter and learned that most of his officers preferred to move against the city's southern gates. Scott and a few others, however, worried that the Mexicans were fully expecting this obvious line of attack, so Scott opted for the western approach.

Coming from the west would have the benefit of surprise because the route was difficult. The army would first need to storm Chapultepec, a 200-foot hill southwest of the city. An old fortress lately used as a military school sat atop Chapultepec, and on September 12, Scott attempted to soften these defenses with an artillery bombardment. To deceive Santa Anna into thinking that the obvious southern approach was the main American thrust, part of General Twiggs's division commenced a noisy demonstration against the south gate on September 13. Another American artillery bombardment presaged the main attack at Chapultepec. In almost two hours of heavy fighting, American soldiers clawed their way up the hill and finally overran the fortress. Casualties were high and more sobering than usual when it was discovered that six military academy cadets—boys, really—had been killed in the assault.[13]

When the Americans had taken Chapultepec, Worth and John A. Quitman moved their divisions through the western gates of Mexico City where fighting continued until nightfall. In the darkness, Santa Anna withdrew his forces north to the town of Guadalupe Hidalgo. On September 14, 188 days after landing at Vera Cruz, Winfield Scott took possession of Mexico City.

The Treaty of Guadalupe Hidalgo

The Mexican government was in flight, so American possession of Mexico City did not mean an end to the war. The longer the delay, the more determined the Polk administration was to extract a larger land cession to defray the conflict's rising costs. Nicholas Trist's seeming inability to end the war also caused Polk and his cabinet to become disenchanted with their handpicked diplomat. Trist's reports, which included the recommendation that the United States should reduce its territorial demands, were especially infuriating to Polk, and he heatedly ordered Trist to come home.

With a victorious army in Mexico City, yet no peace agreement to crown its achievement, the Polk administration was actually entering the most dangerous phase of the war. The president was unwilling to accept anything less than his original territorial goals, but many Americans were beginning to call for considerably more. An "All Mexico" movement was picking up support as many hardcore expansionists opined that the American domain should comprise the entire North American continent. Polk never publicly supported this ambitious vision, but he certainly considered it.

Trist did not obey his order to come home. His negotiations with a newly elected Mexican government were on the verge of a promising breakthrough, so he simply ignored his superiors to remain in Mexico and conclude a treaty. It took a month, but on February 2, 1848, Trist and the Mexican commissioners signed the Treaty of Guadalupe Hidalgo. The treaty called for Mexican recognition of the Rio Grande boundary, the cession of New Mexico and Upper California in exchange for fifteen million dollars, and the assumption by the United States government of Mexico's debts to American citizens.

When the treaty arrived by special messenger in Washington about two weeks later, Polk was inclined to reject it. He was still angry with its author, his irritation over Trist's insubordination unabated by the diplomat's successful perseverance. Polk was also annoyed with the leisurely way the Mexicans had drawn out the peace process and was determined to extract more territory as punishment.

Then, upon the advice of cooler-headed counselors, the president calmed down. Opposition to the war had become a potentially large problem, and in such a climate, rejecting a treaty that satisfied Trist's instructions would be an administrative embarrassment. Polk discussed the situation with his cabinet and finally agreed that the wisest course was to send the treaty to the Senate. After an uncomfortable debate, the Senate ratified the Treaty of Guadalupe Hidalgo by a close vote of 38 to 14, only four votes more than the necessary two-thirds majority.

Conclusion

The exchange of ratifications between the two governments brought the Mexican-American War to a close and presented the victorious United States with a vast new domain full of marvelous opportunities, grave challenges, and serious problems. The discovery of gold in California and the establishment of a Pacific trade that opened diplomatic relations with isolationist Japan were just the beginning of the impressive benefits the Mexican cession would bestow. Yet, they would come at a high price.

Although some Americans continued to envision an ever-expanding American empire eventually stretching into Latin America and the Caribbean, most saw the acquisition of the Pacific realm as the culmination of America's destiny to become a continental power. Moreover, the spirit of the Wilmot Proviso set off arguments about admitting slavery to the new western territories, and the impassioned dispute overshadowed the presidential election of 1848. The Democrats were so divided that the Whig nominee Zachary Taylor won the election. Largely because of the Mexican cession, Taylor would have a troubled presidency, and in 1850 a momentous crisis largely relating to slavery in the western territories nearly split the Union. An ungainly compromise, the last workable one on the slavery issue, averted the crisis, but arguments over slavery continued to dominate almost all public policy discussions.

Some northerners continued to gaze longingly at British Canada, but increasingly expansionism became a program exclusive to southerners eager to extend the reach of slavery and reckless adventurers keen to do their bidding. These latter figures were the filibusterers whose exploits in Latin America were as colorful as they were unrealistic. Filibusterers also unsuccessfully tried to overthrow Spanish control of Cuba, and Madrid's island colony even became a focus of official attempts to revive Manifest Destiny in the 1850s. During his presidency, Polk had tried to purchase it for as much as $100 million, but Spain refused that and all subsequent offers. President Franklin Pierce's administration briefly entertained the idea of taking Cuba by force but quickly abandoned any such scheme when northerners raised violent opposition. Polk was the last president of the period to have the luxury of settling diplomatic frustrations with American military force.

Meanwhile, the necessity of linking the western reaches of the continent to the East gave rise to grand plans for a transcontinental railroad. To facilitate a practical southern route, U.S. minister to Mexico James Gadsden made the last territorial acquisition of the period in 1853. Gadsden dealt with the ever pliant and financially strapped Santa Anna, in charge of Mexico for the eleventh and final time, to obtain an extensive area of northern Mexico for ten million dollars. Yet, the Gadsden Purchase was unpopular because northerners objected to the slaveholding South laying claim to the transcontinental route. Under such conditions, the accord necessary for acquiring additional territory never again materialized for that generation of Americans. The day of Manifest Destiny as a national endeavor was over.

Indeed, efforts to create support for a northern transcontinental railroad would result in plans to organize the large, underpopulated Nebraska region of the Louisiana Purchase. Those efforts produced the ill-fated 1854 Kansas-Nebraska Act. Northerners and Southerners, embroiled in the sectional argument and on an irreversible collision course, became so disagreeable that Lincoln would describe the country as "a house divided."[14] The quarrel was about land and liberty, the tangible core of the American dream. The pioneers who carved out forest clearings, the politicians and armies who drove Indians from their homelands, the Conestoga teamsters who pointed their oxen toward the passes of the Rockies, and the soldiers who brawled their way into Mexico City, all in some way had been impelled by that dream, certain its fulfillment was predestined. Tragically, their very triumph would finally force them to confront that destiny's momentous consequences.

Notes

1. Captain Thorton's bad luck was only beginning. After the Mexicans released him, he rejoined Taylor's army. He was later transferred to Winfield Scott's command, participated in the Mexico City Campaign, and was killed August 18, 1847, in the approach to the Mexican capital.

2. Richardson, *Messages and Papers*, 4:442.

3. The site would become Brownsville, Texas.

4. Bauer, *Mexican War*, 74.

5. Reginald Horsman in *Race and Manifest Destiny: The Origins of American Racial Anglo–Saxonism* (Cambridge: Harvard University Press, 1981) covers this topic most completely. See specifically Chapter 12.

6. Because of his family connections—he was powerful senator Thomas Hart Benton's son-in-law—Frémont was pardoned by President Polk. Frémont nevertheless felt himself so wronged by the experience that he angrily resigned from the army.

7. Colonel F. S. Belton to Mrs. Belton, 12 January 1847, Edmund Kirby Smith Papers, Southern Historical Collection, University of North Carolina, Chapel Hill, NC.

8. Taylor won the presidency in 1848. Jefferson Davis was wounded at Buena Vista and returned to his native Mississippi a hero. He soon embarked on a political career that would culminate with his becoming a president, too—of the Confederate States of America.

9. Medical science neither hypothesized that a mosquito-borne virus causes yellow fever until the early 1880s, nor verified the discovery until 1901. Experience had shown, however, that higher elevations, where coincidentally mosquitoes are rarer, reduced attacks of the disease. Those who contract yellow fever are beset by severe muscle aches, fever, and finally vomiting of blood (hence, the "black vomit"). Yellow fever's rapid destruction of the heart and kidneys usually kills the victim in about a week, but those who survive recover swiftly and are immune to recurrence. The disease is named yellow fever because the liver's rapid deterioration imparts a jaundiced hue to the skin.

10. Jeanne T. Heidler, "The Military Career of David Emanuel Twiggs," Ph.D. dissertation, Auburn University, Auburn, AL, 1988, 116.

11. Ibid., 123.

12. Sometimes the engagement fought here is referred to as Contreras after a nearby town.

13. They would later be immortalized in Mexican national history as *Los Niños Heroicos*—the Heroic Children.

14. Quoted in David Herbert Donald, *Lincoln* (New York: Simon & Schuster, 1995), 206.

BIOGRAPHIES OF PROMINENT PEOPLE IN THE PERIOD

John Quincy Adams (1767–1848)

John Quincy Adams contributed to U.S. expansion by negotiating treaties that led to significant enlargement of the nation's domain. As an aging congressman, in his last years, however, Adams opposed expansion brought by the Mexican War, which he viewed as an attempt to spread slavery.

The son of John Adams, second president of the United States, John Quincy Adams entered the diplomatic service during George Washington's administration. For years, he was U.S. envoy to several European countries until his government named him to the peace delegation that negotiated an end to the War of 1812. At Ghent in 1814, Adams and the other commissioners refused to bow to British demands for an Indian buffer state in the Northwest, thus preserving that area for further U.S. expansion. Following the War of 1812, Adams was named U.S. minister to Great Britain, a post he held until he became James Monroe's secretary of state in 1817.

As secretary of state, Adams persistently tried to acquire Florida from Spain. His talks with Spanish minister Don Luis de Onís, however, foundered in 1818 upon news that Major General Andrew Jackson, sent into Florida to punish Seminole Indians for attacks on the American frontier, had seized St. Marks and Pensacola. Onís broke off negotiations and demanded an explanation, but Adams was not discouraged. As other cabinet members urged Monroe to disavow Jackson's actions, Adams defended the general, insisting that a united American front would convince Spain to renew negotiations. Adams proved correct in his prediction. Onís returned to the negotiating table, and the two diplomats hammered out what would be variously called the Transcontinental Treaty or the Adams-Onís Treaty. The treaty ceded Florida to the United States and established the boundary between the United States and Spanish territory to the Pacific Ocean.

Adams's last great contribution to American expansion as secretary of state occurred in 1823. He persuaded President Monroe that the United States needed to make a policy declaration regarding the threat of further European encroachment in the Western Hemisphere. Specifically, the American government was concerned with French plans to quash Latin American rebellions against Spanish authority. The resulting Monroe Doctrine implicitly claimed United States dominance over the Americas, a belief that would become American policy in subsequent years.

In the contentious election of 1824, Adams narrowly defeated Andrew Jackson when the election went to the House of Representatives. Adams was little concerned with territorial expansion during his presidency. At most, he had limited success in extinguishing Indian land claims in the South. Rather, his Jacksonian enemies set the main theme of his troubled time as chief executive with dogged charges that Adams had secured his office through corrupt politicking. He accordingly lost his bid for reelection to Andrew Jackson in 1828.

Within three years, Adams was back in Washington as a member of the House of Representatives where he would serve until his death in 1848. Adams opposed American expansion in the southwest because of his antagonism toward slavery, but he vehemently supported U.S. claims in Oregon. A peppery foe of Texas annexation and a strong opponent of the Mexican-American War, Adams exemplified the swelling antislavery movement of his native New England that sought to stop the spread of slavery into the western territories.

Stephen Fuller Austin (1793–1836)

Like his father Moses Austin, Stephen Austin typified the wanderlust of many Americans in the early nineteenth century. Before settling in Texas, he lived in Virginia, Connecticut, Kentucky, Missouri, Arkansas, and Louisiana. When Moses died in 1821, Stephen resolved to carry out his father's dream of establishing an American settlement in Texas.

With permission backed by a sizable land grant from the newly independent Mexican republic, Austin set up the first American enclave in 1822 and became the first of the so-called Texas *empresarios,* paving the way for thousands of Americans to move to Texas.

Considered a fair man by most, Austin became the primary leader of Anglo-Texans during these early years of American settlement, and under his direct sponsorship more than a thousand families moved to Texas. By then, many other *empresarios* were receiving similar grants that settled thousands more.

At first, Austin worked well with the Mexican government and even served in the provincial legislature. He maneuvered to mitigate Mexican laws restricting slavery and to prevent strict tariff enforcement, factors that kept a steady stream of American immigrants coming into Texas. The growing number of Anglo-Texans, however, alarmed the Mexican government, especially when they brazenly flouted Mexican law. When Mexican officials began a severe crackdown in the early 1830s, Austin advocated making Texas a separate Mexican state as a solution, an attitude that led to his imprisonment for a year. By the time Austin was released in the summer of 1835, the Mexican government under President Antonio López de Santa Anna was strengthening its centralized control over all of Mexico. Already angry over Austin's imprisonment, Texans reacted to the centralization program with a fury that soon led them to revolt.

Austin became a unifying figure as the revolt became a revolution. He served briefly as the commander of Texas volunteers, but his lack of military aptitude soon convinced both him and his men that he could better serve elsewhere. The Texas provisional government dispatched him to the United States to raise money and volunteers, but by the time he returned in June 1836, independence had been accomplished. In a three-man contest to decide who would be Texas' first elected president, Sam Houston defeated Austin. Austin served as Houston's secretary of state for only two months and then died of pneumonia in December 1836.

A moderate by nature, Austin reluctantly embraced the role of revolutionary. In truth, his course and that of Texas had been set years earlier when he had brought the first American families across the Red River. By the time of Austin's death, Texas was drafting a new chapter of a history that would figure prominently in the annals of American expansion. Austin would be absent from that chronicle, but he had loomed large in its prologue.

John Charles Frémont (1813–90)

John C. Frémont tried several careers before accepting a commission in the United States Army Topographical Corps in the 1830s. In that capacity, he conducted surveys for projected roads, but his role in western exploration garnered him fame. In the late 1830s he was part of a group charting the area west of the upper Mississippi River, a journey that established his reputation as a notable western explorer.

That reputation resulted largely from Frémont's indefatigable habit of self-promotion. Shortly after his return from this first expedition, he was introduced to powerful Missouri senator Thomas Hart Benton, an influential champion of western exploration. When Benton learned that Frémont was courting Benton's teenage daughter Jessie Benton, he separated the couple by having Frémont sent on a mapping expedition to the Iowa Territory. When Frémont returned, however, he secretly married Jessie, briefly infuriating her father. Once he overcame his anger, Benton, aside from Jessie, became Frémont's most energetic promoter.

In 1842, the year after his marriage, Frémont with Benton's help secured the command of an exploratory mission to the northern Rockies to gain information about the Oregon Trail. His report on that expedition (largely ghostwritten by Jessie) did much to popularize the Oregon Trail and encourage settlement in the Pacific Northwest. It also made Frémont a celebrity.

In 1843 another Frémont exploratory party traveled to Oregon, Nevada, and California. In California, he carefully noted Mexican weakness there before returning to St. Louis by way of Bent's Fort. Proponents of Manifest Destiny hailed his report on this journey as opening the way for American expansion to the Pacific.

James K. Polk's election occurred while Frémont was away, but it made possible another expedition to map Utah and the Sierra Nevada Mountains. Frémont claimed later that he had secret instructions to cooperate with the U.S. Navy to seize California in case of war with Mexico, but his behavior at the time was unduly rash and impetuous. When he arrived in California, war had not yet erupted and his June 1846 participation with American settlers in the Bear Flag Revolt preceded any knowledge he could have had about its onset. When the U.S. Navy arrived, Frémont put himself at the service of first Commodore Sloat and then his replacement Commodore Stockton to help seize Los

Angeles. When Mexican forces briefly reclaimed the city, Frémont assisted Brigadier General Stephen Watts Kearny in retaking it.

When Stockton disputed Kearny's authority to assume command in California, Frémont supported Stockton and was rewarded by being named governor of California. Eventually, Washington officially certified Kearny's overarching authority, though, and Frémont accordingly found himself in a great deal of trouble. Eventually convicted by court-martial for insubordination, the explorer was pardoned by the president upon father-in-law Benton's intercession, but Frémont soothed his wounded pride by resigning from the army.

Widely hailed as the Pathfinder of the West, Frémont continued to explore in the employ of wealthy developers, but his 1848–49 expedition into the Sangre de Cristo and San Juan Mountains during the dead of winter was a costly disaster. The misadventure was his last exploration, for soon gold was discovered on land he had acquired in California. He moved there to exploit his new wealth and was elected one of the first U.S. senators for the new state of California.

His wife's excellent public relations skills had turned Frémont's feud with Kearny into a national sensation, and many perceived the Pathfinder as gravely wronged by the episode. In 1856, the new Republican Party nominated him for president. He lost the election to James Buchanan, but his showing was surprisingly strong, and he remained a popular figure. At the outbreak of the Civil War, President Abraham Lincoln had no choice but to offer him a command in the Union army, a post for which Frémont was militarily and politically unsuited. He was eventually removed. After the war he failed in business, lived for a while in California, and served as territorial governor of Arizona. He died in New York.

Andrew Jackson (1767–1845)

Born in the Waxhaws region of South Carolina, an area of rapid colonial expansion, Andrew Jackson lived most of his life on the American frontier. After being orphaned by the American Revolution, Jackson studied law and then moved to the frontier territory of Tennessee. As a rising attorney and politician, he consistently advocated opening more of Tennessee for settlement, primarily by seizing Indian lands.

In 1802, Jackson was elected major general of the Tennessee militia, and though he would not see military action until the War of 1812, he did participate in several episodes connected to territorial expansion before the war. At the end of 1803, fears that Spain would resist the transfer of Louisiana to the United States prompted President Thomas Jefferson to request that Jackson put the Tennessee militia on alert. When it proved unnecessary to march on the Spaniards, a disappointed Jackson continued to view Spain as an enemy. When Aaron Burr approached him the following year with a vague plan to seize Spanish territory west of Louisiana, Jackson eagerly joined the scheme. Although Jackson abandoned the project when indications strongly suggested that Burr also intended to detach part of the southwestern United States, he was slow to drop the idea of invading and annexing Spanish territory.

At the start of the War of 1812 Jackson was still a major general of Tennessee militia with hopes of using it to expand the United States. Initially, he yearned to take his men to the Northwest to cooperate in the conquest of British Canada, but the government regarded him with suspicion for his former connection to Burr. Consequently, the Madison administration all but ignored him, and he fretted that the war would pass him by. Then in the fall of 1812, the War Department ordered him to march his men to Louisiana to help defend New Orleans from an expected British attack. At Natchez, though, additional orders instructed him to pause there. After several months, another War Department message informed Jackson that he should disband his force and go back to Tennessee. Jackson was enraged, especially because he suspected the entire affair was a plot to discredit him. He disobeyed the order to dismiss his men so far from their homes and instead led them back to Tennessee. The gesture and his willingness to endure the same grim hardships as his men earned him their lasting affection and complete loyalty. They began calling him "Old Hickory" after the hardwood that would not bend and never broke.

Jackson still hoped to fight in some capacity, but as he waited for his chance, he became embroiled in a dispute with some of his officers, most notably former protégé, Thomas Hart Benton. During the summer of 1813, a brawl in Nashville with Benton and his supporters left Old Hickory with a serious bullet wound in his shoulder. As Jackson recuperated, word reached Nashville of an Indian massacre perpetrated by Red Stick Creeks in the Mississippi Territory, and Jackson was told to reassemble his men as part of a multifaceted campaign against the Red Sticks.

His wound unhealed, Jackson mobilized his men and in the fall of 1813 marched into what is now Alabama. At Tallushatchee and Taladega, his force defeated numerous Red Stick warriors, but supply shortages and expiring enlistments caused him to stop the campaign until early the next year. In early 1814, Jackson repulsed Red Stick attacks while raiding into their territory, and when he received reinforcements in February, he launched a major campaign against the Red Stick stronghold called Tohopeka or Horseshoe Bend on the Tallapoosa River. On March 27, 1814, Jackson annihilated the Red Sticks gathered there and broke their ability to continue the war. That August, he dictated the Treaty of Fort Jackson to the Creeks, forcing them to cede twenty-three million acres of their land to the United States. It was the United States government's largest land acquisition during the War of 1812.

Fears that the British intended to invade from Spanish West Florida caused Jackson to make a preemptive strike against Pensacola. British plans to attack New Orleans prevented him from consolidating an American hold on West Florida, but Jackson would remember the vulnerability of this Spanish territory and would return in a few years to retake it. At present, he rushed to New Orleans and on January 8, 1815, won what some would argue was the most important battle of the war.

After the war, Jackson remained in the army as a major general in command of the Southern division. His primary responsibility was to guard the southern and southwestern frontiers, but his chief problem was preventing American settlers and Florida Indians (collectively known as Seminoles) from fighting one another. He believed that the only permanent solution was to annex Florida, and when he received orders to chastise Seminoles in Florida for their raids into the United States, he took the opportunity to seize the Spanish fort at St. Marks and the Spanish capital of Pensacola. Although Spain initially halted ongoing negotiations aimed at selling Florida to the United States, the Spanish government ultimately deemed it wiser to sell the province than have it wrested from them.

Jackson's victory at New Orleans and his exploits in Florida made him a national hero, and in 1828, the people made him president. In that office, he continued his efforts to expand the United States, primarily by extracting land cessions from all Indians remaining in the East in exchange for land grants west of the Mississippi. He persuaded

Congress to pass the Indian Removal Act of 1830 that gave his administration the money and the means to bribe or intimidate most eastern tribes into accepting removal treaties. Those who refused to leave their ancestral homes were forced off their land. Thus did the Jackson administration secure for frontier settlers and land speculators millions of additional acres for expansion.

One of Jackson's final predicaments as president was the question of Texas annexation. He had supported the Texas fight for independence from Mexico and would recognize the Texas republic before leaving office, but he rightly calculated that opposition to adding such a large slave area to the Union made such a move politically perilous. Although Jackson left this contest to others, he remained a staunch proponent of Texas annexation. He lived to see it happen, if only barely, dying in 1845 just weeks after John Tyler signed the joint resolution inviting Texas to join the United States.

Stephen Watts Kearny (1794–1848)

Stephen Watts Kearny entered the army as a lieutenant during the War of 1812 and made the service his career. After the war, the young officer served most of his life on the American frontier to participate and lead several exploratory missions well beyond American settlements.

In the early 1830s, Kearny received command of a new branch of the army, the First Dragoons, the country's only mounted regiment. He made his headquarters at Fort Leavenworth and was there when named to command the Third Military Department of the United States. In the spring of 1846, Kearny received orders to march the newly designated Army of the West to seize New Mexico for the United States. While conducting this operation, he received promotion to brigadier general.

Mexican authorities in New Mexico offered no resistance to Kearny's advance; he easily took possession of Santa Fe in August 1846 and began planning to execute the second part of his orders to take California and establish an American government there. With about a third of his original sixteen hundred men, he set out in September for the West Coast. En route, he heard that a combination of United States Navy forces and army topographical engineers under Captain John C. Frémont had already taken possession of California, but the news was partly inaccurate. Commodore Robert Stockton and Frémont had indeed secured most of California's major towns, but Mexican authorities had regrouped not only to retake Los Angeles but also to present Kearny with some stiff resistance as he tried to reach San Diego. Kearny had to fight his way through San Pasqual before he could join forces with Stockton in San Diego and for the last time oust Mexican forces from Los Angeles.

California was back in American hands, but the victors could not decide who was in charge. Kearny's orders from Washington authorized him to form an American government, but Stockton dug in his heels along with his friend and ally Frémont, who was enjoying the power of governor conferred on him by Stockton. Kearny ultimately prevailed and repaid Frémont's impertinence with a lifelong enmity that first manifested itself in the captain's court-martial for insubordination and mutiny. It would prove a costly feud for both men, essentially ending Frémont's military career and gaining Kearny a powerful and unforgiving enemy in Frémont's father-in-law, Democratic senator Thomas Hart Benton.

The old frontier soldier's competence and excellent reputation saved his career, however, and as he was transferred to Vera Cruz, he received a brevet promotion to major general. After the war with Mexico, he assumed command at Jefferson Barracks at St. Louis, but he soon became seriously ill, probably from something picked up in Mexico, and died in October 1848.

Osceola (1800?–38)

Born in the Creek Nation in the early part of the nineteenth century, the young Osceola joined other refugees of the Creek War who fled to Florida following the Treaty of Fort Jackson's massive land cession. He grew to manhood among the Seminoles of Florida and by the 1830s was one of their most respected warriors.

Osceola strongly opposed additional land cessions to the United States and gathered around him a faction of Seminoles determined to resist removal to the West. Branded a troublemaker by American authorities, Osceola was imprisoned by U.S. Seminole Agent Wiley Thompson until he pledged to stop his agitations.

In 1832, a group of Seminole headmen had signed the Treaty of Payne's Landing agreeing to exchange Seminole land in Florida for western lands. The following year, several Seminole leaders, ostensibly on a western tour to inspect their prospective homes, signed the Treaty of Fort Gibson. The treaty determined that in early 1836 Seminoles would gather at Tampa Bay for transport to the West. Osceola resolved to prevent implementation of the treaty, and as a warning to other cooperationists, he killed one of its signers.

As the time for Seminole removal drew near, Osceola organized preemptive strikes against the United States. Dividing his men into two groups, he led a war party on December 28, 1835, to kill Agent Thompson at his agency. The other band ambushed soldiers commanded by Major Francis Dade as they marched from Tampa Bay to Fort King, killing all but 3 of the 110 men. The two incidents began the Second Seminole War.

During the first two years of the war, Osceola proved an excellent combat commander. His rapid maneuvers and hit-and-run tactics completely befuddled the United States Army. Frustrated by the elusive nature of his enemy, General Thomas Jesup summoned Osceola for peace talks. When Osceola came in under a flag of truce in October 1837, Jesup took him prisoner. The Seminole warrior was taken to Fort Moultrie in Charleston Harbor and several months later died of an undetermined illness.

James Knox Polk (1795–1849)

As a Tennessee congressman in the 1820s and 1830s, James K. Polk was a strong Jacksonian and supported the Indian removal policies of Old Hickory. His loyalty to Jackson earned him election as Speaker of the House of Representatives toward the end of Jackson's presidency. In 1839, he was elected governor of Tennessee and served a two-year term.

With the approach of the election of 1844, the Democrats began planning their ticket. Initially it appeared that Martin Van Buren would be the party's standard bearer and Polk would perhaps receive the vice presidential nomination, but Van Buren's opposition to annexing Texas caused many Jacksonians to reject him. Polk, however, voiced strong public support for the acquisition of Texas and the settlement of the Oregon boundary at latitude 54°40'. Partly because of Jackson's behind-the-scenes machinations from his home in Tennessee, Polk received the party's nomination, and in part Polk's stance on United States expansion helped him defeat Henry Clay in the election of 1844.

Congress had already approved Texas annexation before Polk took office, but the new president planned to add more territory to the United States, specifically California. Because war with Mexico might be necessary to accomplish that goal, Polk wanted to avoid conflict with Britain. Consequently, he abandoned the Democratic campaign slogan of "Fifty-four Forty or Fight!" regarding Oregon and instead settled for the forty-ninth parallel.

Buying California and New Mexico was much more preferable than fighting for them. Polk sent John Slidell to Mexico City to negotiate their purchase, but the Mexican government's refusal to treat with Slidell caused Polk to increase military preparations along the Rio Grande. It was a provocative move, because Mexico claimed the territory. Soon, a Mexican attack on an American patrol gave Polk the motive to ask Congress for a declaration of war, and Congress obliged.

As a war president, Polk proved a strong leader, especially in dealing with the egotistical rivals in command of the army. His military policies succeeded in defeating Mexico and gaining a treaty that ceded California and New Mexico to the United States and confirmed the Rio Grande as the Texas-Mexican border. Polk's achievement, however, carried heavy costs. Acquisition of the vast Mexican cession revived the sectional dispute over expansion of slavery, an issue that would not die until civil war resolved it with force.

John Louis O'Sullivan (1813–95)

Trained in the law in New York, John L. O'Sullivan turned to journalism in 1841 when he began editing the *United States Magazine and Democratic Review.* An ardent Democrat, O'Sullivan believed that fervent nationalism should promote rapid territorial expansion. In an 1845 issue of the *Democratic Review,* he coined the phrase "Manifest Destiny" as an expression of his belief that the United States should occupy all of North America.

O'Sullivan was unsatisfied with the extent of territory gained from Mexico in the Mexican War. After that conflict, he urged the acquisition of Cuba and financially supported filibustering expeditions to that island. He was indicted though not convicted of violating United States neutrality laws. During the 1850s, O'Sullivan served as United States minister to Portugal and then lived abroad during the Civil War because of his Confederate sympathies. He returned to the United States in the 1870s, but his days of prominence and prosperity were ended. Ironically, by the time he died in relative obscurity in New York City, a new wave of imperialism—dubbed the "New Manifest Destiny"—was driving U.S. policy to assume the rank of a world power. O'Sullivan might have regarded the move as vindicating his dream of a half-century earlier.

Antonio López de Santa Anna (1794–1876)

Santa Anna, from middle-class origins, entered the Spanish army as a sixteen-year-old cadet in 1810. His support for the Mexican independence movement earned him rapid promotion to brigadier general in 1821, the year the revolution against Spain finally succeeded. Afterward, his courageous actions defending the Mexican coast solidified his reputation with the army and ensured his popularity with the general population, earning him acclaim that nurtured his already swaggering vanity. In 1833, he indulged his conceit with a successful run for the Mexican presidency.

Santa Anna ambitiously and shrewdly exploited Mexico's political factionalism to proclaim himself dictator in 1834. He led the Mexican army north in 1836 to repress the Texas Revolution, not only defeating the Texas defenders of the Alamo but killing them all as well. He also ordered the execution of the entire Texas garrison of Goliad, although those men had surrendered. Such ferocious brutality, apparently meant to overawe Texan revolutionaries, only inspired them to revenge. On April 21, 1836, the commander of Texas troops, Sam Houston, trapped Santa Anna and much of his army on the San Jacinto River, killing most of them and capturing the rest, including Santa Anna. Houston forced him to sign a treaty recognizing Texas independence.

After a brief exile, Santa Anna returned to Mexico where the country's inherent instability and his military reputation again brought him to power as president in 1843. Santa Anna's lavish lifestyle and his regime's fiscal irresponsibility allowed his political enemies to depose him in 1845. He was ordered into exile and ended up in Cuba.

The following year, when the United States and Mexico went to war, Santa Anna offered to end it on American terms if the Polk administration would allow his return to Mexico. President Polk unwisely agreed. As the Mexican government reeled under the weight of military disaster compounded by bureaucratic ineptitude, Santa Anna's glamour again allowed him to resume power, whereupon he promptly broke his pledge to Polk. Instead of ending the war, he raised a large army and marched north to fight Zachary Taylor. Defeated on February 22–23, 1847, at Buena Vista, he brought his shattered army back to Mexico City as General Winfield Scott landed another American army at Vera Cruz.

Santa Anna led his army east to stop Scott but was defeated at Cerro Gordo in April 1847. Forced to fall back to Mexico City, Santa Anna fought delaying actions against Scott throughout August and September 1847, but when the Americans took possession of the commanding hill Chapultepec, Santa Anna withdrew his army from the city. Santa Anna again went into exile, but incredibly he would return to power once more in the 1850s, would be overthrown again, and would finally age into a pathetic figure. At the end, swindlers cynically played on his enduring vanity to strip him of his money. For this prince of scoundrels, who had for years worked a fraud on his country, it was a mocking justice.

Winfield Scott (1786–1866)

Abandoning an unrewarding career at law, Winfield Scott received a captain's commission in the United States Army in 1808. Scott's supreme competence during the War of 1812 gained him promotion to brevet major general. After the war, he traveled to Europe to study the militaries there, and upon his return he attempted to implement European reforms in the American army.

Though rarely stationed on the American frontier, Scott was always available when a frontier clash materialized. He attempted to lead almost 1,000 men to fight in the Black Hawk War in 1832, but his command was felled by cholera and missed the fight. In 1835, he was ordered to assume command of the United States campaign in the Second Seminole War. President Jackson became impatient with Scott's prosecution of the war and removed him from command. In 1838, President Van Buren gave Scott command of the contingent that escorted the Cherokees on what would become known as the Trail of Tears.

In 1841, Scott became commanding general of the United States Army. Over the next two decades, he dedicated himself to improving and enforcing standards in the army, gaining the nickname "Old Fuss and Feathers."

At the outbreak of the Mexican War, Scott was satisfied to give advice to his junior, Zachary Taylor, on prosecuting the initial phases of the war, but increasingly he desired a field command of his own. His ardent support for the Whig Party, however, discredited him with Democrat President Polk who initially refused to allow Scott to take the field. Finally realizing that Taylor's campaign in northern Mexico was bringing the war no closer to conclusion and with no other suitable officer at hand, Polk relented and gave Scott command of the Mexico City campaign.

Scott's landing at Vera Cruz on March 9, 1847, was the United States' first major amphibious invasion of foreign soil. Scott then conducted a brilliant logistical and strategic campaign to the gates of Mexico City. That September he directed the assault on the hill of Chapultepec that gained the Mexican capital for the United States.

With the campaign over, Scott became embroiled in a dispute with some of his subordinates, most notably President Polk's law partner, volunteer general Gideon Pillow. The main point of contention regarded who was most responsible for the successful campaign. Polk sided with Scott's opponents and brought him before a court of inquiry. All charges eventually were dropped.

In 1852, the Whig Party nominated the old war hero for president, but Franklin Pierce defeated him. Remaining at the head of the service, Scott spent the years before the Civil War directing the activities of a largely frontier army. In fact, the army's primary role on the frontier hampered Scott's efforts to arrange the defense of Washington, D.C., during the secession crisis of 1860–61. He provided valuable advice to President Abraham Lincoln in the early months of the Civil War, but poor health forced his retirement in November 1861. He died at West Point, New York, in 1866.

Zachary Taylor (1784–1850)

Born in Virginia and reared in Kentucky, Zachary Taylor spent most of his adult life as an officer in the United States Army, some would say as an instrument of Manifest Destiny. He began his service in 1808 as a first lieutenant in New Orleans and then as captain on the Northwest frontier in the Indiana Territory. At the outbreak of the War of 1812, he commanded Fort Harrison. His defense of that fort in September 1812 earned him a brevet promotion to major.

Taylor fought on the frontier for the remainder of the war, achieving the full rank of major by 1815. In the postwar army reductions, he was offered retention in return for a reduction back to captain, but he refused and temporarily left the service. Taylor returned the following year when offered a major's commission. For fifteen years, he only briefly resided in the East, serving primarily on the northwestern or southwestern frontiers. In 1832, he achieved the rank of colonel.

Taylor fought in the Black Hawk War and for the next few years continued to serve in the West. In 1837, he took command of troops in Florida in the Second Seminole War, a conflict that would establish his reputation. He was more aggressive than his predecessors, defeating the Seminoles at Lake Okeechobee in December 1837, and more deliberate in his planning. He partitioned southern and central Florida into a grid where troops in each section would round up Seminoles. Although Taylor never had the manpower to make his grid system fully functional, he succeeded over his predecessors in capturing Indians for transportation west.

Troubled by not receiving enough support to finish the war in Florida, Taylor asked to be relieved of command and was sent back to the Southwest. In 1845, he received orders to assume command of American troops in newly annexed Texas. Through the remainder of 1845 into 1846, Taylor commanded the Army of Observation, ostensibly in place at the Nueces River to prevent Mexico from invading Texas.

To press claims that the Rio Grande was the Texas-Mexico border, the Polk administration ordered Taylor to take his army south of the Nueces in January 1846. Over the next few months, Taylor watched a Mexican army across the Rio Grande. In April, a Mexican force north of the river attacked an American patrol, and President Polk and Congress used this attack as provocation to declare war.

Taylor, however, had a war on his hands even before the official declaration. Leaving a force to protect the fort he had built opposite Matamoros, Mexico, Taylor moved to Point Isabel on the Gulf of Mexico to establish his supply lines. On his way back, he encountered a Mexican army blocking his path and won the first two battles of the Mexican War at Resaca de la Palma and Palo Alto.

During the early summer, Taylor received reinforcements and orders to invade Mexico. He led his army across the Rio Grande, then up the river before heading inland to the large fortified Mexican city of

Monterrey. Several days of heavy fighting forced an armistice so that negotiations could end the war, but Polk later canceled the arrangement because it had not achieved his objective of acquiring the Southwest.

Taylor was angry that Polk had overruled him. He became even angrier when most of his regulars were transferred to Winfield Scott's campaign that would land at Vera Cruz and march inland to Mexico City. His ranks depleted, Taylor resolved to expand his hold on northern Mexico. He violated his orders by moving out of fortified Monterrey. Mexican president-general Antonio López de Santa Anna learned of Taylor's vulnerability and moved to trap him, but in the resulting Battle of Buena Vista on February 22 and 23, 1847, Taylor dealt Santa Anna a major defeat. Won against heavy odds, the victory added to Taylor's growing reputation to make him a national hero.

Hoping to benefit from Taylor's popularity, the Whig Party nominated him for the presidency in the 1848 election. Taylor proved a prudent candidate, carefully avoiding the volatile issue of slavery expansion into the Mexico cession and winning the presidency amid Democratic disarray. For the one year and four months of his presidency, Taylor, however, faced the turbulent consequences of territorial expansion that he had helped bring about. Slavery became the nation's most divisive issue, and he did little to bring it to peaceful resolution. In the midst of the controversy surrounding the proposed Compromise of 1850, Taylor became ill on July 4, 1850, and died five days later.

PRIMARY DOCUMENTS OF THE PERIOD

Florida and Oregon

The Adams-Onís Treaty

In 1819, the Adams-Onís Treaty was remarkable not only for the American acquisition of Florida, but also for the provisions of Article 3 that extended a line beyond the Florida panhandle to define the U.S.-Spanish boundary all the way to the Pacific Ocean. For this reason, historians frequently refer to the agreement as the Transcontinental Treaty. This extra arrangement was important because it removed all of Spain's claims to the region above the forty-second parallel while recognizing U.S. rights to the area known as the Oregon Country.

Document 1
Treaty of Amity, Settlement and Limits between the United States of America, and His Catholic Majesty

The United States of America and His Catholic Majesty . . . have determined to settle and terminate all their differences and pretensions by a Treaty, which shall designate with precision the limits of their respective bordering territories in North America. . . .

ARTICLE II.

His Catholic Majesty cedes to the United States, in full property and sovereignty, all the territories which belong to him, situated to the Eastward of the Mississippi, known by the name of East and West

Florida. The adjacent Islands dependent on said Provinces, all public lots and squares, vacant Lands, public Edifices, Fortifications, Barracks and other Buildings, which are not private property, Archives and Documents, which relate directly to the property and sovereignty of said Provinces, are included in this Article. The said Archives and Documents shall be left in possession of the Commissaries, or Officers of the United States, duly authorized to receive them.

ARTICLE III.

The Boundary Line between the two Countries, West of the Mississippi, shall begin on the Gulph of Mexico, at the mouth of the River Sabine in the Sea, continuing North, along the Western Bank of that River, to the 32d degree of Latitude; thence by a Line due North to the degree of Latitude, where it strikes the Rio Roxo of Nachitoches, or Red-River, then following the course of the Rio-Roxo Westward to the degree of Longitude, 100 West from London and 23 from Washington, then crossing the said Red-River, and running thence by a Line due North to the River Arkansas, thence, following the Course of the Southern bank of the Arkansas to its source in Latitude, 42. North and thence by that parallel of Latitude to the South-Sea. The whole being as laid down in Melishe's Map of the United States, published at Philadelphia, improved to the first of January 1818. . . . The Two High Contracting Parties agree to cede and renounce all their rights, claims and pretensions to the Territories described by the said Line: that is to say.—The United States hereby cede to His Catholic Majesty, and renounce forever, all their rights, claims, and pretensions to the Territories lying West and South of the above described Line; and, in like manner, His Catholic Majesty cedes to the said United States, all his rights, claims, and pretensions to any Territories, East and North of the said Line, and, for himself, his heirs and successors, renounces all claim to the said Territories forever. . . .

Source: *Treaties and Conventions Concluded Between the United States of America and other Powers since July 4, 1776.* Washington: GPO, 1889. 1013–21.

Treaty of 1818

Three years after the War of 1812, U.S. envoys Albert Gallatin and Richard Rush negotiated a treaty that sought to resolve several remaining differences with Great Britain. In addition to securing New England fishing rights off the Canadian coast, extending commercial arrangements for ten years, and submitting American claims to arbitration, the agreement set the forty-ninth parallel as the Canadian boundary to the Rocky Mountains. Concerning the Pacific Northwest, the treaty arranged for mutual access to the region for ten years. This understanding essentially amounted to a postponement of assigning definite territorial rights to either party. At the time, it was a sensible solution for a thinly populated and distant country.

Document 2
Convention of 1818 between
the United States and Great Britain

The United States of America, and His Majesty The King of the United Kingdom of Great Britain and Ireland . . . have agreed to and concluded the following Articles.

ARTICLE I.

[Provision for defining fishing rights of British North America.]

ARTICLE II.

[Provision for establishing forty-nine degrees as the Canadian boundary from the Lake of the Woods to the Rocky Mountains.]

ARTICLE III.

It is agreed, that any Country that may be claimed by either Party on the North West Coast of America, Westward of the Stony Mountains, shall, together with its Harbours, Bays, and Creeks, and the Navigation of all Rivers within the same, be free and open, for the term of ten Years from the date of the Signature of the present Convention, to the Vessels, Citizens, and Subjects of the Two Powers: it being well understood, that this Agreement is not to be construed to the Prejudice of any Claim, which either of the Two High Contracting Parties may have to any part of the said Country, nor shall it be taken to affect the Claims of any other Power or State to any part of the said Country; the only Object of The High Contracting Parties, in that respect, being to prevent disputes and differences amongst Themselves. . . .

Source: Miller, Hunter, ed. *Treaties and Other International Acts of the United States of America.* 8 vols. Washington: GPO, 1931–38. 2:658–62.

Oregon Treaty of 1846

In 1827, Great Britain and the United States extended the Oregon terms of the 1818 treaty indefinitely. Termination of the extension required twelve months' notice. By the 1840s, a surge of American migration into the Willamette Valley south of the Columbia River required a clear-cut resolution of the border, but differences between Britain and the United States again deferred the matter while tempers on both sides fanned the controversy into a crisis. In April 1846, Congress authorized President James K. Polk to end the 1827 mutual access arrangement after the required wait of a year. The British foreign office chose to use this signal as an opening for renewed negotiations, and with some relief, both sides quickly came to the following arrangement. To protect himself from charges of surrendering American interests in the region, Polk submitted the Oregon Treaty to the Senate for its "advice and consent" before it was signed, a unique event in American diplomatic history.

Document 3
Treaty with Great Britain, in Regard to Limits
Westward of the Rocky Mountains.

THE United States of America and her Majesty the Queen of the United Kingdom of Great Britain and Ireland, deeming it to be desirable for the future welfare of both countries that the state of doubt and uncertainty which has hitherto prevailed respecting the sovereignty and government of the territory on the northwest coast of America, lying westward of the Rocky or Stony Mountains . . . have agreed upon and concluded the following articles:

ARTICLE I.

From the point on the forty-ninth parallel of north latitude, where the boundary laid down in existing treaties and conventions between the United States and Great Britain terminates, the line of boundary between the territories of the United States and those of her Britannic Majesty shall be continued westward along the said forty-ninth parallel of north latitude to the middle of the channel which separates the continent from Vancouver's Island, and thence southerly through the middle of the said channel, and of Fuca's Straits, to the Pacific Ocean: Provided, however, That the navigation of the whole of the said channel and straits, south of the forty-ninth parallel of north latitude, remain free and open to both parties.

Source: Miller, Hunter, ed. *Treaties and Other International Acts of the United States of America.* 8 vols. Washington: GPO, 1931–38. 5:3–5.

Indian Removal

For many years, U.S. policy toward Indians attempted to integrate them into the customs of white society. Such so-called acculturation programs were occasionally successful. The Cherokee Indians' extraordinary acceptance of white traditions was the most famous example. Yet, acculturation frequently failed in the face of Indian ethnic resistance, and in any case, when whites wanted Indian land, neither acculturation nor the U.S. legal system offered any protection. The Cherokees discovered this distasteful reality in one of the most shameful episodes of the period.

As early as 1804, Thomas Jefferson pondered the possibility of using part of the Louisiana Purchase for an Indian enclave, but removal did not become government policy until white settlement burst out of its eastern confines after the War of 1812. President James Monroe formally endorsed it in 1825, and Congress five years later formalized it in the Indian Removal Act. Some in Congress, such as Massachusetts' Edward Everett, expressed dismay over the idea of Indian removal, but such voices could not interrupt a rising chorus of support from land-hungry farmers and gold-seeking prospectors. In the ensuing years, President Andrew Jackson's administration uncompromisingly employed Indian removal to clear tribes from desirable lands. In his second annual message, Jackson explained the policy as benefiting everyone— including the Indians being forced from their homelands. Indian sentiment regarding removal took an entirely contrary view, as the message from Cherokee chief John Ross shows.

Document 4
Indian Removal Act of 28 May 1830

An Act to provide for an exchange of lands with the Indians residing in any of the states or territories, and for their removal west of the river Mississippi.

Be it enacted by the Senate and House of Representatives of the United States of America, in Congress assembled,

That it shall and may be lawful for the President of the United States to cause so much of any territory belonging to the United States, west of the river Mississippi, not included in any state or organized territory, and to which the Indian title has been extinguished, as he may judge necessary, to be divided into a suitable number of districts, for the reception of such tribes or nations of Indians as may choose to exchange the lands where they now reside, and remove there; and to cause each of said districts to be so described by natural or artificial marks, as to be easily distinguished from every other.

Sec. 2 *And be it further enacted,* That it shall and may be lawful for the President to exchange any or all of such districts, so to be laid off and described, with any tribe or nation of Indians now residing within the limits of any of the states or territories, and with which the United States have existing treaties, for the whole or any part or portion of the territory claimed and occupied by such tribe or nation, within the bounds of any one or more of the states or territories, where the land claimed and occupied by the Indians, is owned by the United States, or the United States are bound to the state within which it lies to extinguish the Indian claim thereto.

Sec. 3 *And be it further enacted,* That in the making of any such exchange or exchanges, it shall and may be lawful for the President solemnly to assure the tribe or nation with which the exchange is made, that the United States will forever secure and guarantee to them, and their heirs or successors, the country so exchanged with them; and if they prefer it, that the United States will cause a patent or grant to be made and executed to them for the same: *Provided always,* That such lands shall revert to the United States, if the Indians become extinct, or abandon the same.

Sec. 4 *And be it further enacted,* That if, upon any of the lands now occupied by the Indians, and to be exchanged for, there should be such improvements as add value to the land claimed by any individual or individuals of such tribes or nations, it shall and may be lawful for the President to cause such value to be ascertained by appraisement or otherwise, and to cause such ascertained value to be paid to the person or persons rightfully claiming such improvements. And upon the payment of such valuation, the improvements so valued and paid for, shall pass to the United States, and possession shall not afterwards be permitted to any of the same tribe.

Sec. 5 *And be it further enacted,* That upon the making of any such exchange as is contemplated by this act, it shall and may be lawful for the President to cause such aid and assistance to be furnished to the emigrants as may be necessary and proper to enable them to remove to, and settle in, the country for which they may have exchanged; and also, to give them such aid and assistance as may be necessary for their support and subsistence for the first year after their removal.

Sec. 6 *And be it further enacted,* That it shall and may be lawful for the President to cause such tribe or nation to be protected, at their new residence, against all interruption or disturbance from any other tribe or nation of Indians, or from any other person or persons whatever.

Sec. 7 *And be it further enacted,* That it shall and may be lawful for the President to have the same superintendence and care over any tribe or nation in the country to which they may remove, as contemplated by this act, that he is now authorized to have over them at their present places of residence: *Provided,* That nothing in this act contained shall be construed as authorizing or directing the violation of any existing treaty between the United States and any of the Indian tribes.

Sec. 8 *And be it further enacted,* That for the purpose of giving effect to the provisions of this act, the sum of five hundred thousand dollars is hereby appropriated, to be paid out of any money in the treasury, not otherwise appropriated.

Source: Perdue, Theda, and Michael D. Green, eds., *The Cherokee Removal: A Brief History With Documents.* New York: St. Martin's Press, 1995. 116–17.

Document 5
President Andrew Jackson's
Second Annual Message to Congress, December 6, 1830

It gives me pleasure to announce to Congress that the benevolent policy of the Government, steadily pursued for nearly thirty years, in relation to the removal of the Indians beyond the white settlements is approaching to a happy consummation. Two important tribes have accepted the provision made for their removal at the last session of Congress. . . .

The consequences of a speedy removal will be important to the United States, to individual States, and to the Indians themselves. The pecuniary advantages which it Promises to the Government are the least of its recommendations. . . . It will place a dense and civilized population in large tracts of country now occupied by a few savage hunters. By opening the whole territory between Tennessee on the north and Louisiana on the south to the settlement of the whites it will incalculably strengthen the southwestern frontier and render the adjacent States strong enough to repel future invasions without remote aid. It will relieve the whole State of Mississippi and the western part of Alabama of Indian occupancy, and enable those States to advance rapidly in population, wealth, and power. It will separate the Indians from immediate contact with settlements of whites . . . and perhaps cause them gradually, under the protection of the Government and through the influence of good counsels, to cast off their savage habits and become an interesting, civilized, and Christian community. . . .

Toward the aborigines of the country no one can indulge a more friendly feeling than myself, or would go further in attempting to reclaim them from their wandering habits and make them a happy, prosperous people. . . .

Humanity has often wept over the fate of the aborigines of this country, and Philanthropy has been long busily employed in devising means to avert it, but its progress has never for a moment been arrested, and one by one have many powerful tribes disappeared from the earth. To follow to the tomb the last of his race and to tread on the graves of extinct nations excite melancholy reflections. But true philanthropy reconciles the mind to these vicissitudes as it does to the extinction of one generation to make room for another. . . .

The present policy of the Government is but a continuation of the same progressive change by a milder process. The tribes which occupied the countries now constituting the Eastern States were annihilated or have melted away to make room for the whites. The waves of population and civilization are rolling to the westward, and we now propose to acquire the countries occupied by the red men of the South and West by a fair exchange, and, at the expense of the United States, to send them to a land where their existence may be prolonged and perhaps made perpetual. Doubtless it will be painful to leave the graves of their fathers; but what do they more than our ancestors did or than our children are now doing? To better their condition in an unknown land our forefathers left all that was dear in earthly objects. Our children by thousands yearly leave the land of their birth to seek new homes in distant regions. Does Humanity weep at these painful separations from everything, animate and inanimate, with which the young heart has become entwined? Far from it. It is rather a source of joy that our country affords scope where our young population may range unconstrained in body or in mind, developing the power and faculties of man in their highest perfection. These remove hundreds and almost thousands of miles at their own expense, purchase the lands they occupy, and support themselves at their new homes from the moment of their arrival. Can it be cruel in this Government when, by events which it can not control, the Indian is made discontented in his ancient home to purchase his lands, to give him a new and extensive territory, to pay the expense of his removal, and support him a year in his new abode? How many thousands of our own people would gladly embrace the opportunity of removing to the West on such conditions!

Source: Richardson, James D., comp., *A Compilation of the Messages and Papers of the President, 1789–1908.* Washington: Bureau of National Literature and Art, 1908. 2:519–22.

Document 6
Message of the Principal Chief [John Ross] of the Cherokee Nation to the General Council.
To the Committee and Council in General Council Convened.

Friends and Fellow Citizens,

A majority of you have decided upon the necessity and expediency of holding the General Council at this place for the following reason in part:

1. Because it is clearly demonstrated that the cruel treatment which our citizens have experienced from persons acting under the usurped authority of Georgia has originated from the extraordinary course of policy which the present administration of the General Government has adopted and exercised toward us—

2. Because the proper authorities of this nation are menaced by Georgia with an ignominious punishment in the event of their meeting in General Council at New Echota—

3. It was apprehended that an attempt on the part of the Georgia Troops to arrest the members of the General Council, at the point of the bayonet, amidst as great a concourse of our citizens as would in all

probability have attended at that place, such as seems would have occurred . . . and it being the ardent desire of this nation that the peace and friendship which has so happily existed with the United States, almost half a century should be . . . inviolate, you have therefore, considered it . . . prudent to avoid a conflict with the Georgia Troops on this occasion. . . .

Being fully convinced that President Washington and his successors well understood the constitutional powers of the General Government, and the rights of the individual states, as well as those belonging to the Indian Nations, and that the treaties made under their respective administrations with the Cherokee Nation were intended to be faithfully & honestly regarded on the part of the United States; and that the judicial power would extend to all cases of litigation that might arise under these treaties; it was determined on the expediency of employing legal counsel to defend the rights of the Nation before the Courts of the United States. . . .

. . . You will discover from the accompanying documents that the President [Andrew Jackson] declined making any reply to the important subjects presented by our delegation for his consideration.

Source: *Cherokee Phoenix,* November 19, 1831.

Land Policy

Squatters were a persistent problem as the United States surveyed and opened new lands for sale and settlement. Some squatters spent a lifetime restlessly meandering and roosting on public lands, while others came to stay, putting down homesteads and toiling away at improvements. Regardless of such distinctions, the government had little patience with people unlawfully occupying federal lands. Frontier folk certainly believed Andrew Jackson was one of their own, and they might have expected he would be sympathetic to the plight of squatters, but such was not always the case. Concerning the rich soils of northwestern Alabama, Jackson insisted that land policy be strictly enforced.

Document 7
Proclamation Regarding Public Lands Near Huntsville, Alabama; March 30, 1830

By the President of the United States of America.
A Proclamation.

Whereas it has been represented that many uninformed or evil-disposed persons have taken possession of or made a settlement on the public lands of the United States within the district of lands subject to sale at Huntsville, in the State of Alabama . . .

I, Andrew Jackson, President of the United States, have thought proper to issue this my proclamation, commanding and strictly enjoining all persons who have unlawfully taken possession of or made any settlement on, or who now unlawfully occupy, any of the public lands within the district . . . to remove therefrom; and I do hereby further command and enjoin the marshal, or officer acting as marshal, in that State . . . to remove, from and after the 1st day of September, 1830, all or any of the said unlawful occupants; and to effect the said service I do hereby authorize the employment of such military force as may become necessary in pursuance of the provisions of the act of Congress aforesaid, warning the offenders, moreover, that they will be prosecuted in all such other ways as the law directs. . . .

Done at the city of Washington, the 6th day of March, A.D. 1830, and of the Independence of the United States of America the fifty-fourth.

ANDREW JACKSON.
By the President:
M. VAN BUREN,
Secretary of State.

Source: Richardson, James D., comp. *A Compilation of the Messages and Papers of the President, 1789–1908.* Washington: Bureau of National Literature and Art, 1908. 2:494–95.

Texas

Independence

In 1836, American emigrants as well as native *tejanos* in the Mexican province of Texas rose up in revolt against the centralized government of Antonio López de Santa Anna. While Santa Anna's army besieged the small garrison at the Alamo in San Antonio, Texas delegates met at Washington on the Brazos to determine the course and the extent resistance would take. Acting quickly, a five-man drafting committee produced a declaration of independence that the convention approved the next day. Its authors modeled the document on the United States Declaration of Independence of 1776. Although the Alamo would fall, its example inspired Texans to fight through to victory at San Jacinto the following April.

Document 8
The Texas Declaration of Independence, March 2, 1836

The Unanimous Declaration of Independence made by the Delegates of the People of Texas in General Convention at the town of Washington on the 2nd day of March 1836.

When a government has ceased to protect the lives, liberty and property of the people, from whom its legitimate powers are derived, and for the advancement of whose happiness it was instituted, and so far from being a guarantee for the enjoyment of those inestimable and inalienable rights, becomes an instrument in the hands of evil rulers for their oppression.

When the Federal Republican Constitution of their country, which they have sworn to support, no longer has a substantial existence, and the whole nature of their government has been forcibly changed, without their consent, from a restricted federative republic, composed of sovereign states, to a consolidated central military despotism, in which every interest is disregarded but that of the army and the priesthood, both the eternal enemies of civil liberty, the ever ready minions of power, and the usual instruments of tyrants.

When, long after the spirit of the constitution has departed, moderation is at length so far lost by those in power, that even the semblance of freedom is removed, and the forms themselves of the constitution discontinued, and so far from their petitions and remonstrances being regarded, the agents who bear them are thrown into dungeons, and mercenary armies sent forth to force a new government upon them at the point of the bayonet.

When, in consequence of such acts of malfeasance and abdication on the part of the government, anarchy prevails, and civil society is dissolved into its original elements. In such a crisis, the first law of nature, the right of self-preservation, the inherent and inalienable rights of the people to appeal to first principles, and take their political affairs into their own hands in extreme cases, enjoins it as a right towards themselves, and a sacred obligation to their posterity, to abolish such government, and create another in its stead, calculated to rescue them from impending dangers, and to secure their future welfare and happiness.

Nations, as well as individuals, are amenable for their acts to the public opinion of mankind. A statement of a part of our grievances is therefore submitted to an impartial world, in justification of the hazardous but unavoidable step now taken, of severing our political connection with the Mexican people, and assuming an independent attitude among the nations of the earth. . . .

These, and other grievances, were patiently borne by the people of Texas, until they reached that point at which forbearance ceases to be a virtue. We then took up arms in defence of the national constitution. We appealed to our Mexican brethren for assistance. Our appeal has been made in vain. Though months have elapsed, no sympathetic response has yet been heard from the Interior. We are, therefore, forced to the melancholy conclusion, that the Mexican people have acquiesced in the destruction of their liberty, and the substitution therefor of a military government; that they are unfit to be free, and incapable of self government.

The necessity of self-preservation, therefore, now decrees our eternal political separation.

We, therefore, the delegates with plenary powers of the people of Texas, in solemn convention assembled, appealing to a candid world for the necessities of our condition, do hereby resolve and declare, that our political connection with the Mexican nation has forever ended, and that the people of Texas do now constitute a free, Sovereign, and independent republic, and are fully invested with all the rights and attributes which properly belong to independent nations; and, conscious of the rectitude of our intentions, we fearlessly and confidently commit the issue to the decision of the Supreme arbiter of the destinies of nations.

Richard Ellis, President of the Convention and Delegate from Red River. [Document signed by 56 delegates.]

Source: Jenkins, John H., ed. *The Papers of the Texas Revolution, 1835–1836.* 10 vols. Austin, TX: Presidial Press, 1973. 4:493–97.

Annexation

After independence, many in Texas wanted to become part of the United States. American southerners especially insisted that incorporating the region into the Union was as logical as it was desirable. Yet, northern antislavery forces made Texas annexation mathematically impossible because their numbers in the Senate could thwart the required two-thirds majority to ratify an annexation treaty with the Lone Star Republic.

The standoff continued until the 1840s when concerns about England's interest in Texas revived the annexation debate. A perilous political climate then affected the 1844 presidential election. Henry Clay's irresolute stand on Texas annexation cost him the election and placed expansionist Democrat James K. Polk in the presidency, although Polk's margin of victory was extremely narrow.

Nonetheless, lame-duck John Tyler and Secretary of State John C. Calhoun interpreted Polk's victory as a mandate for acquiring Texas. With just days left in its existence, the Tyler administration resolved the Senate ratification problem by having the measure enacted by a joint resolution of Congress, a procedural stratagem that required only simple majorities in both houses. The measure passed, but the political consequences were as enduring as they were grim. The antislavery movement was especially incensed at the addition of so large a slave region to the country. Note that section 3 includes provisions for making the region into as many as five states. Although it would never be applied, the stipulation could have resulted in ten new slave state senators.

Document 9
Joint Resolution of the Congress of the United States, March 1, 1845
28th Congress, Second Session

Resolved by the Senate and House of Representatives of the United States of America in Congress assembled, That Congress doth consent that the territory properly included within, and rightfully belonging to the Republic of Texas, may be erected into a new state, to be called the state of Texas, with a republican form of government, to be adopted by the people of said republic, by deputies in Convention assembled, with the consent of the existing government, in order that the same may be admitted as one of the states of this Union.

2. *And be it further resolved,* . . . New states, of convenient size, not exceeding four in number, in addition to said state of Texas, and having

sufficient population, may hereafter, by the consent of said state, be formed out of the territory thereof, which shall be entitled to admission under the provisions of the federal constitution. And such states as may be formed out of that portion of said territory lying south of thirty-six degrees thirty minutes north latitude, commonly known as the Missouri compromise line, shall be admitted into the Union with or without slavery, as the people of each state asking admission may desire. And in such state or states as shall be formed out of said territory north of said Missouri compromise line, slavery, or involuntary servitude, (except for crime,) shall be prohibited.

3. *And be it further resolved,* That if the President of the United States shall in his judgment and discretion deem it most advisable, instead of proceeding to submit the foregoing resolution to the Republic of Texas, as an overture on the part of the United States for admission, to negotiate with that Republic; then, Be it resolved, that a state, to be formed out of the present Republic of Texas, with suitable extent and boundaries, and with two representatives in Congress, until the next apportionment of representation, shall be admitted into the Union, by virtue of this act, on an equal footing with the existing states, as soon as the terms and conditions of such admission, and the cession of the remaining Texan territory to the United States shall be agreed upon by the governments of Texas and the United States. . . .

Source: Miller, Hunter, ed. *Treaties and Other International Acts of the United States of America.* 8 vols. Washington: GPO, 1931–1938. 4:689–90.

War with Mexico

The United States Declaration

When Polk took office in March 1845, he inherited troubled Mexican-American relations that rapidly turned more acrimonious. Mexico broke off diplomatic relations after the U.S. annexation of Texas. Polk tried to repair the breach so that he could coax Mexico to a bargain over California, but the Mexicans rebuffed his efforts and refused to meet with his envoy. Frustrated and impatient, Polk sought to apply pressure by dispatching a military force under Zachary Taylor to the Rio Grande. The president embraced Texan claims that the Rio Grande, rather than the Nueces River, was the Mexican border, and he claimed that Taylor's "Army of Observation" was necessary to protect American lives and property.

These provocative moves did not immediately produce a sufficiently angry Mexican response, and Polk began drafting a message to Congress that implausibly cited Mexico's diplomatic snub as adequate cause for a declaration of war. The arrival of Zachary Taylor's report that Mexican forces had fired on him, however, changed everything. Polk concluded his message with a description of the clash. He insisted that the war was already underway. Congress agreed.

Document 10
Polk's War Message, 1846

The existing state of the relations between the United States and Mexico renders it proper that I should bring the subject to the consideration of Congress. . . .

The strong desire to establish peace with Mexico on liberal and honorable terms, and the readiness of this Government to regulate and adjust our boundary and other causes of difference with that power on such fair and equitable principles as would lead to permanent relations of the most friendly nature, induced me in September last to seek the reopening of diplomatic relations between the two countries. . . . An envoy of the United States repaired to Mexico with full powers to adjust every existing difference. But though present on the Mexican soil by agreement between the two Governments, invested with full powers, and bearing evidence of the most friendly dispositions, his mission has been unavailing. The Mexican Government not only refused to receive him or listen to his propositions, but after a long-continued series of menaces have at last invaded our territory and shed the blood of our fellow-citizens on our own soil. . . .

In my message at the commencement of the present session I informed you that upon the earnest appeal both of the Congress and convention of Texas I had ordered an efficient military force to take a position "between the Nueces and the Del Norte." This had become necessary to meet a threatened invasion of Texas by the Mexican forces, for which extensive military preparations had been made. The invasion was threatened solely because Texas had determined, in accordance with a solemn resolution of the Congress of the United States, to annex herself to our Union, and under these circumstances it was plainly our duty to extend our protection over her citizens and soil. . . .

The Army moved from Corpus Christi on the 11th of March, and on the 28th of that month arrived on the left bank of the Del Norte opposite to Matamoras, where it encamped on a commanding position, which has since been strengthened by the erection of fieldworks. A depot has also been established at Point Isabel, near the Brazos Santiago, 30 miles in the rear of the encampment. The selection of his position was necessarily confided to the judgment of the general in command.

The Mexican forces at Matamoras assumed a belligerent attitude, and on the 12th of April General Ampudia, then in command, notified General Taylor to break up his camp within twenty-four hours and to retire beyond the Nueces River, and in the event of his failure to comply with these demands announced that arms, and arms alone, must decide the question. But no open act of hostility was committed until the 24th of April. On that day General Arista, who had succeeded to the command of the Mexican forces, communicated to General Taylor that "he considered hostilities commenced and should prosecute them." A party of dragoons of 63 men and officers were on the same day dispatched from the American camp up the Rio del Norte, on its left bank, to ascertain whether the Mexican troops had crossed or were preparing to cross the river, "became engaged with a large body of these troops, and after a short affair, in which some 16 were killed and wounded, appear to have been surrounded and compelled to surrender."

. . . The cup of forbearance had been exhausted even before the recent information from the frontier of the Del Norte. But now, after reiterated menaces, Mexico has passed the boundary of the United States, has invaded our territory and shed American blood upon the American soil. She has proclaimed that hostilities have commenced, and that the two nations are now at war.

As war exists, and, notwithstanding all our efforts to avoid it, exists by the act of Mexico herself, we are called upon by every consideration of duty and patriotism to vindicate with decision the honor, the rights, and the interests of our country.

Source: Richardson, James D., comp. *A Compilations of the Messages and Papers of the President, 1789–1908.* Washington: Bureau of National Literature and Art, 1908. 4:437–43.

The Mexican Cession

By 1847, Mexico was defeated in the field and in political chaos. The latter circumstance presented General Winfield Scott and U.S. diplomatic envoy Nicholas Trist with a significant problem. Unwisely, Trist and Scott consented to an armistice so that Mexican authorities could gather themselves to make peace. More injudiciously, the Americans attempted to bribe their way to a hasty settlement, and when Santa Anna reacted to both gestures with characteristic bad faith, President Polk furiously questioned both the judgment and integrity of Trist. Although the president recalled him and thereby stripped him of all power to negotiate any settlement with Mexico, Trist seized upon an opportunity to end the war anyway. The treaty he negotiated was signed outside Mexico City in the village of Guadalupe Hidalgo. He returned with it to Washington where Polk grudgingly admitted that it contained every provision he desired. The president never forgave Trist for his alleged apostasy, however, and the unfortunate envoy was summarily dismissed from government service.

Document 11
The Treaty of Guadalupe-Hidalgo

ARTICLE V

The boundary line between the two Republics shall commence in the Gulf of Mexico, three leagues from land, opposite the mouth of the Rio Grande, otherwise called Rio Bravo del Norte, or Opposite the mouth of its deepest branch, if it should have more than one branch emptying directly into the sea; from thence up the middle of that river, following the deepest channel, where it has more than one, to the point where it strikes the southern boundary of New Mexico; thence, westwardly, along the whole southern boundary of New Mexico (which runs north of the town called Paso) to its western termination; thence, northward, along the western line of New Mexico, until it intersects the first branch of the river Gila; (or if it should not intersect any branch of that river, then to the point on the said line nearest to such branch, and thence in a direct line to the same); thence down the middle of the said branch and of the said river, until it empties into the Rio Colorado; thence across the Rio Colorado, following the division line between Upper and Lower California, to the Pacific Ocean. . . .

The boundary line established by this article shall be religiously respected by each of the two republics, and no change shall ever be made therein, except by the express and free consent of both nations, lawfully given by the General Government of each, in conformity with its own constitution. . . .

ARTICLE XII

In consideration of the extension acquired by the boundaries of the United States, as defined in the fifth article of the present treaty, the Government of the United States engages to pay to that of the Mexican Republic the sum of fifteen millions of dollars. . . .

ARTICLE XIV

The United States do furthermore discharge the Mexican Republic from all claims of citizens of the United States, not heretofore decided against the Mexican Government, which may have arisen previously to the date of the signature of this treaty; which discharge shall be final and perpetual, whether the said claims be rejected or be allowed by the board of commissioners provided for in the following article, and whatever shall be the total amount of those allowed.

ARTICLE XV

The United States, exonerating Mexico from all demands on account of the claims of their citizens mentioned in the preceding article, and considering them entirely and forever canceled, whatever their amount may be, undertake to make satisfaction for the same, to an amount not exceeding three and one-quarter millions of dollars. . . .

ARTICLE XVI

Each of the contracting parties reserves to itself the entire right to fortify whatever point within its territory it may judge proper so to fortify for its security. . . .

Source: Miller, Hunter, ed. *Treaties and Other International Acts of the United States of America.* 8 vols. Washington: GPO, 1931–1938. 5:207–36.

The Slavery Controversy

As the United States expanded after the War of 1812, the specter of slavery overshadowed every territorial acquisition. Sometimes it took form in sharp disagreements, as when Missouri sought statehood in 1819. New York Representative James Tallmadge declared his famous amendment to the Missouri Enabling Bill and touched off one of the first and most prominent slavery debates in American political history. The resulting Missouri Compromise sought not only to resolve the immediate controversy but also to establish a principle—the so-called Missouri Compromise Line of 36°30'—as a guide to avoid future problems. It was a hopeless plan, for the debate over slavery would not be silenced.

Document 12
The Tallmadge Amendment, February 13, 1820

And provided, That the further introduction of slavery or involuntary servitude be prohibited, except for the punishment of crimes, whereof the party shall have been fully [duly] convicted; and that all children born within the said State, after the admission thereof into the Union, shall be free at the age of twenty-five Years.

Source: *Annals of Congress*, 15th Cong., 2nd sess. 1170.

As abolitionist agitation and free soil advocacy became more vocal, any acquisition of new territory fell prey to this all-encompassing argument. The debate had a profound effect on expansion, threatening to stall it in the Southwest. In 1845, Lawyer and journalist John L. O'Sullivan wrote an editorial proclaiming Americans' "manifest destiny to overspread the continent allotted by Providence for the free development of our yearly multiplying millions." In the same piece, O'Sullivan disputed the charge that Texas expansion was a plot to advance the slave interests. Unsurprisingly, his arguments failed to sway antislavery activists.

Document 13
John L. O'Sullivan on Annexation and the Slave Issue

Nor is there any just foundation for the charge that Annexation is a great pro-slavery measure—calculated to increase and perpetuate that institution. Slavery had nothing to do with it. Opinions were and are greatly divided, both at the North and South, as to the influence to be exerted by it on Slavery and the Slave States. That it will tend to facilitate and hasten the disappearance of Slavery from all the northern tier of the present Slave States, cannot surely admit of serious question. The greater value in Texas of the slave labor now employed in those States, must soon produce the effect of draining off that labor southwardly, by the same unvarying law that bids water descend the slope that invites it. Every new Slave State in Texas will make at least one Free State from among those in which that institution now exists—to say nothing of those portions of Texas on which slavery cannot spring and grow—to say nothing of the far more rapid growth of new States in the free West and Northwest, as these fine regions are overspread by the emigration fast flowing over them from Europe, as well as from the Northern and Eastern States of the Union as it exists. On the other hand, it is undeniably much gained for the cause of the eventual voluntary abolition of slavery, that it should have been thus drained off towards the only outlet which appeared to furnish much probability of the ultimate disappearance of the negro race from our borders. The Spanish-Indian-American populations of Mexico, Central America and South America, afford the only receptacle capable of absorbing that race whenever we shall be prepared to slough it off—to emancipate it from slavery, and (simultaneously necessary) to remove it from the midst of our own. Themselves already of mixed and confused blood, and free from the "prejudices" which among us so insuperably forbid the social amalgamation which can alone elevate the Negro race out of a virtually servile degradation even though legally free, the regions occupied by those populations must strongly attract the black race in that direction; and as soon as the destined hour of emancipation shall arrive, will relieve the question of one of its worst difficulties, if not absolutely the greatest.

Source: *United States Magazine and Democratic Review* July 1845.

> When war broke out with Mexico, southerners such as John C. Calhoun had their worst fears realized. Calhoun opposed Polk's aggressive stand against Mexico because he feared a war would reanimate northern objections to slavery. Pennsylvania Democrat David Wilmot fulfilled the prophecy when he attached a provisional amendment to the administration's request for money to offer Mexico as an alternative to war. To the great alarm of southerners, the Wilmot Proviso twice passed the House of Representatives, but the Senate always defeated the measure. The growing

momentum of antislavery continued to frighten southerners in the years after the Mexican cession and eventually led them out of the Union and caused the Civil War.

Document 14
The Wilmot Proviso, August 12, 1846

Provided, That, as an express and fundamental condition to the acquisition of any territory from the Republic of Mexico by the United States, by virtue of any treaty which may be negotiated between them, and to the use by the Executive of the moneys herein appropriated, neither slavery nor involuntary servitude shall ever exist in any part of said territory, except for crime, whereof the party shall first be duly convicted.

Source: Congressional Globe, 29th Cong., 1st sess. 1217.

GLOSSARY

Acculturation Policy. U.S. Indian policy before the adoption of Indian removal that strove to educate Indian cultures about and adapt them to white agricultural, economic, political, and social customs. Uneven in its achievements, acculturation was most avidly adopted by the Cherokees.

Arbitration. In diplomacy, the act of submitting an international dispute to a disinterested third party for resolution. Arbitration is supposed to endorse the claim of one side over the other, as contrasted to mediation, which seeks to find a middle course between conflicting positions.

Bear Flag Republic. The brief governmental entity established by the small American insurrection in California during the Mexican War; so named because its flag featured a grizzly; U.S. authority superseded the Bear Flag Republic almost as soon as it had been proclaimed.

BUS. The acronym for the Second Bank of the United States (1816–36) that also distinguished it from its predecessor, the Bank of the United States (1791–1811).

Cockboat. A small auxiliary boat usually employed in ship tending.

Confederation Congress. The national unicameral legislative body that operated under the Articles of Confederation before the U.S. Constitution replaced it with the present bicameral legislature.

Crackers. A disparaging name for extremely poor whites in the rural South.

Distribution. The idea of disbursing proceeds from public land sales to the states. Distribution was briefly enacted in 1841 under a formula linking it to tariff schedules that virtually ensured its quick repeal.

Empresario. Roughly translated as "a director of an enterprise," the term denoted a person who entered into contracts with the Mexican government to settle immigrants in Texas.

Factor. A business agent who manages the affairs and represents the interests of a client or a company. John McLoughlin, chief factor for the Hudson's Bay Company in the Oregon Country, was similar to today's corporate regional manager.

Filibusterer. A corruption of the Dutch word *vrijbuiter,* which means freebooter, meaning someone who plunders for "free booty." The Spanish variation is *filibustero,* and from that is derived the English filibusterer. In the mid-1800s, filibusterers were Americans who sought personal fortune and the extension of U.S. influence by trying to overthrow Latin American governments.

Joint Resolution. A congressional measure whose passage requires only a simple majority in the House of Representatives and the Senate.

Minister. One who fulfills a diplomatic function. The United States did not appoint ambassadors to foreign capitals until the late nineteenth century, believing the rank was a vestige of aristocracy.

Northwest Ordinance. The Ordinance of 1787, which specifically pertained to organizing governments for the Old Northwest. Its procedures for gaining statehood established the system still in use for transforming territories into co-equal members of the Union.

Old Northwest. During the early nineteenth century, the region that extended from the Allegheny Mountains to west of the Great Lakes.

Preemption. The plan for allowing squatters the first chance to purchase land they have inhabited and improved, regardless of the legitimacy of their original claim.

Range (n.). The U.S. land survey's method of charting and organizing public lands for sale and distribution. A range consists of townships between meridians placed six miles apart. Ranges are numbered from east to west starting with the survey's prime (or starting) meridian, whereas townships are numbered from north to south starting from a base line.

Red Sticks. A faction of the Creek Indians who took up arms against white acculturation policies to wage the Creek War of 1813–14. They were called Red Sticks because of the Creek practice of counting down days to an important event (such as a battle) using bundles of red wooden rods.

Sauk-Fox. Algonquian Indians whose close relationship began in the early eighteenth century when they allied to fight the French. By the early nineteenth century, the tribes had melded into virtually one entity under Black Hawk.

Squatters. Settlers who claim ownership of land by merely inhabiting it.

Tejano. A Texan of Mexican descent.

Township. A designation within a range, six square miles in area and divided into thirty-six square mile sections, designed to promote the orderly settlement of public lands.

Ukase. Under the Russian tsars, an imperial decree that carried the force of law.

Young America. An expression that described, encouraged, and celebrated an ardent U.S. nationalism during the mid-1800s. Extolling the virtues of capitalism, individualism, democracy, and territorial expansion, it helped to shape the aggressive foreign policy embraced by proponents of Manifest Destiny.

ANNOTATED BIBLIOGRAPHY

Biographies

Andrew, John A. *From Revivals to Removal: Jeremiah Evarts, the Cherokee Nation, and the Search for the Soul of America*. Athens: University of Georgia Press, 1992.

Well-researched analysis of Evarts' desire to transform Cherokee nation into Christian community.

Barker, Eugene Campbell. *The Life of Stephen F. Austin, Founder of Texas, 1793–1836*. New York: Da Capo, 1968.

Massive account of Austin's efforts to establish the colony and Republic of Texas.

Bass, Altha Leah Bierbower. *Cherokee Messenger*. Foreword by William L. Anderson. Norman: University of Oklahoma Press, 1936. Reprint, 1996.

Details Worcester's long life among the Cherokees while making excellent contribution to Cherokee history.

Bauer, K. Jack. *Zachary Taylor: Soldier, Planter, Statesman of the Old South*. Baton Rouge: Louisiana State University Press, 1985.

Excellent biography that analyzes Taylor's military career and short, though pivotal presidency.

Bergeron, Paul H. *The Presidency of James K. Polk*. Lawrence: University of Kansas Press, 1987.

Generally positive overview of Polk's presidency.

Bogue, Allan G. *Frederick Jackson Turner: Strange Roads Going Down*. Norman: University of Oklahoma Press, 1998.

Excellent evaluation of Turner's life and importance to the historical profession.

Campbell, Randolph, and Oscar Handlin. *Sam Houston and the American Southwest.* New York: HarperCollins, 1993. Reprint, New York: Longman, 2002.

Part of Library of American Biography series that examines Sam Houston's life in the light of American expansion.

Cantrell, Gregg. *Stephen F. Austin, Impresario of Texas.* New Haven: Yale University Press, 1999.

Scholarly examination of Austin's mission to colonize Texas and to protect his creation.

Cunningham, Noble E., Jr. *The Presidency of James Monroe.* Lawrence: University of Kansas Press, 1996.

Detailed look at crises of expansion (Missouri and Florida) that occurred during Monroe's presidency as well as how the Monroe Doctrine shaped Americans' views toward North America.

Cutrer, Thomas W. *Ben McCulloch and the Frontier Military Tradition.* Chapel Hill: University of North Carolina Press, 1993.

Comprehensive biography of frontiersman who did much to shape the image of Texans.

De Bruhl, Marshall. *Sword of San Jacinto: A Life of Sam Houston.* New York: Random, 1993.

Highly readable, laudatory account of Houston's life.

Eisenhower, John S. D. *The Life and Times of Winfield Scott.* New York: Free Press, 1997. Reprint, Norman: University of Oklahoma Press, 1999.

Engagingly written biography of the early nineteenth century's greatest soldier.

Elliott, Charles W. *Winfield Scott: The Soldier and the Man.* New York: Macmillan, 1937.

Detailed biography of Scott.

Gabriel, Ralph Henry. *Elias Boudinot, Cherokee & His America.* Norman: University of Oklahoma Press, 1941.

Comprehensive biography of Cherokee editor.

Gregory, Jack, and Rennard Strickland. *Sam Houston with the Cherokees, 1829–1833.* Austin: University of Texas Press, 1967. Reprint, Norman: University of Oklahoma Press, 1996.

An account of the four years Sam Houston lived with the Cherokees after resigning as governor of Tennessee.

Haley, James L. *Sam Houston.* Norman: University of Oklahoma Press, 2002.

Intimate look at Houston's entire life.

Hartley, William B., and Ellen Hartley. *Osceola, the Unconquered Indian.* New York: Hawthorn, 1973.

Biography of Osceola set primarily in the Second Seminole War.

Hudson, Linda S. *Mistress of Manifest Destiny: A Biography of Jane McManus Storm Cazneau, 1807–1878.* Austin: Texas State Historical Association, 2001.

Exciting look at the life of a strong, adventurous frontier woman.

Hughes, William J. *Rebellious Ranger: Rip Ford and the Old Southwest.* Norman: University of Oklahoma Press, 1964.

Biography of an early Texan who came from Tennessee to fight in the Texas Revolution and became one of Texas's most adventurous pioneers.

James, Marquis. *The Raven: A Biography of Sam Houston.* Indianapolis: Bobbs–Merrill, 1929.

Excellent, though somewhat dated biography of the hero of the Texas Revolution.

Johnson, Timothy D. *Winfield Scott: The Quest for Military Glory.* Lawrence: University Press of Kansas, 1998.

A thorough analysis of Scott's military career and his impact on the United States military.

Kieffer, Chester L. *Maligned General: The Biography of Thomas Sidney Jesup.* San Rafael, CA: Presidio Press, 1979.

Solid defense of Jesup's conduct in the Second Seminole War.

Launius, Roger D. *Alexander William Doniphan: Portrait of a Missouri Moderate.* Columbia: University of Missouri Press, 1997.

Comprehensive biography of Doniphan's entire career.

May, Robert E. *John A. Quitman: Old South Crusader.* Baton Rouge: Louisiana State University Press, 1985.

Standard biography of Mexican-American War general and proponent of national expansion.

Moulton, Gary E. *John Ross, Cherokee Chief.* Athens: University of Georgia Press, 1978.

Excellent biography of a man whose life spanned much of Cherokee history in the nineteenth century.

Nevins, Allan. *Frémont: Pathmarker of the West.* New York: Harper & Brothers, 1928. Reprint, Lincoln: University of Nebraska Press, 1992.

Admiring but well-researched and well-written biography.

Nichols, Roy Franklin. *Franklin Pierce: Young Hickory of the Granite Hills.* Philadelphia: University of Pennsylvania Press, 1958.

Definitive biography of New England expansionist and Mexican-American War volunteer general.

Niven, John. *Martin Van Buren: The Romantic Age of American Politics.* New York: Oxford University Press, 1983.

Standard biography of Van Buren.

Ohrt, Wallace. *Defiant Peacemaker: Nicholas Trist in the Mexican War.* College Station: Texas A&M University Press, 1997.

Full biography of Trist with a focus on his peacemaking activities during the war.

Remini, Robert V. *Andrew Jackson and the Course of American Democracy, 1833–1845.* New York: Harper, 1984.

Third part of trilogy covers Jackson's second term to his death.

————. *Andrew Jackson and the Course of American Empire, 1767–1821.* New York: Harper & Row, 1977.

First part of trilogy offers a laudatory examination of Jackson's early life and military career.

————. *Andrew Jackson and the Course of American Freedom, 1822–1832.* New York: Harper & Row, 1981.

Second part of trilogy examines Jackson's push for the presidency and his first term.

Roberts, David. *A New World: Kit Carson, John C. Frémont, and the Claiming of the American West.* New York: Simon & Schuster, 2000.

Holds that these two explorers were responsible for United States gaining Southwest and California.

Schlesinger, Arthur M., Jr. *The Age of Jackson.* New York: Little, Brown and Company, 1945.

Extremely laudatory look at Jacksonian Democracy equating Jacksonianism with Franklin Roosevelt's New Deal.

Sellers, Charles Grier. *James K. Polk: Continentalist, 1843–1846.* Princeton: Princeton University Press, 1966.

Examination of Polk's political career with an emphasis on his run for the presidency to the outbreak of the Mexican-American War.

————. *James K. Polk, Jacksonian, 1795–1843.* Princeton: Princeton University Press, 1957.

First part of biography that emphasizes Polk's early political career in Congress through his governorship of Tennessee.

Smith, Gene A. *Thomas Ap Catesby Jones: Commodore of Manifest Destiny.* Annapolis: Naval Institute Press, 2000.

Definitive biography of career naval officer who made a premature attempt to seize part of California.

Ward, John William. *Andrew Jackson: Symbol for an Age.* New York: Oxford University Press, 1977.

An examination of Jackson's influence on the Early Republic.

Wilkins, Thurman. *Cherokee Tragedy: The Story of the Ridge Family and the Decimation of a People.* New York: Macmillan, 1970.

The destruction of the Cherokee nation through the eyes of one of its most prominent families.

Williams, John Hoyt. *Sam Houston: The Life and Times of the Liberator of Texas, an Authentic American Hero*. New York: Simon & Schuster, 1993.

Flattering portrait of Sam Houston.

General

Beers, Henry Putney. *The Western Military Frontier, 1815–1846*. Philadelphia: Porcupine, 1975.

Thorough examination of army's efforts to maintain peace in the Southwest and Northwest to the outbreak of the Mexican-American War.

Belohlavek, John M. *"Let the Eagle Soar!": The Foreign Policy of Andrew Jackson*. Lincoln: University of Nebraska Press, 1985.

Study of a frequently unexamined part of Jackson's presidency.

Billington, Ray Allen. *Westward Expansion: A History of the American Frontier*. New York: Macmillan, 1974.

Designed primarily as a textbook on the westward movement.

Boime, Albert. *The Magisterial Gaze: Manifest Destiny and American Landscape Painting, c. 1830–1865*. Washington: Smithsonian, 1991.

Examines impact of American expansion on American painting.

Brauer, Kinley J. *Cotton Versus Conscience: Massachusetts Whig Politics and Southwestern Expansion, 1843–1848*. Lexington: University of Kentucky Press, 1967.

Division of Whig Party centered on the Mexican conflict.

Coffman, Edward M. *The Old Army: A Portrait of the American Army in Peacetime, 1784–1898*. New York: Oxford University Press, 1986.

A social history of the United States Army; focuses primarily on the frontier.

Colorado Historical Society. *The Santa Fe Trail: New Perspectives*. Denver: Colorado Historical Society, 1987.

Series of essays presented at a symposium about the trail.

Dangerfield, George. *The Awakening of American Nationalism, 1815–1828*. New York: Harper & Row, 1965.

Sees nationalism as driving force in post–War of 1812 America.

Dary, David. *The Santa Fe Trail: Its History, Legends, and Lore*. New York: Knopf, 2000.

Well-written social history of the trail.

Davis, William C. *The American Frontier: Pioneers, Settlers, & Cowboys, 1800–1899*. Norman: University of Oklahoma Press, 1999.

Well-illustrated look at trans-Mississippi West.

DeConde, Alexander. *The Affair of Louisiana.* New York: Scribner, 1976.

Views Louisiana Purchase as part of overall trend toward expansion.

DeVoto, Bernard. *The Course of Empire.* Boston: Houghton Mifflin Company, 1952.

Account of colonial and early national exploration.

Foreman, Grant. *Pioneer Days in the Early Southwest.* Cleveland: Clark, 1926. Reprint, Lincoln: University of Nebraska Press, 1994.

Account of the movement of settlers into the southwest including Texas.

Foust, James D. *The Yeoman Farmer and Westward Expansion of U.S. Cotton Production.* New York: Arno 1975.

An economic explanation for the spread of cotton agriculture into the southwest.

Freehling, William W. *Slavery, the Civil War, and the Reintegration of American History.* New York: Oxford University Press, 1990.

Essays that examine different aspects of the slavery debate including its expansion.

Gates, Paul W. *The Farmer's Age: Agriculture, 1815–1860.* New York: Torchbooks-Harper, 1968.

Excellent overview from series on economic history of the United States.

Gibson, Arrell Morgan. *The West in the Life of the Nation.* Lexington, MA: Heath, 1976.

Dated but good overview by expert on western expansion.

Goetzmann, William H. *Exploration and Empire: The Explorer and the Scientist in the Winning of the American West.* Austin: Texas State Historical Association, 1994.

Examination of the systematic exploration of the American West in the early nineteenth century.

———. *New Lands, New Men: America and the Second Great Age of Discovery.* New York: Viking, 1986.

Puts American exploration into the context of European exploration.

———. *When the Eagle Screamed: The Romantic Horizon in American Diplomacy, 1800–1860.* New York: Wiley, 1966.

Traditional look at American expansion.

Graebner, Norman A. *Empire on the Pacific: A Study in American Continental Expansion.* New York: Ronald, 1955.

Sees American settlement on the Pacific as key to expansionism in 1840s.

———. *Manifest Destiny.* Indianapolis: Bobbs-Merrill, 1968.

Primary documents with commentary on the contemporary views of the 1840s and 1850s on American expansionism.

Holt, Michael F. *Political Parties and American Political Development: From the Age of Jackson to the Age of Lincoln.* Baton Rouge: Louisiana State University Press, 1992.

Essays that deal with political parties in the middle period, including the impact of expansion.

————. *The Rise and Fall of the American Whig Party: Jacksonian Politics and the Onset of the Civil War.* New York: Oxford University Press, 1999.

Comprehensive look at the entire existence of the Whig Party.

Horsman, Reginald. *Race and Manifest Destiny: The Origins of American Racial Anglo–Saxonism.* Cambridge, MA: Harvard University Press, 1981.

Traces the evolution of a feeling of racial superiority among white Americans from colonial times through the Mexican-American War.

Johannsen, Robert Walter, Sam W. Haynes, and Christopher Morris. *Manifest Destiny and Empire: American Antebellum Expansionism.* College Station: Texas A&M University Press, 1997.

Lectures by established and young historians on subjects from Texas to filibusterers.

Jones, Howard, and Donald A. Rakestraw. *Prologue to Manifest Destiny: Anglo–American Relations in the 1840s.* Wilmington, DE: SR Books, 1997.

Details the diplomatic relations between the United States and Great Britain culminating with the settlement of the Oregon boundary.

Katz, William Loren. *The Black West: A Documentary and Pictorial History of the African American Role in the Westward Expansion of the United States.* New York: Simon & Schuster, 1996.

An attempt to address the dearth of information on African-Americans in the West.

Knupfer, Peter B. *The Union As It Is: Constitutional Unionism and Sectional Compromise, 1787–1861.* Chapel Hill: University of North Carolina Press, 1991.

Important analysis of the role moderates played in the sectional crises of the country.

Kohl, Lawrence F. *The Politics of Individualism: Parties and the American Character in the Jacksonian Era.* New York: Oxford University Press, 1989.

Looks at political rhetoric of Jacksonian period and determines that Jacksonian Democrats were the conservatives.

Kolodny, Annette. *The Land Before Her: Fantasy and Experience of the American Frontiers, 1630–1860.* Chapel Hill: University of North Carolina Press, 1984.

Taken from letters and diaries, story looks at frontier experience from women's viewpoints.

Kownslar, Allan O. *Manifest Destiny and Expansionism in the 1840's*. Boston: Heath, 1967.

Classroom reader part of New Dimensions in American History series.

Krenn, Michael L., ed. *Race and U.S. Foreign Policy from Colonial Times through the Age of Jackson*. New York: Garland, 1998.

Essays that determine the evolution of ideas regarding race and its impact on Early Republic's dealings with foreign powers.

Jones, Dorothy V. *License for Empire: Colonialism by Treaty in Early America*. Chicago: University of Chicago Press, 1982.

Attempts to examine Indian-white relations from both sides.

Leckie, Robert. *From Sea to Shining Sea: From the War of 1812 to the Mexican War, the Saga of American Expansion*. New York: HarperCollins Publishers, 1993.

Using the two wars as bookends, Leckie examines the evolution of American expansion.

Merk, Frederick. *Manifest Destiny and Mission in American History: A Reinterpretation*. New York: Knopf, 1963.

Examines public expressions, primarily newspapers and pamphlets, of the spirit of Manifest Destiny.

Meyer, Larry L. *Shadow of a Continent: The Prize that Lay to the West, 1776*. Palo Alto, CA: American West, 1975.

Morrison, Michael A. *Slavery and the American West: The Eclipse of Manifest Destiny and the Coming of the Civil War*. Chapel Hill: University of North Carolina Press, 1997.

Examines the evolution of political debate on western expansion over the issue of slavery.

Myers, Marvin. *The Jacksonian Persuasion: Politics and Belief*. Stanford, CA: Stanford University Press, 1957.

Insightful look at inherent agrarian conservatism of Jacksonians.

Nevins, Allan. *Ordeal of the Union. Fruits of Manifest Destiny, 1847–1852*. New York: Scribner, 1975.

Readable look at the results of American expansion in the first half of the nineteenth century.

Nobles, Gregory H. *American Frontiers: Cultural Encounters and Continental Conquest*. New York: Hill & Wang, 1997.

Collision of cultures that resulted when European Americans encountered Indians and the resultant harm to Indian cultures.

Owsley, Frank Lawrence, and Gene A. Smith. *Filibusters and Expansionists: Jeffersonian Manifest Destiny, 1800–1821*. Tuscaloosa: University of Alabama Press, 1997.

Examination of presidential expansion in the Early Republic.

Peavy, Linda S. *Women in Waiting in the Westward Movement: Life on the Home Frontier.* Norman: University of Oklahoma Press, 1994.

Case studies of frontier women's experiences when left behind while husbands sought their fortunes.

Perkins, Bradford. *The Creation of a Republican Empire, 1776–1865.* Cambridge: Cambridge University Press, 1993.

Examination of American foreign relations during its formative years.

Pessen, Edward. *Jacksonian America: Society, Personality, and Politics.* Homewood, IL: Dorsey, 1969.

Views Jacksonian America as far less democratic than many supposed.

Prucha, Francis Paul. *Broadax and Bayonet: The Role of the Army in the Development of the Northwest, 1815–1860.* Lincoln: University of Nebraska Press, 1953.

The army's impact on settlement of the Northwest.

———. *The Sword of the Republic: The United States Army on the Frontier, 1783–1846.* Toronto: Macmillan, 1969.

An overview of the army's impact on the American frontier.

Segal, Charles M., and David C. Stineback. *Puritans, Indians, and Manifest Destiny.* New York: Putnam, 1977.

Views New England expansion as part of Puritan belief in divine mission.

Sellers, Charles G. *The Market Revolution: Jacksonian America, 1815–1846.* Princeton: Princeton University Press, 1991.

A political, economic, social overview of the entire period.

Skelton, William B. *An American Profession of Arms: The Army Officer Corps, 1784–1861.* Lawrence: University Press of Kansas, 1992.

A comprehensive look at the development of the American officer corps.

Stephanson, Anders. *Manifest Destiny: American Expansionism and the Empire of Right.* New York: Hill and Wang, 1995.

Short, provocative look at American expansionism through the twentieth century.

Stuart, Reginald C. *United States Expansionism and British North America, 1775–1871.* Chapel Hill: University of North Carolina Press, 1988.

Looks at United States-Canadian relations in the wake of tremendous United States growth.

Utley, Robert M. *A Life Wild and Perilous: Mountain Men and the Paths to the Pacific.* New York: Holt, 1997.

Well-researched look at importance of these men in the first half of the nineteenth century.

Watson, Harry L. *Liberty and Power: The Politics of Jacksonian America.* New York: Farrar, Straus, & Giroux, 1990.

Discusses expansion onto Indian land and fits it into seeming conflict between preservation of liberty and exercise of power.

Weinberg, Albert Katz. *Manifest Destiny; A Study of Nationalist Expansionism in American History.* Gloucester, MA: P. Smith, 1958.

Dated but excellent overview of the movement.

Wiebe, Robert H. *The Opening of American Society: From the Adoption of the Constitution to the Eve of Disunion.* New York: Vintage, 1984.

Contends that the United States was remade in the nineteenth century by an increase in democracy and territorial expansion.

Wilson, Major L. *The Presidency of Martin Van Buren.* Lawrence: University Press of Kansas, 1984.

Revisionary analysis of Van Buren as an effective president.

———. *Space, Time, and Freedom: The Quest for Nationality and the Irrepressible Conflict, 1815–1861.* Westport, CT: Greenwood, 1974.

War of 1812

Coles, Harry L. *The War of 1812.* Chicago: University of Chicago Press, 1965.

Straightforward account from History of American Civilization series.

Elting, John R. *Amateurs, to Arms! A Military History of the War of 1812.* Chapel Hill: Algonquin, 1991.

Uneven military examination of the War of 1812.

Heidler, David S., and Jeanne T. Heidler. *The War of 1812.* Westport, CT: Greenwood, 2002.

Topical approach that examines military, political, and diplomatic aspects of the war.

Hickey, Donald R. *The War of 1812: A Forgotten Conflict.* Urbana: University of Illinois Press, 1989.

Standard narrative of the war.

Pratt, Julius W. *Expansionists of 1812.* New York: Macmillan, 1925.

Argues that war was caused by American expansionism.

Stagg, J. C. A. *Mr. Madison's War: Politics, Diplomacy, and Warfare in the Early American Republic, 1783–1830.* Princeton: Princeton University Press, 1983.

Places War of 1812 into the context of the politics of the Early Republic.

Wright, J. Leitch. *Britain and the American Frontier, 1783–1815.* Athens: University of Georgia Press, 1975.

Outlines patterns of British relations with Indians from the end of the Revolution through the War of 1812.

Florida

Heidler, David S., and Jeanne T. Heidler. *Old Hickory's War: Andrew Jackson and the Quest for Empire.* Mechanicsburg, PA: Stackpole, 1996. Reprint, Baton Rouge: Louisiana State University Press, 2003.

    The only book-length, scholarly study of Jackson's invasion of Florida in 1818.

Peters, Virginia Bergman. *The Florida Wars.* Hamden, CT: Archon, 1979.

    A short look at all of the Florida Seminole wars.

Rowland, Eron Opha Moore. *Andrew Jackson's Campaign Against the British, or The Mississippi Territory in the War of 1812, Concerning the Military Operations of the Americans, Creek Indians, British, and Spanish, 1813–1815.* New York: Macmillan, 1926.

    Primarily deals with War of 1812 but contains interesting sections on Jackson's Indian wars.

Smith, Joseph Burkholder. *The Plot to Steal Florida: James Madison's Phony War.* New York: Arbor, 1983.

    Outlines Madison's attempts before and during the War of 1812 to secure Florida.

Indian Removal

Anderson, William L. *Cherokee Removal: Before and After.* Athens: University of Georgia Press, 1991.

    Essays by experts on various aspects of removal and its impact.

Braund, Kathryn E. Holland. *Deerskins & Duffels: The Creek Indian Trade with Anglo-America, 1685–1815.* Lincoln: University of Nebraska Press, 1993.

    Tremendously important study of the impact of European trade on Creek culture.

Buker, George E. *Swamp Sailors: Riverine Warfare in the Everglades, 1835–1842.* Gainesville: University Presses of Florida, 1975.

    An examination of the impact of the navy on the Second Seminole War.

Chapman, George. *Chief William McIntosh: A Man of Two Worlds.* Atlanta, GA: Cherokee, 1988.

    General biography of controversial Creek who favored removal.

Coe, Charles H. *Red Patriots: The Story of the Seminoles.* Edited by Charlton W. Tebeau. Gainesville: University Presses of Florida, 1974.

    Reprint of late-nineteenth-century look at Seminoles as freedom fighters.

Covington, James W. *The Seminoles of Florida.* Gainesville: University Presses of Florida, 1993.

    Comprehensive study of the Seminole people.

Debo, Angie. *The Road to Disappearance*. Norman: University of Oklahoma Press, 1941.

Classic history of the Creek Indians.

Ehle, John. *Trail of Tears: The Rise and Fall of the Cherokee Nation*. New York: Doubleday, 1988.

Well-written popular account of Cherokee removal.

Fairbanks, Charles Herron. *The Florida Seminole People*. Phoenix: Indian Tribal Series, 1973.

Examination of Seminoles by leading anthropologist.

Filler, Louis, and Allen Guttmann, eds. *The Removal of the Cherokee Nation: Manifest Destiny or National Dishonor?* Boston: Heath, 1962.

Primary sources on removal.

Foreman, Grant. *The Five Civilized Tribes*. Norman: University of Oklahoma, 1934.

History of the Creek, Cherokee, Choctaw, Chickasaw, and Seminole Indians.

———. *Indian Removal: The Emigration of the Five Civilized Tribes of Indians*. Norman: University of Oklahoma Press, 1953.

Groundbreaking look at removal.

Francke, Arthur E. *Fort Mellon, 1837–1842: A Microcosm of the Second Seminole War*. Miami: Banyan, 1977.

A look at the war from the perspective of the garrison of one fort.

Giddings, Joshua R. *The Exiles of Florida; or the Crimes Committed by Our Government Against the Maroons Who Fled from South Carolina and Other States, Seeking Protection under Spanish Laws*. Gainesville: University of Florida Press, 1964.

Contemporary look at the plight of the Seminoles by a prominent abolitionist and opponent of expansion.

Halliburton, R., Jr. *Red over Black: Black Slavery Among the Cherokee Indians*. Westport CT: Greenwood, 1977.

Good overview in series on African-American history.

Hoig, Stan. *Night of the Cruel Moon: Cherokee Removal and the Trail of Tears*. New York: Facts on File, 1996.

Good overview and interesting narrative of events surrounding removal.

King, Duane H., ed. *The Cherokee Indian Nation: A Troubled History*. Knoxville: University of Tennessee Press, 1979.

Comprehensive history of the Cherokees from colonial period to the twentieth century.

Laumer, Frank. *Massacre!* Gainesville: University of Florida Press, 1968.

Account of the attack on Francis Dade's command that started the Second Seminole War.

———. *Dade's Last Command.* Gainesville: University Press of Florida, 1995.

Revision of Laumer's earlier work which holds that the attack on Dade's command occurred as an effort to protect runaway slaves from recapture.

Littlefield, Daniel F. *Africans and Seminoles: From Removal to Emancipation.* Westport, CT: Greenwood, 1977. Reprint, Oxford: University Press of Mississippi, 2001.

Account of the role of African-Americans in Seminole society and their activities in the Second Seminole War and removal.

Lumpkin, Wilson. *The Removal of the Cherokee Indians from Georgia.* 2 vols. New York: Arno, 1969.

Look at the issue by Georgia politician during removal.

Mahon, John K. *History of the Second Seminole War, 1835–1842.* Gainesville: University Presses of Florida, 1991.

Narrative of the causes and conduct of the war with some background on the Seminole people.

Mails, Thomas E. *The Cherokee People: The Story of the Cherokee from Earliest Origins to Contemporary Times.* Tulsa, OK: Council Oak, 1992.

A social history of the Seminoles.

Malone, Henry Thompson. *Cherokees of the Old South: A People in Transition.* Athens: University of Georgia Press, 1956.

Short look at Cherokees focusing on removal period.

Mancall, Peter C., and James H. Merrell, eds. *American Encounters: Natives and Newcomers from European Contact to Indian Removal, 1500–1850.* New York: Routledge, 2000.

Twenty-five essays taken from other sources on issues of contact.

Martin, Joel W. *Sacred Revolt: The Muskogees' Struggle for a New World.* Boston: Beacon, 1991.

Views the Creek War as primarily a spiritual difference within the Creek Nation.

McEwan, Bonnie G., ed. *Indians of the Greater Southeast: Historical Archaeology and Ethnohistory.* Gainesville: University Presses of Florida, 2000.

Contains several articles by experts on southeastern Indians during the removal period.

McLoughlin, William Gerald. *After the Trail of Tears: The Cherokees' Struggle for Sovereignty, 1839–1880.* Chapel Hill: University of North Carolina Press, 1993.

Takes Cherokees from removal through the Civil War and looks at the devastation that conflict caused.

————. *Cherokee Renascence in the New Republic.* Princeton: Princeton University Press, 1986.

Examines the relationship between the Cherokees and white governments before removal.

————. *The Cherokees and Christianity, 1794–1870: Essays on Acculturation and Cultural Persistence.* Athens: University of Georgia Press, 1994.

Essays that examine various Cherokee reactions to attempts to Christianize them.

————. *The Cherokee Ghost Dance: Essays on the Southeastern Indians, 1789–1861.* Macon, GA: Mercer University Press, 1984.

Essays by leading scholars on various aspects of southeastern Indian culture.

McReynolds, Edwin C. *The Seminoles.* Norman: University of Oklahoma Press, 1957.

Overview of Seminole history from the Civilization of the American Indian series.

Perdue, Theda, and Michael D. Green. *The Cherokee Removal: A Brief History with Documents.* Boston: Bedford-St. Martin, 1995.

Overview with pertinent documents. Good for class use.

Perdue, Theda. *Slavery and the Evolution of Cherokee Society, 1540–1866.* Knoxville: University of Tennessee Press, 1979.

Author believes the introduction of slavery had a profound impact on Cherokee culture.

Remini, Robert V. *Andrew Jackson and His Indian Wars.* New York: Penguin-Viking, 2001.

Largely an apologia for Jackson's actions toward Southeastern Indians.

————. *The Legacy of Andrew Jackson: Essays on Democracy, Indian Removal, and Slavery.* Baton Rouge: Louisiana State University Press, 1988.

Three lectures that praise Jackson's role in American history.

Rensi, Raymond Charles. *Gold Fever: America's First Gold Rush.* Atlanta: Georgia Humanities Council, 1988.

Episodic look at the gold rush as well as its impact on the Indian population.

Satz, Ronald N. *Tennessee's Indian Peoples: From White Contact to Removal, 1540–1840.* Knoxville: University of Tennessee Press, 1979.

Examination of how white contact, beginning with De Soto, changed Southeastern Indian cultures.

Saunt, Claudio. *A New Order of Things: Property, Power, and the Transformation of the Creek Indians, 1733–1816.* New York: Cambridge University Press, 1999.

Impact of private property, particularly slaves and cattle on Creek culture.

Shoemaker, Nancy, ed. *Negotiators of Change: Historical Perspectives on Native American Women*. New York: Routledge, 1995.

Series of essays by prominent experts on Indian women's history detailing the cultural impact on women and their influence on Indian culture during the period of white American expansion through the twentieth century.

Southerland, Henry deLeon, and Jerry Elijah Brown. *The Federal Road Through Georgia, the Creek Nation, and Alabama, 1806–1836*. Tuscaloosa: University of Alabama Press, 1989.

The Federal Road's effect on the Creeks and the subsequent conflict it caused.

Van Every, Dale. *Disinherited: The Lost Birthright of the American Indian*. New York: Morrow, 1966.

Analysis of causes and conduct of Indian removal.

Wallace, Anthony F. C. *The Long Bitter Trail: Andrew Jackson and the Indians*. New York: Hill and Wang, 1993.

Study centers on the Indian Removal Act of 1830 and its implications for American history.

Walton, George H. *Fearless and Free: The Seminole Indian War, 1835–1842*. Indianapolis: Bobbs-Merrill, 1977.

Account of Second Seminole War as revolving around slavery.

Wardell, Morris L. *A Political History of the Cherokee Nation, 1838–1907*. Norman: University of Oklahoma Press, 1938.

Older work from the Civilization of the American Indian series.

White, Richard. *The Middle Ground: Indians, Empires, and Republics in the Great Lakes Region, 1650–1815*. New York: Cambridge University Press, 1991.

Examines the uneasy cooperation between cultures around the Great Lakes and how that cooperation ended.

Williams, David. *The Georgia Gold Rush: Twenty-niners, Cherokees, and Gold Fever*. Columbia: University of South Carolina Press, 1993.

Ties discovery of gold to Georgia's insistence on Indian removal.

Wright, J. Leitch. *Creeks & Seminoles: The Destruction and Regeneration of the Muscogulge People*. Lincoln: University of Nebraska Press, 1986.

Attempts to explain the diversity of the Creek and Seminole people.

Young, Mary Elizabeth. *Redskins, Ruffleshirts and Rednecks; Indian Allotments in Alabama and Mississippi, 1830–1860*. Norman: University of Oklahoma Press, 1961.

Work on the division of Indian lands during and after removal.

Texas

Adams, Ephraim Douglass. *British Interests and Activities in Texas, 1838–1846*. Gloucester, MA: P. Smith 1963.

> Lectures given in early twentieth century on this topic.

Bannon, John Francis. *The Spanish Borderlands Frontier, 1513–1821*. Albuquerque: University of New Mexico Press, 1974.

> Emphasis on development of Mexico through its independence.

Barr, Alwyn. *Black Texans: A History of African Americans in Texas, 1528–1995*. Norman: University of Oklahoma Press, 1996.

> Traces black experience in Texas from colonial exploration to American frontier settlement.

Chipman, Donald E. *Spanish Texas, 1519–1821*. Austin: University of Texas Press, 1992.

> Comprehensive look at Spanish dominion over Texas.

Fehrenbach, T. R. *Lone Star: A History of Texas and the Texans*. New York: Macmillan, 1968.

> Well-written narrative of Texas history.

Frantz, Joe Bertram. *Texas: A Bicentennial History*. New York: Norton, 1976.

> Short, well-written history of the state.

Hardin, Stephen L. *Texian Iliad: A Military History of the Texas Revolution, 1835–1836*. Austin: University of Texas Press, 1994.

> Exhaustively researched analysis of the military events of the Texas Revolution.

Keating, Bern. *An Illustrated History of the Texas Rangers*. Chicago: Rand McNally, 1975.

> As title would indicate, well-illustrated but also well-written history of the Rangers.

Lack, Paul D. *The Texas Revolutionary Experience: A Political and Social History, 1835–1836*. College Station: Texas A&M University Press, 1992.

> Looks at the background of the revolution and then analyzes the different groups involved.

Merk, Frederick. *Slavery and the Annexation of Texas*. New York: Knopf, 1972.

> Puts race at the center of annexation debates.

Nackman, Mark E. *A Nation Within a Nation: The Rise of Texas Nationalism*. Port Washington, NY: Kennikat, 1975.

> Author emphasizes its leaders in this look at Texas history from Mexican independence to the Civil War.

Nance, Joseph Milton. *After San Jacinto: The Texas-Mexican Frontier, 1836–1841*. Austin: University of Texas Press, 1963.

> Account of border difficulties between the Republic of Texas and Mexico.

Nance, Joseph Milton. *Attack and Counter Attack: The Texas–Mexican Frontier, 1842*. Austin University of Texas Press, 1964.

Texas-Mexican relations on the eve of statehood.

Nofi, Albert A. *The Alamo and the Texas War of Independence, September 30, 1835 to April 21, 1836: Heroes, Myths, and History*. Conshohocken, PA: Combined, 1992.

Objective look at the war with an emphasis on the Alamo and the myths surrounding it.

Richardson, Rupert Norval. *Texas, The Lone Star State*. Englewood Cliffs, NJ: Prentice-Hall, 1981. Rev. ed., 2000.

Comprehensive textbook history of Texas.

Siegel, Stanley. *A Political History of the Texas Republic, 1836–1845*. Austin: University of Texas Press, 1956.

An intimate look at the personal differences within the Texas government.

Tijerina, Andres. *Tejanos and Texas Under the Mexican Flag, 1821–1836*. College Station: Texas A&M University Press, 1994.

An examination of the diversity of views of Mexican Texans before independence.

Tinkle, Lon. *13 Days to Glory: The Siege of the Alamo*. College Station: Texas A&M University Press, 1996.

Fast-paced account of the siege.

Utley, Robert M. *The First Century of the Texas Rangers*. New York: Oxford University Press, 2002.

Balanced look at this controversial group.

Vigness, David M. *The Revolutionary Decades, the Saga of Texas, 1810–1836*. Austin, TX: Steck-Vaughn, 1965.

Background to American settlement of Texas and account of the Revolution.

Oregon

Kushner, Howard I. *Conflict on the Northwest Coast: American-Russian Rivalry in the Pacific Northwest, 1790–1867*. Westport, CT: Greenwood, 1975.

Good section on disputes in 1830s and 1840s over Oregon.

Lavender, David Sievert. *Westward Vision: The Story of the Oregon Trail*. New York: McGraw-Hill, 1963.

Beginning with early western explorers, author examines all aspects of the famous trail.

Parkman, Francis. *The Oregon Trail; Sketches of Prairie and Rocky–Mountain Life*. New York: Dodd, Mead, 1964.

Well-written romanticized view from one of the first great U.S. historians.

Williams, Jacqueline B. *Wagon Wheel Kitchens: Food on the Oregon Trail.* Lawrence: University Press of Kansas, 1993.

Comprehensive look at how pioneers ate on the trail.

Mexican-American War

Bauer, K. Jack. *The Mexican War, 1846–1848.* New York: Macmillan, 1974.

Standard history that compares opposition to the Mexican War to opposition during Vietnam.

Brack, Gene M. *Mexico Views Manifest Destiny, 1821–1846: An Essay on the Origins of the Mexican War.* Albuquerque: University of New Mexico Press, 1975.

Evolution of Mexican hostility toward the United States.

Chidsey, Donald Barr. *The War with Mexico.* New York: Crown, 1968.

Short overview of the war.

Dawson, Joseph G., and Joseph G. Dawson, III. *Doniphan's Epic March: The 1st Missouri Volunteers in the Mexican War.* Lawrence: University Press of Kansas, 1999.

Looks at how Doniphan's leadership style brought success to the 1st Missouri.

Eisenhower, John S. D. *So Far From God: The U.S. War with Mexico, 1846–1848.* New York: Random House, 1989.

Sweeping narrative history of the war.

Francaviglia, Richard V., and Douglas Richmond. *Dueling Eagles: A Reinterpreting of the Mexican-American War, 1846–1848.* Fort Worth: Texas Christian University Press, 2000.

Essays by leading American and Mexican historians on different aspects of the war.

Goetzmann, William H. *Sam Chamberlain's Mexican War: The San Jacinto Museum of History Paintings.* Austin: Texas State Historical Association, 1993.

The war through the eyes of a private who painted striking scenes of the war.

Griswold del Castillo, Richard. *The Treaty of Guadalupe Hidalgo: A Legacy of Conflict.* Norman: University of Oklahoma Press, 1990.

Analyzes the treaty's impact on Hispanic Americans.

Johannsen, Robert. *To the Halls of the Montezumas: The Mexican War in the American Imagination.* New York: Oxford University Press, 1985.

Examination of the American perceptions of the Mexican-American War.

McCaffrey, James M. *Army of Manifest Destiny: The American Soldier in the Mexican War, 1846–1848*. New York: New York University Press, 1992.

Social history of American soldiers in the war.

Pletcher, David M. *The Diplomacy of Annexation: Texas, Oregon, and the Mexican War.* Columbia: University of Missouri Press, 1975.

Examines United States-British-Mexican relations.

Price, Glenn W. *Origins of the War with Mexico: The Polk–Stockton Intrigue.* Austin: University of Texas Press, 1967.

Seeks to prove that Polk conspired to persuade Texas to make war on Mexico before annexation so that when annexation occurred, Polk could use the war as a pretext to take California.

Ricketts, Norma Baldwin. *The Mormon Battalion, U.S. Army of the West, 1846–1848*. Logan: Utah State University Press, 1996.

Comprehensive account of the trek of this unit to California during the Mexican-American War.

Santoni, Pedro. *Mexicans at Arms: Puro Federalists and the Politics of War, 1845–1848*. Fort Worth: Texas Christian University Press, 1996.

Analyzes the complicated political situation in Mexico during the Mexican-American War.

Schroeder, John H. *Mr. Polk's War: American Opposition and Dissent, 1846–1848*. Madison: University of Wisconsin Press, 1973.

Examination of peace movements during Mexican-American War.

Singletary, Otis A. *The Mexican-American War.* Chicago: University of Chicago Press, 1960.

Short, straightforward narrative of the war.

Smith, Justin. *War with Mexico*. 2 vols. Gloucester, MA: P. Smith, 1963.

The most comprehensive treatment of the war.

Stephenson, Nathaniel W. *Texas and the Mexican War; A Chronicle of the Winning of the Southwest*. New Haven: Yale University Press, 1921.

Nice overview in older Chronicles of America series.

Stevens, Peter F. *The Rogue's March: John Riley and the St. Patrick's Battalion.* Washington: Brassey's, 1999.

Argues that nativism pushed Irish-Americans to desert the U.S. Army.

Vogel, Victor H. *Soldiers of Manifest Destiny: The Army of the West in the Mexican War, 1846–1848*. Fredericktown, MO: Foundation for Historic Preservation, 1990.

Winders, Richard Bruce. *Mr. Polk's Army: The American Military Experience in the Mexican War.* College Station: Texas A&M University Press, 1997.

Examines the social and cultural origins of the American army in Mexico.

Memoirs, Diaries, Papers

Bembrose, John. *Reminiscences of the Second Seminole War.* Ed. John K. Mahon. Gainesville: University of Florida Press, 1966. Reprint, Gainesville: University of Tampa Press, 2001.

Memoirs of doctor during war.

Benton, Thomas H. *Thirty Years' View; Or, A History of the Working of the American government for Thirty Years, from 1820 to 1850.* 2 vols. New York: Appleton, 1856.

Memoirs by one of the most important politicians of the day.

Boudinot, Elias. *Cherokee Editor: The Writings of Elias Boudinot.* Ed. Theda Perdue. Knoxville: University of Tennessee Press, 1983. Reprint, Athens: University of Georgia Press, 1996.

Excellent collection with good overview by editor.

Castaneda, Carlos Eduardo, ed. *The Mexican Side of the Texan Revolution (1836) by the Chief Mexican Participants, General Antonio Lopez de Santa-Anna, D. Ramon Martinez Caro . . . General Vicente Filisola, General Jose Urrea, General Jose Maria Tornel.* Dallas, TX: Turner, 1928.

Collection of firsthand accounts from Mexican perspective.

Cohen, Myer M. *Notices of Florida and the Campaigns.* Gainesville: University of Florida Press, 1964.

Personal account of some of the early military campaigns of the Second Seminole War.

Dickens, Asbury, and Forney, John W., editors. *American State Papers: Military Affairs.* 7 vols. Washington, D.C.: Gales and Seaton, 1832–61.

Government documents of army on the frontier before the Civil War.

Doubleday, Abner. *My Life in the Old Army: The Reminiscences of Abner Doubleday: From the Collections of the New York Historical Society.* Edited by Joseph E. Chance. Fort Worth: Texas Christian University Press, 1998.

Large section on Doubleday's activities in the Mexican-American War.

Ford, John Salmon. *Rip Ford's Texas.* Austin: University of Texas Press, 1963.

Reminiscences of a Texas Ranger during the Republic and Texas statehood.

General Scott and His Staff: Comprising Memoirs of Generals Scott, Twiggs, Smith, Quitman, Shields, Pillow, Lane, Cadwalader, Patterson and Pierce; Colonels Childs, Riley, Harney, and Butler, and other distinguished officers attached to General Scott's army. Philadelphia: Grigg, Elliot & Col., 1848.

Good collection of primary sources.

Halleck, Henry W. *The Mexican War in Baja California: The Memorandum of Captain Henry W. Halleck Concerning His Expeditions in Lower California, 1846–1848.* Ed. Doyce B. Nunis, Jr. Los Angeles: Dawson, 1977.

Halleck's diary and commentary on his experiences in California during the Mexican-American War.

Hitchcock, Ethan Allen. *Fifty Years in Camp and Field: Diary of Major General Ethan Allen Hitchcock, U.S.A.* Ed. W. A. Cruffut. Freeport, N.Y.: Books for Libraries, 1971.

Insightful memoir by one of the army's most observant officers.

Holley, Mary Austin. *Texas; Observations, Historical, Geographical and Descriptive.* New York: Arno, 1973.

Reprint of recruiting document for Texas settlement.

Holmes, Kenneth L., and David Duniway, eds. *Covered Wagon Women: Diaries & Letters From the Western Trails, 1840–1890.* 8 vols. Glendale, CA: A. H. Clark, 1983.

Volume 1 details diaries of women from 1840 to 1849.

Houston, Sam. *The Autobiography of Sam Houston.* Ed. Donald Day and Harry Herbert Ullom. Norman: University of Oklahoma Press, 1954. Reprint, Westport, CT: Greenwood Press, 1980.

Interesting editorial job of arranging Houston's writings into an autobiography.

——. *The Personal Correspondence of Sam Houston.* 4 vols. Edited by Madge Thornal Roberts. Denton, TX: University of North Texas Press, 1996–2001.

Much of Houston's surviving correspondence up to his death in 1863 and some family letters after 1863.

Hughes, John T. *Doniphan's Expedition: An Account of the U.S. Army Operations in the Great Southwest.* Chicago: Rio Grande, 1962.

Memoir of one of the participants in Kearny's and Doniphan's expeditions in the Southwest during the Mexican-American War.

Jenkins, John H. *The Papers of the Texas Revolution, 1835–1836.* 10 vols. Austin, TX: Presidial, 1973.

Excellent collection of official papers of the revolution.

Jones, Anson. *Memoranda and Official Correspondence Relating to the Republic of Texas, Its History and Annexation; Including a Brief Autobiography of the Author.* Chicago: Rio Grande, 1966.

Deals primarily with annexation concerns.

Moquin, Wayne, ed. *Great Documents in American Indian History.* New York: Praeger, 1973.

Documentary history that covers colonial period to twentieth century.

Morgan, Dale Lowell. *Overland in 1846; Diaries and Letters of the California-Oregon Trail.* Georgetown, CA: Talisman, 1963.

Good primary sources.

Motte, Jacob Rhett. *Journey into Wilderness; an Army Surgeon's Account of Life in Camp and Field During the Creek and Seminole Wars, 1836–1838.* Ed. James F. Sunderman. Gainesville: University of Florida Press, 1953.

Memoir of the first three years of the Second Seminole War.

Peña, Jose Enrique de la. *With Santa Anna in Texas: A Personal Narrative of the Revolution.* Ed. Carmen Perry. College Station: Texas A&M University Press, 1975.

Mexican officer's account of the fall of the Alamo. Interesting account of the death of Davy Crockett.

Polk, James K. *Correspondence of James K. Polk.* 9 vols. Edited by Herbert Weaver, Wayne Cutler, and Paul Bergeron. Nashville: Vanderbilt University Press, 1969–1996.

Comprehensive collection of Polk letters.

———. *The Diary of James K. Polk During His Presidency, 1845 to 1849.* 4 vols. Chicago: McClurg, 1910.

Comprehensive diary kept by Polk during his presidency.

Potter, Woodburne. *The War in Florida.* Ann Arbor: University Microfilms, 1966.

A memoir of the first year of the Second Seminole War.

Preuss, Charles. *Exploring with Frémont; the Private Diaries of Charles Preuss, Cartographer for John C. Frémont on his First, Second, and Fourth Expeditions to the Far West.* Ed. Erwin G. Gudde and Elisabeth K. Gudde. Norman: University of Oklahoma Press, 1958.

Good firsthand accounts of Frémont's early explorations.

Prince, Henry. *Amidst a Storm of Bullets: The Diary of Lt. Henry Prince in Florida, 1836–1842.* Ed. Frank Laumer. Tampa, FL: University of Tampa Press, 1998.

Interesting look at the Second Seminole War through the eyes of a West Point graduate.

Ross, John. *The Papers of Chief John Ross.* 2 vols. Ed. Gary E. Moulton. Norman: University of Oklahoma Press, 1985.

Comprehensive collection of Cherokee chief's papers.

Santa Anna, Antonio Lopez de. *The Eagle: The Autobiography of Santa Anna.* Ed. Ann Fears Crawford. Austin, TX: Pemberton, 1967.

Interesting view of American expansion through the eyes of Santa Anna.

Scott, Winfield. *Memoirs of Lieut. General Scott, L.L. D., Written by Himself.* 2 vols. New York: Sheldon, 1864.

Somewhat self-serving, but interesting perspective on the nation to the Civil War.

Smith, George Winston, and Charles Judah. *Chronicles of the Gringos: The U.S. Army in the Mexican War, Accounts of Eyewitnesses and Combatants.* Albuquerque: University of New Mexico Press, 1968.

American soldiers' accounts of the war.

Sprague, J. T. *The Origin, Progress, and Conclusion of the Florida War.* Gainesville: University of Florida Press, 1964.

Contemporary view of the war with appendices on casualties and exceptional performance.

Stuart, Robert. *The Discovery of the Oregon Trail: Robert Stuart's Narratives of His Overland Trip Eastward from Astoria in 1812–1813.* Edited by Philip Ashton Rollins. Lincoln: University of Nebraska Press, 1995.

Diary of perceptive explorer.

Vogel, Virgil J. *This Country Was Ours: A Documentary History of the American Indian.* New York: Harper & Row, 1972.

Important documents in Indian history.

Washburn, Wilcomb E., ed. *The American Indian and the United States; A Documentary History.* 4 vols. New York: Random House, 1973.

Good collection of documents primarily by whites who interacted with Indians.

Films, Computer Discs

100% Educational Videos (Producer). (1998). *The Oregon Trail* [Videocassette]. Orangevale, CA: Chip Taylor Communications.

Documentary about the use of the Oregon Trail during the first half of the nineteenth century.

Bosner, Paul (Producer). (1987). *Manifest Destiny* [Videocassette]. Mesquite, TX: RMI Media Productions.

Focuses primarily on the westward expansion that led to the Mexican-American War.

Burns, Ken (Producer). (1997). *Lewis & Clark—The Journey of the Corps of Discovery* [Television broadcast]. Burbank, CA: PBS.

Blends contemporary accounts with modern historical interpretation.

Dallas County Community College District (Producer). (1988). *American adventure* [Television series]. Austin, TX: PBS.

Series on development of the United States. Episode 15 deals with expansionism and Manifest Destiny.

Dobbs, Frank Q. (Producer). (1986). *Gone to Texas* [Videocassette]. United States: Worldvision Home Video.

Biography of Sam Houston.

Drooker, Arthur (Producer). (1992). *The battle of the Alamo* [Videocassette]. United States: Arts and Entertainment Network.

Contemporary pictures and interviews with scholars bring to light lives of defenders and attackers and examines the place of the Alamo in Texas's war for independence.

Hughes, Robert (Writer/Narrator). (1996). *The Wilderness and the West* [Videocassette]. Alexandria, VA: PBS Video.

Discusses the art and artists of Manifest Destiny.

Hutchison, Sonny (Producer). (1995). *How the West was Lost* [Videocassette]. Santa Monica, CA: Discovery Channel.

Explores the displacement of American Indians. 100 minutes.

Ives, Stephen (Producer). (1996). *Empire Upon the Trails* [Home video]. Alexandria, VA: PBS.

Covers the early phases of nineteenth-century American expansionism.

Leustig, Jack (Producer). (1995). *500 Nations: Stories of the North American Indian Experience* [Home video]. Burbank, CA: Warner Home Video.

Eight-part history of American Indians. 390 minutes.

Matthews, Stan (Producer). (1986). *The West of the Imagination: The Golden Land* [Videocassette]. Princeton, NJ: Films for the Humanities.

Examines the Manifest Destiny of the 1840s and 1850s through the eyes of artists.

Thompson, Linwood C. (Producer). (2001). *Early American History, Native Americans through the Forty-Niners* [Videocassette series]. Springfield, VA: Teaching Company.

In six tapes (1,200 minutes) takes American history from pre-Columbian Indians through the California Gold Rush.

Tranchin, Robert (Producer). (1998). *The U.S.-Mexican War (1846–1848)* [Videocassette]. Dallas, TX: KERA and PBS Video.

Views war as one of aggression on the part of the U.S. 240 minutes.

Westward Expansion [Computer optical disc]. (1998). Woodbridge, CT: Primary Source Media.

More than 200 primary documents and 500 illustrations.

Web Pages

http://www.pbs.org/usmexicanwar/

Good overview, a companion to PBS video, *The U.S.-Mexican War.*

http://sunsite.unam.mx/revistas/1847/

Uneven site in Spanish and English with useful documents on the Mexican-American War.

http://www.acusd.edu/~rleisse/index.html

A look at California history with interesting section on American expansion maintained by University of San Diego.

http://www.army.mil/cmh–pg/

Good source for information on army's participation, maintained by the U.S. Army Center for Military History.

http://cdl.library.cornell.edu/moa/ Cornell University's "Making of America" site. Great place to locate sources for research and view digitized sources.

Bibliographies

Fehrenbacher, Don Edward, comp. *Manifest Destiny and the Coming of the Civil War.* New York: Appleton, 1970.

Bibliography of sources on expansion as a cause of the Civil War.

Garrett, Jenkins, and Katherine Goodwin, eds. *The Mexican-American War of 1846–1848: A Bibliography of the Holdings of the Libraries, the University of Texas at Arlington.* College Station: Published for the University of Texas at Arlington by the Texas A&M University Press, 1995.

Good look at available unpublished sources.

Green, Michael D., ed. *The Creeks: A Critical Bibliography.* Bloomington: Indiana University Press, 1979.

Good, though dated source guide.

Kidwell, Clara Sue, ed. *The Choctaws: A Critical Bibliography.* Bloomington: Indiana University Press, 1980.

Good, though dated source guide.

Prucha, Francis Paul, ed. *A Bibliographical Guide to the History of Indian-White Relations in the United States.* Chicago: University of Chicago Press, 1977.

Dated look at important sources on Indian-white relations.

———. *United States Indian Policy: A Critical Bibliography.* Bloomington: Indiana University Press, 1977.

Annotated, though old bibliography from government perspective.

Tutorow, Norman E., ed. *The Mexican-American War: An Annotated Bibliography.* Westport, CT: Greenwood, 1981.

Reference

Byrnes, Mark Eaton, ed. *James K. Polk: A Biographical Companion.* Santa Barbara, CA: ABC–Clio, 2001.

Contains documents and selection of encyclopedia-like entries related to Polk's life.

Crawford, Mark, ed. *Encyclopedia of the Mexican-American War.* David S. Heidler and Jeanne T. Heidler, consulting editors. Santa Barbara, CA: ABC-Clio, 1999.

Good, short reference.

Frazier, Donald S., ed. *The United States and Mexico at War: Nineteenth-Century Expansionism and Conflict.* New York: Macmillan, 1998.

Good reference that puts Mexican conflict in perspective of American expansion.

Hatch, Thom, ed. *Encyclopedia of the Alamo and the Texas Revolution.* Jefferson, NC: McFarland, 1999.

Good reference on rather short period of history.

Heidler, David S., and Jeanne T. Heidler, eds. *Encyclopedia of the War of 1812.* Santa Barbara, CA: ABC-Clio, 1997.

Only comprehensive reference work on the war.

Heitman, Francis B., comp. *Historical Register and Dictionary of the United States Army.* 2 vols. Washington: GPO, 1903.

Most complete source on frontier army officers.

Moseley, Edward H., ed. *Historical Dictionary of the United States-Mexican War.* Lanham, MD: Scarecrow, 1997.

Good reference to begin research on the war.

Wexler, Alan, ed. *Atlas of Westward Expansion.* New York: Facts on File, 1995.

Looks at western expansion through maps from colonial period through the nineteenth century.

INDEX

About the Authors

DAVID S. HEIDLER is an independent scholar. He is the author of *Pulling the Temple Down: The Fire-eaters and the Destruction of the Union.*

JEANNE T. HEIDLER is Professor of History at the United States Air Force Academy and, along with her husband David, is co-author/editor of *Old Hickory's War: Andrew Jackson and the Quest for Empire, The Encyclopedia of the War of 1812,* the award winning *The Encyclopedia of the American Civil War: A Social, Political, and Military History,* and *The War of 1812* (Greenwood, 2002).